Felton & Fowler's
FAMOUS AMERICANS
YOU NEVER KNEW EXISTED

OTHER BOOKS BY THE AUTHORS:

Felton & Fowler's Best, Worst, and Most Unusual
Felton & Fowler's More Best, Worst, and Most Unusual

Felton & Fowler's FAMOUS AMERICANS YOU NEVER KNEW EXISTED

Bruce Felton and Mark Fowler

.SB

A SCARBOROUGH BOOK
STEIN AND DAY/*Publishers*/New York

For Judy, with love, from Bruce
For FJF and MHF—Mark

FIRST SCARBOROUGH BOOKS EDITION 1981

Felton & Fowler's Famous Americans You Never Knew Existed
was originally published in hardcover by Stein and
Day/*Publishers*.

Copyright © 1979 by Bruce Felton and Mark Fowler
All rights reserved
Designed by Ed Kaplin
Printed in the United States of America
STEIN AND DAY/*Publishers*/Scarborough House
Briarcliff Manor, N.Y. 10510

Library of Congress Cataloging in Publication Data

Felton, Bruce.
    Felton & Fowler's Famous Americans you never knew
existed.

        1. United States—Biography.   I.   Fowler, Mark,
joint author.   II. Title.   III. Title: Famous
Americans you never knew existed.
CT215.F44 1979   920´.073   78-56944
ISBN 0-8128-6108-6

Contents

Introduction   vii

Blunderers, Dreamers, and Enthusiasts   1

Derring-Doers   14

Deceivers   38

Evildoers   50

Food Faddists and Gourmands   67

Inventors and Innovators   91

Lawmakers, Plaintiffs, and Defendants   127

Money-Makers   151

Overdoers   166

Performing and Creative Artists   183

Physical Specimens   204

Prophets and Moralists   212

Scientific Figures   222

Sexy People   256

Sports Heroes   273

Index   287

ACKNOWLEDGMENTS

Special thanks to Jay Acton, Benton Arnovitz, Mary Greene, picture researcher Jessica Kaplan, Lois Klein, Susan Mc-Kanna, Daphne Hougham, Mark Scherzer, Anne Schooler, and the staff of the Rye (New York) Free Reading Room for their assistance in the compilation and writing of this book. The authors would also like to express their appreciation to the individuals and institutions whose names accompany the photo captions.

Introduction

History has not done right by Alferd Packer. Surely one would expect that America's only tried-and-true cannibal—the man who was jailed in 1874 for eating most of the Democratic Party of Hinsdale County, Colorado—would have been forevermore enshrined in the national memory, have public holidays, high schools and turnpike service areas named in his honor. Yet Packer remains essentially unknown today, as do such other one-time luminaries as Sylvester Graham, the great nineteenth-century apostle of vegetarianism and bowel regularity; Edward Hyde, the transvestite governor of New York; Solyman Brown, poet laureate of American dentists; and Dr. Robert J. White, transplanter of heads. Their accomplishments are impressive; their fame is scant.

Felton & Fowler's Famous Americans You Never Knew Existed has been compiled to exhume these and some 400 other overlooked Americans from colonial times to the present from the burial crypts of history. It is a field guide to rare birds, a first step toward a comprehensive who's who of homegrown cranks, quacks, blunderers, fanatics, dreamers, heroes, saints, evildoers and eccentrics of all stripes who somehow got lost in the shuffle. Few of these singular characters can be found in any of the standard biographical reference volumes. By and large they've been overlooked or in some cases, deliberately snubbed. Some may strike you as wildly improbable.

All the same, the men and women who inhabit these pages are all very real, and many have made an ineradicable mark on American life. Joseph Gayetty, for one, invented toilet paper, and Hanson Gregory was the man who put the hole in the doughnut. There are explorers (John Cleves Symmes planned a journey to the center of the earth and nearly persuaded Congress to finance the expedition), politicians (David Rice Atchison is acknowledged by some to be the twelfth president of the United States), athletes (major league catcher "Mule" Sprinz successfully handled a base-ball dropped from a hovering blimp), entertainers (vaude-villian Hadji Ali was billed as "The Amazing Regurgitator"), artists (John Banvard painted a landscape three miles long), composers (a Bostonian named Greeler set the entire United States Constitution to music), religious figures (Theophilus Gates founded a nineteenth-century sect that worshiped in the nude), and men of science (Dr. John Brinkley made a fortune transplanting "goat glands" into the elderly to renew their sexual vigor). You will also meet the original Mother Goose, the original Phileas Fogg, and the original Uncle Sam, who were by no means mythical figures.

Oddly, one of the stars of these pages, madwoman-essayist Delia Bacon, is in fact listed in the *Dictionary of American Biography,* which notes with some sadness that apart from a single unnamed acquaintance of Nathaniel Hawthorne's, there is no record of anyone, anywhere, ever having read the one book she spent her entire life producing.

Sad indeed. But perhaps in *Famous Americans* she will receive, at long last, the fair hearing she so richly deserves.

Bruce Felton
Mark Fowler
September 1978

Felton & Fowler's
FAMOUS AMERICANS
YOU NEVER KNEW EXISTED

Blunderers, Dreamers, and Enthusiasts

WILLIAM G. CRUSH What's in a name? In 1896, William G. Crush, an enterprising executive with the Missouri, Kansas & Texas Railway, staged what was billed as the most sensational train crash of the century. Thirty thousand people were on hand along an isolated stretch of track in Texas to watch two locomotives come together head-on at 60 miles per hour. On the whole the crowd was delighted with the spectacle, which proved even more destructive than anticipated. Flying shrapnel killed one onlooker and maimed two photographers.

William Crush's planned train wreck *(From* The Katy Railroad, *by V.V. Masterson, copyright 1952 by the University of Oklahoma Press)*

1

IGNATIUS DONNELLY The legend of Atlantis can be traced back to no less an authority than Plato. In an unfinished dialogue, *Kritias,* composed in 335 B.C., the philosopher describes "a great and wonderful empire," larger than Libya and Asia Minor put together, that was completely destroyed in a single day and night by "violent earthquakes and floods." For the next 22 centuries not much was added to the story of the Lost Continent. Then in 1882 the House of Harper published a weighty and erudite volume entitled *Atlantis: The Antediluvian World* by a fourth-term United States Congressman, Ignatius Donnelly (1831–1901).

Few men are more difficult to pigeonhole than Donnelly. On the one hand he was a brilliant orator and radical politician, the founder and leader of the Populist party, and an advocate of such progressive reforms as universal suffrage, antitrust regulation, nationalization of railroads, and the 40-hour week. On the other hand he propounded some of the wildest and most enduring nonsense of the nineteenth or any other century.

According to Donnelly, civilization was born on Atlantis, the true Garden of Eden, thence spread out to all the other continents. As proof he cited similarities in archaeology, architecture, and folklore among such ancient and far-distant cultures as Mexico, Egypt, and China. The kings of Atlantis, he said, were identical with the pagan gods worshiped by later civilizations. *(See also:* Augustus Le Plongeon.)

Thousands of readers here and abroad were fascinated and persuaded by Donnelly's book, which went through 50 printings, the most recent in 1960. One distinguished convert was William E. Gladstone, the British prime minister, who asked the Treasury to fund an expedition to the Azores, which Donnelly claimed were the tops of sunken Atlantean mountains. While sympathetic, the Exchequer declined to spend public money to look for submerged continents; England was overmuch engaged with conquering the existing ones.

Donnelly was an eccentric but not a monomaniac; he quickly turned his attentions to several other notions. In 1883

2

he came out with *Ragnarok: The Age of Fire and Gravel* in which he attributed the world's deposits of clay, gravel, silt, and sand to a celestial traffic accident with a mighty comet.

And finally there was Donnelly's magnum opus, *The Great Cryptogram,* wherein he expanded on a hypothesis first advanced by Delia Bacon (q.v.) of Talmadge, Ohio. With more wit and better scholarship than Miss Bacon ever mustered, he sought to prove, by means of a diabolically ingenious cipher, that Sir Francis Bacon wrote all of the works usually ascribed to Shakespeare. Then, as if that weren't enough, he went on to show that Bacon had also dashed off Marlowe's plays, Montaigne's essays (in French), and Burton's *Anatomy of Melancholy.* A literary war ensued and once again a number of important figures lined up on Donnelly's side, to the detriment of their later reputations.

The British writer Patrick Moore has recently offered what should be the last word on the Shakespeare controversy: "It is transparently obvious to any scholar," he says, "that William Shakespeare's plays were written not by William Shakespeare but by another author of the same name."

KEN GIDNEY Ken Gidney has his nine children and thirteen grandchildren helping him in the booming business he started in 1956 in La Mirada, California: selling ants at a penny apiece to a manufacturer of ant farms. By his own figuring Gidney has trapped and sold nearly 30 million of the wee beasties over the years.

WILLIAM HOPE HARVEY What Tutankhamen did for Egypt, what the Aztec princes did for Mexico, William Hope "Coin" Harvey (1851–1936) dreamed of doing in the Ozarks. Trained as a lawyer, Harvey exercised his greatest influence on American life in the field of economics rather than sepulchral architecture. His *Coin's Financial School* (1894) attempted to explain Populist economics in simple terms that every voter could understand. William Jennings Bryan's famous "cross of gold" speech in 1896 embodied many of Harvey's radical ideas on free coinage of silver.

As it is with most men, he turned his attention to pyramid building rather late in life. Lacking the arrogance or the resources of a Pharaoh, he planned a modest, four-sided structure encompassing a mere 3,600 square feet at the base. The blueprints called for the apex to rise 130 feet into the air, less than a third the height of Cheops, and his architects advised him to use concrete and steel in place of limestone blocks in the construction. Inside, instead of mummies, there would be examples of the greatest cultural treasures of our age, including an autographed copy of *Coin's Financial School.*

A site was selected in an isolated valley near Monte Ne, Arkansas, and soon Harvey raised enough cash to sink a shaft into the bedrock and begin laying a foundation. Then, as he had been forecasting for decades, the economy collapsed in a great depression. The flow of contributions dried up overnight. To save the pyramid and to save the country, supporters prevailed upon "Old Coin" to make a run for the presidency against Herbert Hoover and Franklin Delano Roosevelt. The results are history: Franklin Delano Roosevelt, 22,829,501; Herbert Hoover, 15,760,684; Coin Harvey, 800.

JOE HAYDEN At the age of 17, Joe Hayden announced he would play 180 simultaneous chess matches against 180 opponents at a Cardiff, New Jersey, shopping mall in 1977. But there were only 20 takers and Hayden was trounced by all but two of them. Among the 18 victors was seven-year-old Stowell Fulton who polished the teenager off in a half-dozen moves. One of the two Hayden beat was his own mother.

STEPHEN HOLCOMB The 100,000-mark German banknote Stephen Holcomb offered to the National Bank and Trust Company of Traverse City, Michigan, seemed legitimate in all ways, and the officers gladly paid him the going exchange rate of $39,700 cash. Holcomb, a 32-year-old window-washer, left the bank to embark on a two-week spree during which he purchased, among other items, a $7,000

4

delivery truck, a shotgun, a Panamanian cockatoo and a pistol. He also tipped a hotel elevator operator $900 before the police arrived to end the binge.

The problem was not with the bill's validity but rather its age. It had been printed in 1923, during the height of postwar inflation in Germany. Its value in 1976 was less than a penny.

Too embarrassed to discuss the matter, bank officials nonetheless sued Mr. Holcomb for the $18,177 he had spent. The outcome is so far unknown.

AUGUSTUS LE PLONGEON What Dr. Augustus Le Plongeon (1826–1908) didn't know about archaeology could fill several books—and did. A French-born "physician" with a self-conferred medical degree, Le Plongeon conceived an interest in ancient civilizations and was the first to excavate the Mayan ruins of the Yucatan. The marvels he found there were made even more marvelous by his over-active imagination. He claimed, for instance, to have translated the strange hieroglyphics found on the walls of Chichen Itza. They told the history of Mu, the queen of Atlantis, who had fled to Egypt when her kingdom sank beneath the waves, bringing with her the advanced Atlantean technology that made possible the construction of the pyramids. Other survivors of the inundation came to Mexico and intermarried with the Indians. Even more astonishing was Le Plongeon's discovery that Christ spoke Mayan on the Cross! There was only one problem: when anyone else tried to read the Mayan writings, even using the key provided by Le Plongeon, he got nowhere. Archaeology's greatest fiction writer married an American woman and settled in Brooklyn, where he authored a number of volumes denouncing with ever increasing bitterness those who questioned his singular theories.

JAMES MARSHALL On January 24, 1848, James Marshall, a workman from New Jersey spotted nuggets in Sutter's mill race near Sacramento, sparking the California gold rush. Thereafter he had trouble finding enough yellow metal to fill a rotten tooth. Other prospectors, thinking he was lucky, followed him around and staked out claims right next to his, to no avail. All around him men were getting rich, but Marshall remained dirt poor. The irony drove him out of his mind. He developed the delusion that he was the true and rightful owner of all the gold in California and finally caused such a fuss that he was forcibly excluded from most mining camps.

GLENN MOORE Gluttony, thy name is Glenn Moore: as a promotion gimmick a California eatery offered patrons "all the beer you can drink for a dollar." Wiseguy Moore downed two gallons in a little over four hours and then dropped dead.

DANIEL PRATT For half a century Daniel Pratt (1809–87), vagrant extraordinary, roamed the cities and backwoods of the United States headed nowhere in particular. He called himself the Great American Traveler, an epithet he earned by walking over two hundred thousand miles, visiting 27 states and 16 Indian tribes. For food and shelter he relied on the generosity of the people he met along the way, repaying them with wild stories about his troubles and adventures.

People said he was "brainsick," incurably insane; and it was true. During one of his 17 walks to Washington he arrived at the notion that he had been elected president and was being denied his rightful office by a conspiracy of his political rivals. His constituency was formed of students at the New England colleges he regularly visited. They listened intently to his eccentric lectures on "The Four Kingdoms," "The Harmony of the Human Mind," "The Solar System," and "The Vocabulaboratory of the Human Mind," admiring his oratorical style even if what he said didn't make much sense. Moreover, they were fiercely loyal to him, at times defending him with force when college officials sought to throw him off campus. At Dartmouth, a group of students and faculty expressed their affection for Pratt by conferring on him the honorary degree of COD: collect on delivery.

6

WAYNE REYNOLDS A police officer in Brooklyn, New York, Wayne Reynolds accidentally shot himself in the leg while dropping his gunbelt and pants in the stationhouse men's room.

ROSCOE SAPP Let us not be too harsh in our judgment of Roscoe Sapp, a would-be suicide of uniquely weak resolve. Sapp shinnied atop a 150-foot high construction crane in New York City's Times Square, intent on jumping to his death. Within minutes police talked him into abandoning his plans and climbing down in exchange for beer and crullers. He was served the snack at Bellevue Hospital, where he was taken for observation.

EUGENE SCHEIFFLIN Hail to thee, Eugene Scheifflin! Bird thou never wert. But please forgive us if we keep our hats on as we salute you.

In the 1880s and '90s, Scheifflin was a key member of the Acclimatization Society, those wonderful people who gave you starlings. It was the Acclimatization Society's chief mission to bring to American shores all manner of exotic fauna which Americans would otherwise never see. On March 6, 1890, Scheifflin led a crew of well-meaning Acclimatizers to New York City's Central Park, where they released 80 European starlings, driven by a desire to introduce to Americans at least one of every bird mentioned in Shakespeare's plays. ("I'll have a starling that shall be taught to speak nothing but 'Mortimer' ": *Henry IV.)*

Starlings, of course, have since grown to become a major health hazard for the very people Scheifflin hoped to enlighten, showering the nation's byways with their excretions, decimating wheat fields with the fury of a combine harvester, and spreading bacteria and calamity wherever they go. They are also dogged nesters who won't be displaced by other animals or seasonal changes. On April 25, 1891, Scheifflin released an additional squadron of starlings; soon thereafter, 20 of them were spotted in Staten Island several miles away. Starlings were nesting in Brooklyn by 1896, in Connecticut and New Jersey by 1898, and in Pennsylvania, Delaware, Long Island, and upstate New York by 1910. If Eugene Scheifflin were alive today, he'd doubtless protest, "It seemed like a good idea at the time."

GENERAL JOHN SEDGWICK   In his Civil War diary, *Touched With Fire,* Oliver Wendell Holmes, the elder, wistfully recalls the last words of General John Sedgwick. While supervising the emplacement of Union artillery during the battle of Spottsylvania, Sedgwick rebuked some men who were cowering to avoid enemy fire. "Come! Come!" he said, "Why, they couldn't hit an elephant at this dist. . . . "

WILLIAM JAMES SIDIS   Boris Sidis, a Russian-born professor of abnormal psychology, believed that geniuses are made and not born, and to prove his theories he was determined to mold his son into one of the greatest minds of the century. When his son William James Sidis (named for the famous Harvard psychologist) was just six months old, Boris turned the nursery into a laboratory, dangled alphabet blocks over the crib, hypnotized the child, and began to teach him how to read. By the age of three, baby William was composing stories in English and French on the typewriter. And by five he had mastered Latin and Greek, authored a treatise on anatomy, and developed a method for calculating the day of the week on which any date had fallen during the past ten thousand years.

In 1908, at the age of nine (and having recently proposed a new table of logarithms employing 12 rather than the usual 10 as the base), the wonder child was presented for matriculation at Harvard. But the admissions committee, while conceding that he was academically quite well prepared, deemed him emotionally too immature for college life. Come back when you're 11, they suggested. And so, shortly after his 11th birthday, when he was still wearing Little Lord Fauntleroy short pants and high-button shoes, the prodigious William James Sidis became the youngest Harvard freshman in history, supplanting Cotton Mather who was admitted in 1674 at the ripe old age of 12.

During his first year in college, he astounded the science faculty with a lecture on "Four-Dimensional Bodies." His teachers foresaw a brilliant future for the boy and predicted that he would soon be out-thinking Einstein. Then something came unhinged. Sidis suffered a nervous breakdown and for a time was institutionalized in his father's sanitorium at Portsmouth, New Hampshire. He returned to school, graduated *magna cum laude* at the age of sixteen, and briefly held a professorship at a university in Texas. Then suddenly he gave up all academic and intellectual pursuits and became a legendary underachiever. He made every effort to hide his past accomplishments, took only the most menial of jobs, and refused all promotions. He occupied his powerful intelligence with three subjects to the exclusion of all else: the culture of the Okamakammessett Indian tribe, the submerged continent of Atlantis, and—most obsessively—streetcar transfers.

He collected thousands of transfers from transportation systems all over the world, carefully preserving and cataloging each one. He haunted airports and train stations hoping to pick up rare transfers discarded by travelers from distant cities. At his own expense, he published an encyclopedic work entitled *Notes on the Collection of Transfers,* which sold fewer than fifty copies; and for a while he issued an irregular newsletter, *The Peridromophile.* ("Peridromophile" is a word he coined, meaning one who loves finding his way about.) Sidis once maintained that the greatest achievement of his life was a 15-hour continuous journey on the streetcars of New York during which he acquired 40 transfers—riding the entire distance on one fare.

In 1937 *The New Yorker* ran a "Where Are They Now?" story about his peculiar life. Sidis sued the magazine on the grounds that by reminding the public of his childhood as a prodigy the article made it impossible for him to get work as a clerk or dishwasher. Sidis protested that he had become

9

"an ordinary man" and was willing to undergo intelligence tests to prove it. The judge would not agree that Sidis was ordinary in any sense of the word, and the case was dismissed.

Once a reporter cornered him late in life and asked him how he felt about the prediction of Professor Daniel F. Comstock in 1910 that the little boy who lectured on the fourth dimension would "grow up to be a great mathematician, a famous leader in the world of science." "It's strange," said William James Sidis with a grin, "but, you know, I was born on April Fools' Day."

ELIZABETH TASHJIAN Elizabeth Tashjian's uncommon fondness for nuts dates back to her childhood. "My family always had large bowls of nuts on the tables in our home," she recalls. "Then one day I realized they were more than cold fossils. They're examples of primeval existence because they look ancient but are constantly new."

Today Miss Tashjian is the owner and curator of the na-

Elizabeth Tashjian, curator of the Nut Museum *(Kyn Tolson Photo)*

tion's one and only Nut Museum, located in Old Lyme, Connecticut (the Nutmeg State). The avowed purpose of this remarkable institution, housed in a gabled Victorian mansion with acorn cornices, is to educate people "on the worth of nuts, to give a fresh view of their importance." The price of admission is one nut and a one dollar contribution.

Few museums are so wonderfully odd. An eight-foot nutcracker hangs above the entranceway, and Miss Tashjian personally ushers all her visitors through the extensive collection of nut jewelry, doll house furniture carved from nuts, hooked rugs and paintings displaying nut motifs, as well as books and sheet music on nutty themes. In a gallery called "The Nutcracker Suite" dozens of rare antique nutcrackers are on display. And, of course, there are nuts—hundreds of them—from every corner of the world: commonplace filberts, cashews, and pistachios; exotica such as a Chinese horn chestnut and a heart nut from Japan; and even the world's largest nut, a thirty-five pound *coco de mer* from the Seychelles Islands in the Indian Ocean.

A graduate of the National Academy School of Fine Arts in New York, Miss Tashjian has been depicting nuts in oils since the 1930s. Like Georgia O'Keeffe, she scales up her subjects dramatically. "Nuts loom large in my vision, so I paint them large," she explains. She cuts a dramatic figure herself in the purple silk Armenian robe she often wears when conducting tours, and she is a walking repository of nut wisdom and lore. One learns, for instance, that King Solomon had walnut trees in his garden; that Swedes use walnuts for fish bait; that there are some forty ways to chew betel nuts; and that the female beechnut floats, while the male sinks like a stone.

In the past nuts have been the subject of scorn and derision, but Miss Tashjian is determined to change all that. "Do you realize that in 1950 it was forbidden for anyone at NBC to call someone a nut?" she asks indignantly. But while championing the virtues of nuts, she can hardly bring herself to serve them. "I shell a nut and suddenly I see that it's beautiful, and I lay it aside. I have to close my eyes to eat

11

them." Others have no such scruples. The Nut Museum has long been plagued by marauding squirrels and chipmunks, which make their nests in the walls, and on occasions have devoured some of the exhibits. The tolerant curator cannot bring herself to call the exterminator. "The squirrels may be starting a nut museum of their own," she says.

It's an improbable line of work, to be sure; and in 1974 when Miss Tashjian appeared on the quiz show "To Tell the Truth" she stumped the panel. She dreams of one day constructing a new museum building in the shape of a walnut. There would be arbors of sweet chestnuts, beeches, and pecans, and perhaps even a fountain with a squirrel that spouts water. Noting that the United States now has a peanut farmer as its president, she allows herself to hope that "Nuts are a subject whose time has come."

And maybe there is a kernel of truth in that.

CAPTAIN JAMES IREDELL WADDELL The history books say the Civil War ended when Lee surrendered to Grant at Appomattox Court House on April 9, 1865. Don't believe a word of it. When President Jefferson Davis heard the bad news he issued a proclamation stating that the South had "now entered on a new phase of the struggle, the memory of which is to endure for all ages." The final land battle of the war was fought at Palmetto Ranch near the Rio Grande—and the Confederates won!

Captain James Iredell Waddell (1824–86), commander of the C.S.S. *Shenandoah,* had heard of Lee's surrender, but he had also read Davis's Danville Proclamation urging loyal Southerners to fight on with renewed vigor. Waddell took the President at his word. He continued to follow his original, somewhat preposterous, orders to destroy Yankee whaling ships in the Pacific, cutting off the Union's supply of ambergris, blubber, and sperm oil. Before her voyage was over, the *Shenandoah* had sailed 70,000 miles, captured 38 vessels, destroyed $1.3 million worth of Union shipping, and taken 1,053 prisoners—most of this accomplished after hostilities were officially over.

From one captured whaler, Waddell learned that the port of San Francisco was guarded by a single ironclad gunboat, and he conceived a bold plan to take the city from the sea, enlist Confederate sympathizers into an army, and detach California from the Union. The *Shenandoah* was on her way to carry out the attack when she fell in with the British merchantman *Barracouta* a thousand miles west of Acapulco. Waddell asked for the latest news of the war.

"What war?" replied the puzzled skipper.

It was August 2, 1865, when Captain Waddell was finally forced to admit he had just been whistling Dixie for the past five months. He also realized that he and his crew were in a tough jam; if they landed in a United States port they would probably be hanged for piracy. The captain resolved to sail for England by way of Cape Horn, and on November 6, 1865, the *Shenandoah* surrendered to British authorities in Liverpool. Her ensign was the last flag of the Confederacy to be lowered and the only one to circumnavigate the globe.

WILLIAM H. WINDER General Winder first demonstrated his mettle at the Battle of Stony Creek, during the War of 1812. Backed by an American troop force triple the size of the opposing British contingent, he still managed to blow the contest and get himself taken prisoner. The British ultimately released Winder, no doubt realizing there was no more potent way of subverting America's military strength.

They were right. The following year, as the Britons hammered at Washington, D.C., commander Winder's resolve collapsed like a house of cards and he fled for his life. The British strolled languorously into the nation's capital and burned it to a crisp.

Derring-Doers

Steve Brodie jumped off the Brooklyn Bridge *(New York Public Library, Picture Collection)*

STEVE BRODIE   Steve Brodie was a Manhattan newsboy who wanted nothing more in this world than to make front-page headlines in the papers he sold. He finally made the evening editions on July 23, 1886, by jumping from the Brooklyn Bridge 130 feet into the East River—and living to tell the tale. Reporters dubbed him "the man who took a chance." An overnight celebrity, Brodie gave up his street corner stand, put together a vaudeville act, and toured theaters from Maine to California recreating his famous leap. With a cry of "I'll save the girl!" he would hop six feet from a cardboard bridge down onto the stage, while the propman provided a well-timed splash of confetti. Audiences loved it.

Time and again, Brodie was offered fabulous sums to repeat his dive off the Brooklyn Bridge, so photographers could snap pictures of the death-defying descent. "Nope," Brodie said. "Once is enough." Some people began to accuse him of cowardice. To bolster his sagging reputation, he once again consented to risk life and limb, this time by swimming the violent rapids below Niagara Falls. On September 7, 1889, dressed in an India rubber suit reinforced with steel bands, he plunged into the chilly waters and fought his way one-half mile downstream before being hauled ashore bruised and nearly drowned. The Brodie legend was secured.

An old story has survived about the time Jim Corbett's father ran into Steve Brodie in a bar. "So you're the fellow that jumped over the Brooklyn Bridge," the elderly gentleman said. "No, I jumped off it," Brodie corrected. "Ah," Corbett said with obvious disappointment, "I thought you jumped over it. Any damn fool could jump off it."

Whether he realized it or not, playwright Dan Cameron Rodill pulled a "brodie" (defined in *Webster's* as "a suicidal leap, hence a fall or flop"), when he alerted the news media and vaulted off the Brooklyn Bridge, August 21, 1977. His objective was to attract attention to his unproduced drama about the Vietnam War entitled *The Dry Season.* "I would like to have landed feet first, as I planned," he later told a *New York Times* reporter. Instead he hit the water in "the twentieth century's biggest belly flop." Authorities fished him out of the river with 13 broken ribs and severe lung damage. He spent a month in the hospital recuperating. Thus far the stunt has not paid off. A number of theaters have expressed interest in *The Dry Season,* but it has yet to be staged.

RONALD CHAMPLAIN Ronald Champlain—Master Chi to his followers—works best under pressure. On New Year's Day, 1976, he was at the Guinness World Records Exhibit Hall in New York to set a new record for major league masochism. He succeeded: Champlain had 1,410 pounds of weight lowered on him as he lay sandwiched like a slab of boiled ham between two beds of nails. He emerged unscathed. (His pregame practice drills consisted of having his assistants assault him wildly with an axe and a steel spike. The axe scratched him, the spike did not.)

"Pain is only when you accept it," Mr. Champlain later philosophized, announcing his intention of having himself run over by a 44-passenger schoolbus and jumping, without a parachute, from an airplane a mile over the water.

ANTHONY DiSTASIO With disaster movies like *Earthquake* and the *Towering Inferno* doing so well at the box-office, maybe the time is right for a blockbuster film based on that ghastly, mucilaginous, real-life catastrophe—The Great Boston Molasses Flood. It was extremely cinematic. At 12:30 P.M. on January 15, 1919, a giant storage vat at the Purity Distilling Company on Commercial Street ruptured, spilling 2.5 million gallons of black molasses (enough to make one gingerbread man for every man, woman, and child in the United States) into Boston's crowded business district. Silently, inexorably, a tremendous wall of hot treacle, 15 feet deep and 100 yards wide, oozed toward the sea, destroying everything in its path.

Six small children from the Michelangelo School, on their way home to lunch, were caught by surprise and drowned. The Atlantic Avenue elevated line was demolished only seconds after a train bound for Charlestown passed overhead. Six city workers suddenly found themselves in syrup over their heads and died a cloying death. A fireman lost his life when a station house collapsed. The freight yard of the Bay State Railway was engulfed in goo and destroyed. And by the time the black tide subsided 21 persons had lost their lives in pancake topping.

If Hollywood does make a movie of the tragedy, the hero will be Anthony DiStasio (a perfect part for Charlton Heston). When the wave of molasses hit him, DiStasio somehow had the presence of mind to slosh his way to the crest. Then, in a superhuman effort, he body-surfed all the way through Boston's North End until the molasses poured into Boston Harbor. Pitched from the hot molasses into the freezing water, he lapsed into unconsciousness. When his body, coated like a caramel apple, was recovered from the harbor, a doctor on the scene pronounced him dead. A police ambulance carried him to the city morgue and his sisters were summoned to identify him. But when the coroner drew back the sheet, DiStasio regained his senses and sprang to his feet, gluey and dizzy—but alive.

ARCHIBALD C. EVERETT   When his investments turned to mush before his very eyes, Archibald C. Everett, a Wall Street stockbroker in the late 1800s, boarded the nearest whaling ship and some months later found himself on Arorai, in the Gilbert Islands. There, among the banana fronds and the soulful call of the *chikchak,* he quickly made friends with King Roraka, who as quickly offered him his daughter's hand.

Soon thereafter, Roraka died and Everett became king. He lived in apparent bliss among the cannibals of Arorai forevermore, returning once to New York, as King Everett I, on a state visit in the spring of 1911. At that time he told a *New York Sun* reporter that he'd acquired over 200 wives since his coronation, far more than he would have preferred, but that he found himself unable to refuse any woman who offered to be his bride.

ANGELO FATICONI   Faticoni, alias "The Human Cork," swam from Manhattan's West Side across the Hudson River to New Jersey—bound fast to a chair laden with 40 pounds of lead.

ZOE GAYTON   In the summer of 1890 the West Coast newspapers were asplash with reports of a daring, perhaps suicidal expedition: The first horseback ride across the United States, just completed by a New York City hotelkeeper and a professor of penmanship. But a young San Franciscan named Zoe Gayton read the news and sneered.

She could make the same trip on *foot,* she boasted, and set out from Oakland on August 27, accompanied by two men and a pair of poodles.

Rather than chance getting lost, Miss Gayton & co. trod the railway tracks all 3,400 miles. It was dangerous business and one of the two dogs was squashed by a train. But Miss Gayton's fame preceded her and brakemen and engineers took special pains to ensure her safety, dubbing her the "Sunset Special." Carrying a suitcase packed with linens and other items, she traveled at a good clip, once covering 193 miles in a single week, and arrived in New York's Franklin Square on April 9, 1891.

CARL HAFFKE Bored with his job as a Western Union messenger in Omaha, Carl Haffke joined the navy and served in Manila under Admiral Dewey. He remained in the Philippines after his discharge, where he worked as a court reporter. Always the diplomat, Haffke got on the good side of a band of Ilocano chieftains involved in a legal dispute arbitrated in his court; when a cholera epidemic wiped out that tribe's royal line he was invited to become their king.

The German-born Haffke was crowned King Carlos I of the Ilocanos. He introduced modern farming techniques to his people and then left for Nebraska after a year to marry his fiancée. Despite his promises to return with his bride, King Carlos found Omaha more to his liking than the Philippines. He married, started a law firm, and remained there for the rest of his life.

JAMES HARDEN-HICKEY There lay Trinidad, lush, verdant Trinidad, 700 miles off the coast of Brazil, in the South Atlantic, six miles wide, ten miles long, and just crying out for some elegantly dressed Caucasian to bring order and good table manners to its dark-skinned peoples. So in 1893, James A. Harden-Hickey, satirist, Catholic-turned-Buddhist, and husband of a Standard Oil heiress, bought a full-rigged schooner, printed postage stamps bearing his likeness, fashioned himself a gold crown, and proclaimed himself king, president, and military dictator of the tiny island (not to be confused with its larger, Caribbean namesake). He established a colony of 40 Americans there and made plans to mine the island's rich stores of bat guano. But in 1895 Great Britain took over the island, elbowing Harden-Hickey aside without so much as a nod of thanks, and in 1896 Brazil took it over from Britain. And Harden-Hickey, who called himself Baron, was a dictator without a country.

At this juncture the Baron returned to his native New York and took up the pensive life. His most famous work, *Euthanasia: The Aesthetics of Suicide,* was published by the Truth Seeker Company, an antireligious society and publishing house that had also offered such works as *What Would Christ Do About Syphilis?* In presenting his book to a world-weary public, the Baron assembled some 400 quotations from the world's greatest thinkers, claiming only to have written the preface. (He lied: most of the quotes he made up himself.) The point of it all was that suicide is good for you. The Baron suggested that there were 88 poisons and 51 instruments that could be used for dispatching oneself in style, although he was partial to wolfsbane and scissors. One illustration shows a well-dressed dandy in his death throes, a drained tumbler of poison beside him. Another shows a full-dressed man sitting contemplatively on the edge of his bed, holding a pistol to his head.

"May this little work contribute to the overthrow of the reign of fear," Harden-Hickey wrote. "May it nerve the faltering arm of the poor wretch to whom life is loathsome. . . . The only remedy for a life of misery is death; if you are tired and weary, if you are the victim of disease or misfortune, drop the burden of life, fly away!" In 1898, depressed over his father-in-law's inexplicable unwillingness to lend him the money he would need to launch an invasion of England, the Baron ended his own life with an overdose of morphine.

HUGH HURST When the engine on his 1960 Ford Falcon conked out, 63-year-old Hugh Hurst of Amenia, New York, prevailed upon his wife to drive him to the train station each morning in time for him to catch the 5:19 to Brewster. There he would change for the 6:09 to New York City, 90 miles to the south, where he worked as a loan officer at the Manufacturers Hanover Trust Company.

But Mrs. Hurst soon grew weary of playing predawn chauffeur, whereupon her husband dispensed with her services and assumed what is unquestionably the most heroic commuting grind in modern history. From March, 1977, through his retirement a year later, Hurst traveled an Odyssean ten hours a day to and from work, powered by shoe leather, thumb, and commutation ticket. The day's labors typically began at 3:15 A.M., when he arose, showered, donned multiple layers of sweaters, a pair of rubber hunting boots, and a Seven Dwarfs woolen cap for visibility's sake. By four he would be hiking out to the highway thence to head south, thumb extended, hoping for a ride to the Dover Plains station, where he would pick up the 5:19. Motorists would be scarce at that hour, and Mr. Hurst mustered all the resourcefulness he could so as not to blow potential rides. "When the temperature rises above 20 degrees," he told the *Wall Street Journal,* "I take off my overcoat so people can see my business suit. That way I avoid being mistaken for an escapee from the State Mental Hospital along the route."

Two mornings out of four Mr. Hurst would land a ride that would get him to the Brewster station in time to make the 5:19. "The real adventure begins when I miss the 5:19," he said. "At that time of day only four or five cars pass by in an hour." With luck Mr. Hurst would flag one down en route to a station south of Dover Plains, where he could catch up with the missed train. In his first seven months he rendezvoused with the 5:19 at 11 different railroad stations.

Whatever his luck at Dover Plains, Mr. Hurst invariably caught up with the southbound train and would arrive at Grand Central Station in midtown Manhattan around 7:30. He would hang out in a coffee shop for a bit, then get back on a *northbound* for the ten-minute ride back to his job in East Harlem.

20

The commute home was equally grueling: a 5:10 train would get Mr. Hurst to Brewster in time for the 7:01 to Dover Plains. Arriving there at 7:47, he'd hike a half-mile to Highway 22 and try to thumb a ride back to Amenia. Some nights he'd be home by nine, just in time to say good-night to his eight-year-old son. Other times he'd give it till ten, then call his wife to pick him up. He would watch an hour of TV and retire at 11—supperless—setting the alarm for 3:15.

As tortuous as his daily travels might seem, no one was bending Mr. Hurst's arm. His wife told friends that her husband "thrived" on the ten-hour commute and Hurst rejected suggestions that he simply repair his car and dispense with the hitchhiking. "I'm not sure I want to give up the adventure and the interesting people I'm meeting by commuting this way," he said. Besides, there was always the perverse thrill of being rescued from the subzero chill by a passing motorist.

Eventually, Hurst became something of a celebrity and even a minor legend in Amenia and environs. One man who'd picked him up recalls the eerie circumstances surrounding his first predawn encounter with Hurst: "It was dark when I picked him up and dark when I dropped him off and his story was so strange that I recall wondering later that day whether I had imagined the whole thing." But the driver saw Hurst that evening hitchhiking once again in Dover Plains, "so I had to believe it."

JOHN DAVIS MURRAY   John Murray's first job after he was graduated from Purdue University in 1891 with a degree in mechanical engineering was with the British-based Phosphate Mining and Shipping Company. The company's holdings included the Christmas Islands, 250 miles southwest of Java, and young Murray was sent there to supervise the phosphate mining operations carried on by natives in the employ of the company. To ensure that Murray's directions would be followed the company made him king of the Christmas Islands, investing him formally with the title at a great ceremony. In addition to riding herd on the miners and seeing that excavations went smoothly, he adminstered the laws, held court, settled labor disputes, and in general ruled gently, justly—and absolutely.

Murray didn't die a regent. As King John he visited London in 1910, fell in love and got married. Living among the savages, even as their queen, did not strike his wife as the way she'd like to spend the rest of her life, and rather than argue her down or leave her, King John abdicated his throne for the woman he loved and settled in England.

WALTER NILSSON On a dare from Robert "Believe-It-or-Not!" Ripley, bicycling great Walter Nilsson attempted to pedal from New York City to the West Coast in 1934 atop an 8.5-foot unicycle. Nilsson covered the 3,306 miles in 117 days without falling once and when he wobbled into San Francisco crowds mobbed him as if he were a second Lindbergh. Unfortunately, the trip was so grueling that Nilsson suffered back pains for the rest of his life.

DAVID O'KEEFE The sea was David O'Keefe's life and his livelihood as well, so his wife and infant daughter hardly protested when he left them behind in Savannah, Georgia, in 1871 and boarded a China-bound ship. But O'Keefe never reached Shanghai; he was shipwrecked near the Yap Islands in the South Pacific. Seduced by the balmy quiet and promise of a life of indolence, O'Keefe remained in Yap long enough to befriend the natives, build a home, make himself popular, and acquire real estate. Within a few years he had muscled aside Yap's ruling chieftains, taken their property, and declared himself King David of Yap. He built a castle, designed a new flag—the letters "O'K" figured prominently in it—and dutifully sent his wife a portion of his income twice a year. He also promised her repeatedly that he would soon come home.

But returning seemed unlikely. King David took a Yapian wife, an obese, giggling virgin hand-picked by the island's elders and forced on the "bachelor" king. Dubbed Queen Dollyboy, she bore seven children. Still he persisted in his vows to return to Savannah. In 1901, he set out for Hong Kong with two of his sons aboard the royal schooner *Santa Cruz*. Whether he finished the journey is uncertain, but he and his two boys were never heard from again.

The king's will was read two years later by a Philadelphia lawyer who journeyed to Yap at the first Mrs. O'Keefe's asking. Although he left over a million dollars, she was cut out without a cent. But her daughter, Queen Dollyboy, and Queen Dollyboy's sons profited handsomely.

ELM FARM OLLIE On February 18, 1939, Elm Farm Ollie became the first American cow to fly in an airplane. She was accompanied by an army of newsmen who watched in delight as she was milked in midflight, and the milk sealed in paper containers and dropped by parachute over St. Louis.

ANNIE SMITH PECK Never was there a more unlikely-looking mountaineer. Far from being the Amazon everyone imagined, Annie Smith Peck (1850–1935) was slight, feminine, and bookish—the very picture of a classics professor, which indeed she was for nine months of the year. But from the moment she first saw "the frowning walls" of the Matterhorn, Annie Peck was consumed by an insatiable passion to stand atop the highest peaks in the world.

After scaling a number of formidable mountains in Europe and California, she became the first woman to reach the top of the Matterhorn, a feat which brought her instant fame and instant scandal. Her outfit, consisting of knickerbockers, hip-length tunic, woolen hose, and a soft felt hat with a veil, was considered even more daring than her ascent. In 1895, with woman suffrage still 25 years away, it was thought a Smith College professor should climb in skirts and a whalebone corset, if at all.

Sexist criticism only fired her ambition to conquer "some height where no *man* has previously stood." She went hunting for virgin peaks among the far-flung ranges of Europe, Mexico, and South America. Following two unsuccessful attempts, she became the first person of either sex to reach the apex of 21,812-foot Mount Huascarán, then thought to be the highest point in the Americas. (In 1927 the Lima Geographical Society named the treacherous north peak of Huascarán "Aña Peck" in her honor.) Well beyond her sixtieth birthday, Miss Peck continued to tackle mountains that men had never climbed, planting "Votes for Women" pennants on the summits.

FRANK PERKINS Frank Perkins recently established a new world record for pole sitting, staying aloft 399 days from June 1, 1975, to July 4, 1976, in San Jose, California. He had plenty to think about while perched in an eight-foot square box mounted on a fifty-foot telephone pole: the company sponsoring the stunt went out of business, his telephone and utilities were shut off, and his girlfriend left him for another man.

GEORGE POLLEY Decades before George Willig wriggled up the side of New York City's World Trade Center, George Polley had scaled some 2,000 office buildings from Boston to Seattle, earning the title "The Human Fly." But unlike Willig, Polley's motives were not always the loftiest. His fee for climbing a building was $200 and his skill was much in demand among department store owners, theater managers, and publicity-mad mayors.

In his prime Polley conquered such towers as Boston's 500-foot-tall Custom House and the 57-story Woolworth Building in lower Manhattan, then the tallest building in the world. On a particularly busy day in Hartford he bagged three buildings, and once in Providence he made it to the top of a flagpole blindfolded.

But Polley was no madman. He was compulsive about taking proper safety precautions and never attempted a structure of any sort before submitting it to a rigorous pre-climb check. He did enjoy giving the crowds a thrill, though, and was not above faking a slip. But it wasn't his work that was his undoing. He died of a brain tumor, in bed, at the age of 29.

OWEN J. QUINN In the summer of 1975, leisure-time skydiver Owen J. Quinn disguised himself as a construction worker and thereby slipped past security guards manning the doors to the roof of New York City's 110-story-high World Trade Center. Briefly eyeing the city below him, he changed into jumping gear—sweatshirt, shorts, helmet, and parachute—and jumped.

In the two minutes it took Quinn to fall the 110 stories, he was slammed against the side of the building repeatedly by heavy winds. But the biggest scare came when he pulled his rip-cord after free-falling 600 feet and nothing happened. "I knew that might happen on a jump from that altitude, because you don't have a lot of speed built up," Quinn later said. "It was a bit of a shock, but I just sort of looked at it and at that instant it opened."

Shortly after landing, setting himself aright and limping away from the point of impact, he was handcuffed by police, put in a wheelchair, and taken directly to Beekman Downtown Hospital, where psychiatrists deemed him mentally competent. While at the hospital, he told physicians and reporters that his jump was less a lark than a political statement.

"If people decided not to eat once a month," he said, "and to send the money to the needy poor, then it would help the situation."

ARNO RUDOLPHI They said it would never last, but on August 25, 1940 at the New York World's Fair Grounds, Arno Rudolphi and Ann Hayward became the first couple in history to be married in a parachute. Floating earthward, the bride-and-groom-to-be were wedded by the Reverend Homer Tomlinson of the Church of God (Jamaica, N.Y.) who accompanied them in his own chute, as did the maid of honor, the best man, and a four-piece band.

THOMAS STEVENS Thomas Stevens had never owned a bicycle and didn't know how to ride one; he was, in fact, a most unpromising candidate to become the most famous wheelman in the world. Nonetheless, after just a few short days of practice on an awkward highwheeler, he left San Francisco on April 22, 1884, bound for. . . . San Francisco.

His arduous transcontinental route took him east through mountains, deserts, and forests on rugged trails where covered wagons had passed not many years before. He pedaled across this difficult terrain high atop his boneshaking "ordinary," a cumbersome seventy-five pound machine with a front wheel measuring 50 inches in diameter and a back wheel 17 inches in diameter. For long stretches he pushed or carried his bicycle as often as it carried him. Steering around tight curves was next to impossible, and when racing down the Sierras at speeds up to 50 miles an hour his brake spoons glowed red hot. Worst of all, the smallest pothole could send the precariously perched cyclist toppling headfirst into the roadway. As a matter of self-preservation, Stevens practiced taking headfalls until he could tumble off his saddle as gracefully as a circus gymnast.

All in all it was an adventurous crossing. He was pursued by packs of howling coyotes, cursed by horsemen whose steeds bolted at the sight of him, and on one occasion forced to ride through an obstacle course of pool tables for the entertainment of a bunch of drunken cowpokes who fired bullets through his spokes. His closest call came in the Rockies when, halfway across a railroad bridge, he met a barreling locomotive coming the other way; he dangled from the side of the trestle, bicycle and all, until the train passed.

When Stevens arrived in Boston exactly 103.5 days after setting out from the West Coast, he was a hero and he was broke. For several months it appeared he would have to content himself with being the first person to cross the continent on a bike, giving up his around-the-world dream. Then Colonel A. A. Pope, a prosperous bicycle manufacturer, came forward and agreed to bankroll the remainder of the expedition. Stevens immediately set sail for Europe.

He pedaled on mile after mile through England, France, Germany, Austria-Hungary, Serbia, Turkey, Persia, India, China, and Japan, while back home thousands of Americans followed his progress in the newspapers. In remote areas of Asia he attracted crowds numbering in the tens of thousands who had never seen a bicycle. Eastern potentates loaded him down with valuable gifts that slowed his pace. Finally, on January 4, 1887, he arrived back in San Francisco on board the *City of Peking*, having made about 13,500 miles on his own power in less than three years.

ROY C. SULLIVAN If you ever visit Shenandoah National Park, don't stand next to Park Ranger Roy C. Sullivan. Or at least check the weather forecast before you do. Known as the "Human Lightning Rod," Sullivan has been struck seven times by forked high-tension bolts (the first in 1942, the most recent in 1977) and miraculously survived. For some reason no one has been able to explain, Sullivan attracts electrical discharges the way some people attract mosquitoes. The "current events" have left a trail of scars. Over the years, he has lost a big toenail, had his hair and eyebrows set on fire, suffered severe burns on his shoulders and stomach, and had several Ranger hats cremated right on top of his head.

JOHN CLEVES SYMMES In 1823 Captain John Cleves Symmes, a hero of the War of 1812, brought his extraordinary case to Congress. "I declare," he declared, "the earth is hollow and habitable within, containing a number of solid concentric spheres, and that it is open at the poles twelve or sixteen degrees." All he asked of the lawmakers was a ship and a few brave scientists to accompany him in the descent through the "Symmes Hole" at the North Pole, where "we will find a warm and rich land, stocked with thrifty vegetables and animals, if not men. . . . We'll plant Old Glory on those interior planets," he promised.

Captain Symmes was an immensely popular figure on the lecture circuit and thousands of Americans, moved by his marvelous arguments, petitioned Congress to help "our modern-day Columbus" finance his journey to the center of the earth. Richard M. Johnson of Kentucky (q.v.), who later became vice-president, championed Symmes's cause on the House floor and finally forced the question to a vote. The proposal was defeated, but 25 visionary representatives did vote in favor of the subterranean expedition.

Circumventing the legislative branch, John J. Reynolds, an influential Symmes disciple, persuaded the secretaries of the navy and treasury under President John Quincy Adams to outfit three ships to be placed at the explorer's disposal. Before the adventurers could set sail, however, Andrew Jackson came into office and scuttled the plan.

Captain Symmes died in 1829, but his vacuous theory survived him, inspiring a short story by Edgar Allan Poe ("Narrative of A. Gordon Pym") and Jules Verne's famous novel about the underground world. In 1878 the captain's son, Americus Vespucius Symmes, edited his father's collected works, and hypothesized that the inhabitants of the inner earth were the ten lost tribes of Israel. Symmes's theory continued to interest unconventional thinkers until Robert Peary reached 90° N in 1909 and found no hole.

ANNA EDSON TAYLOR   If such things must be proved, Anna Edson Taylor, a 43-year-old widowed schoolteacher, established once and for all, in front of a thousand witnesses, that a woman can be as reckless as a man, and more so. On October 24, 1901, she squeezed into a specially constructed barrel measuring four-and-a-half-feet high and three feet in diameter. For protection she had leather shoulder straps and cushions; at her feet was a 100-pound blacksmith's anvil to keep the craft upright in the water. Her air supply came through a rubber hose connected to a small opening near the lid.

A boat towed the barrel and passenger out into the turbulent Niagara River to a point near Grass Island. Then at exactly 4:05 P.M. the line was cut and the barrel shot downstream, bobbing crazily. At 4:23 it reached the brink of

Anna Edson Taylor, rescued after going over Niagara Falls in a barrel *(New York Public Library, Picture Collection)*

Horseshoe Falls on the Canadian side, poised there for a reluctant moment, and plummeted 158 feet straight down into the swirling eddies below. For sixty long seconds the barrel disappeared from sight before it finally popped up several hundred yards below the falls. Seventeen minutes later a team of men recovered the barrel, which had to be sawed apart to extricate the dizzy female daredevil. She had been knocked unconscious and blood was pouring from a three-inch gash on her forehead. When she had recovered enough to speak, Mrs. Taylor warned others never to attempt "the foolish thing I have done"; good advice from the first person ever to go over Niagara Falls and survive.

Bobby Leach didn't listen. In 1911 he became the first man to equal Mrs. Taylor's feat. It took him six months to recover. Jean Lussier made the treacherous descent on July 4, 1928, traveling first class in a 750-pound rubber ball fully equipped with emergency oxygen tanks. The giant Spaulding cost him $1,485 to construct.

John A. "Snowshoe" Thomson
(Rita L. Moroney/United
States Postal Service)

JOHN A. (SNOWSHOE) THOMSON   To the snowbound miners of the high Sierras the sight of John A. Thomson sweeping down the mountainside on his "gliding shoes" was as welcome as four aces in a poker game. During January and February it was not uncommon for 25-foot snowdrifts to pile up in the main streets of little towns like Meadow Lake and Poker Flat, cutting off all communication with the outside world. Then in 1856 the postmaster in Sacramento put out a call for an able-bodied man to carry the mail between Hangtown (now Placerville), California, on the west side of the Sierra range, and Genoa, Nevada, on the east; a distance of ninety frozen miles through the Carson Pass. It had been tried before. Three years earlier "Daddy" Dritt and "Cock-Eye" Johnson had attempted the dangerous crossing on "snowshoes" (as skis were called in that region) and had nearly lost their lives. John Thomson was made of better stuff.

He was born Jon Thoreson Rue in Telemark, Norway, but

in 1837 at the age of ten he emigrated with his parents to America. In 1851 he joined the gold rush to Diamond Springs and Hangtown, arriving after all the richest deposits had been claimed. He never managed to pan much gold, nor was he very successful as a rancher. But owing to the skills he had learned on the steep Norwegian slopes he became the most famous postman in the Old West.

Thomson set out from Hangtown with a 100-pound letter sack on his back and a pair of 12-foot wooden slats strapped to his feet. He coated the underside of his skis with "dope," a waxy concoction that enabled him to attain giddy speeds of up to 90 miles per hour on the downhill. For braking and maneuvering he carried a single spruce pole. En route he ate nothing but pemmican and crackers; he melted snow for his drinking water. At night he slept in the open with his feet toward a burning stump and his head resting on his mailbag. When he arrived in Genoa, his red beard was glazed with ice. It had taken him just three days to complete a journey no man had ever made before in midwinter. On his return trip to Hangtown he cut his time to two days.

For the next 13 years, until the Central Pacific Railroad was completed in 1869, Thomson was the only wintertime postal link between California and the rest of the Union. His compensation was minimal; he charged a dollar for each letter he delivered when the addressee could afford it, which wasn't often. In his spare time he organized the first downhill races in this country. Obscure towns like Port Wine and La Porte became hotbeds of competitive skiing, with the miners wagering thousands of dollars in gold dust on inter-city events.

"Snowshoe" Thomson was a hero in the Carson Valley, and when the railroad put him out of business, the settlers of the Sierra highlands drew up a petition asking Congress to grant their skiing mailman a $6,000 pension for his services. Before Congress could act, Thomson was dead at the age of 49. The bargirls of Genoa donated their best black velvet dresses to line his coffin.

George Francis Train, the model for Phileas Fogg *(The Library Of Congress)*

GEORGE FRANCIS TRAIN   George Francis Train (1829–1904) was a man of many accomplishments, great and small. He was the first to put rubber erasers on the tips of pencils and the first to suggest that postage stamps be perforated for easier tearing. He went to Melbourne during the gold rush, where he introduced canned goods, Fourth of July celebrations, and bowling. When a band of miners rebelled against the British Crown, they offered Train the presidency of the independent Australian republic they were trying to establish. He wisely declined the honor. He made a colossal fortune in the shipping business, and another by organizing the Credit Mobilier scheme to finance construction of the Union Pacific Railroad. Soon the Credit Mobilier collapsed in scandal, but by that time Train had gone on to bigger and more splendid scandals.

It was from a Dublin jail cell, during one of the 15 sentences he served for assorted political crimes, that he announced his intention to seek high elective office in the

United States: "I am that wonderful, eccentric, independent, extraordinary genius and political reformer of America, who is sweeping off all the politicians before him like a hurricane, your modest, diffident, unassuming friend, the future President of America—George Francis Train." He had no trouble financing his aggressive campaign. He simply charged admission to the more than one thousand speeches he delivered. When the votes were counted in November, 1872, Train finished a distant last, trailing even the prohibitionist James Black and the feminist, free-love candidate Victoria Woodhull. But he was $90,000 richer for the effort.

In the midst of the presidential race he took time out for a whirlwind trip around the world, delighting in the mixed public baths of Yokohama, and joining the Communards in their revolution against the Third Republic in France. He was arrested, nearly sent before a firing squad, and ultimately deported. Arriving back in the United States, he recounted his adventures for the benefit of newspaper reporters. A French novelist named Jules Verne was fascinated by Train's fabulous journey and used him as the model for Phileas Fogg in *Around the World in Eighty Days.*

In 1873 Train's old radical rival Victoria Woodhull was jailed for publishing the sordid details of the Reverend Henry Ward Beecher's adulterous relationship with Elizabeth Tilton. Gallantly rising to Woodhull's defense, Train printed three columns of sexy quotations culled from the Old Testament in his newspaper, *The Train Ligne.* "Every verse I used was worse than anything published by these women," he said. Law enforcement officials agreed and he was promptly jailed for obscenity. Against Train's wishes, his attorney entered a plea of not guilty by reason of insanity. (After all, William Lloyd Garrison, the abolitionist leader, had once denounced him as a "crack-brained harlequin and semi-lunatic.") Train was freed. In protest he walked out of jail wearing nothing but an umbrella.

Train again circumnavigated the globe in 1892 and "eclipsed all previous records," making it in sixty days flat. "I have lived fast," he declared. "I have ever been an advocate of speed. I was born into a slow world, and I wished to oil the wheels and gear, so that the machine would spin faster and, withal, to better purposes." Ever hasty, he dictated his autobiography in 1902 in just 35 hours. During his last years, for reasons known only to himself, the man who styled himself the "Champion Crank" spurned all conversation with adults and would only speak to little children he met in the park.

EDWARD PAYSON WESTON   As a young man of seventeen Edward Payson Weston (1839–1929) joined the circus and became a drummer in the band. Not long afterward he was struck by lightning, which he took as a sign that God did not approve of circus life. He returned to his parents' home in Providence, Rhode Island, where he subsisted by peddling his mother's novels *(Kate Felton* was her chef-d'oeuvre) door-to-door, some days walking as far as 50 miles to make a sale.

During the presidential campaign of 1860 Weston wagered a friend that Stephen Douglas would defeat Abraham Lincoln; under the terms of the bet the loser was to walk from Boston to Washington, a distance of 478 miles, to attend the victorious candidate's inauguration. True to his word, Weston started down the State House steps at exactly one o'clock on February 22, 1861. For the next ten days he set a steady pace of three-and-a-quarter miles per hour. He plodded through foot-deep snow banks in Leicester, Massachusetts; he ate his breakfast and lunch on the hoof, usually doughnuts and sandwiches proffered by well-wishers as he strode past; many nights he slept alongside the road. On reaching Philadelphia, however, he treated himself to a room in the plush Continental Hotel. A bellboy tried to usher him into the new steam elevator, but Weston declared, "I will not alter my mode of travel," and climbed the stairs instead. As he neared his destination, Weston attracted more and more attention. The newspapers wondered how a man who weighed just 130 pounds could exhibit such endurance. In one town he was mobbed by young ladies who requested

Edward Weston (right) during the six-day walking match *(New York Public Library, Picture Collection)*

that their kisses be relayed to the president. Driving rains and muddy roads plagued him on the last leg of his journey. He arrived at the Capitol steps on March 4, at 5 P.M., just ten days and four hours after leaving Boston, but too late to witness the swearing-in ceremony. Still, he was in time to attend the Inauguration Ball where he danced all night and magnanimously shook Lincoln's hand.

For his trouble Weston earned a bag of peanuts—another provision of the original wager—and a job as a police reporter with the *New York Herald.* In those days before telephones his speed and endurance afoot gave him a competitive edge over his fellow journalists.

Wanderlust eventually led him to quit the *Herald* and begin a colorful career as a combination professional athlete and gambler. On October 29, 1867, he began a trek from Portland, Maine, to Chicago, a distance of 1,326 miles, wagering $10,000 he could make State Street in 26 days. He cut a colorful figure with his red velvet tunic, high gaiters, silk derby, and a "swagger stick" he used to smack unfriendly dogs. Soon Weston was so far ahead of schedule that he could spare the time to deliver temperance lectures along the way and attend church services every Sunday. He easily won his bet and the newspapers were filled with stories of "The Great Pedestrian Feat." (Forty years later he walked the same route out of nostalgia and bettered his record by 29 hours.)

Once he walked 100 measured miles in Westchester County, New York, in 21 hours, 19 minutes, and 10 seconds. And in 1879 he captured the Astley Belt, the world championship of walking, by defeating "Blower" Brown, England's finest, on a London track. Weston covered 550 miles in six days and copped a $2,500 side bet from Sir John Astley himself. But his remarkable achievement came in 1909 when he crossed from New York to San Francisco *and back,* 7,495 miles, in 181 days, a record that stands to this day; he was seventy years old at the time.

In 1927, while strolling down a Brooklyn street, Edward Weston, history's greatest pedestrian, was struck by a taxicab and paralyzed; two years later he died of complications resulting from the accident.

BRUCE WILLIAMS Now for a true-life story of rare personal courage and determination to overcome a crippling disability. According to the Associated Press, alleged holdup man Bruce Williams was shot and paralyzed from the waist down during a reported attempted motel robbery in Cleveland on May 3, 1977. A lesser man might have given up and resigned himself to an invalid's life. But Williams was made of sterner stuff. Within a year he was charged with five additional crimes, including robbery, theft, and kidnapping, all committed from the confines of his wheelchair. From the descriptions provided by the victims, Cleveland police had little difficulty in locating their suspect. Following his arrest, Williams voiced loud objection to the way the law enforcement system treats the handicapped. "They pick on me," he said.

PLENNIE L. WINGO Like Edward Weston (q.v.), Plennie L. Wingo of Abilene,Texas, was an inveterate pedestrian. On April 15, 1931, he left Santa Monica, California, bound east while looking west. He arrived in Istanbul, Turkey, on October 24, 1932, having traversed an 8,000 mile route across two continents, walking the entire distance *backward.* For hindsight he wore a pair of specially designed reflective glasses.

Then, in 1977, at the age of 81, he celebrated the forty-fifth anniversary of his marathon reverse promenade by hiking backward from Santa Monica to San Francisco, a trek of 452 miles in a leisurely 85 days.

Deceivers

CASSIE CHADWICK It all began when Mrs. Cassie Chadwick, the wife of a respected Cleveland physician, chanced to bump into a talkative Ohio attorney named Dillon in the lobby of New York's posh Holland House hotel. They chatted for a few minutes about mutual friends, then Mrs. Chadwick asked if he would be so kind as to accompany her to her father's home, where she had a brief appointment that afternoon. Dillon chivalrously agreed. A carriage was summoned. And 50 minutes later the lawyer was flabbergasted to find himself parked in front of the palatial Fifth Avenue mansion belonging to Andrew Carnegie, probably the richest man in the world.

While Dillon waited and wondered outside, Mrs. Chadwick entered the front door of the Carnegie abode and remained inside for nearly half an hour before emerging with a fond wave to a well-dressed man at the window, presumably the steel tycoon himself. Lost in thought, Cassie stumbled momentarily as she climbed back into the carriage and a slip of paper fell from her hand. Dillon leaned down, retrieved the paper, glanced at it casually, and nearly split a gut. There, in his hand, he was holding a $2 million promissory note bearing Andrew Carnegie's own signature.

During the trip back to the hotel, Dillon pressured the flustered matron into revealing her sordid family history. She was, she confessed, Andrew Carnegie's illegitimate daughter. The note Dillon happened to see was just one of many, amounting to over $7 million, that the rich old fornicator had given her out of a sense of guilt. Her own shame and fear of scandal had kept her from drawing on them, or even depositing them in a bank. Finally, after pledging Dillon to hold these disclosures in strictest confidence, she tearfully explained that she would inherit $400 million when Carnegie died.

Sworn to silence, Dillon returned to Cleveland and promptly told everyone he knew about the heretofore secret Chadwick fortune. At length, he convinced Cassie to put her notes (previously stashed in a desk drawer) into a local bank for safe keeping. Informed beforehand by Dillon that he was dealing with Cassie *Carnegie* Chadwick, the bank officer issued a receipt without even bothering to look inside the envelope. Other bankers viewed her as an easy mark and encouraged her to take out loans of up to $1 million a year at usurious 25 percent interest rates. They never even asked that the interest be paid, preferring instead to let the debts compound until Cassie came into her father's millions.

Meanwhile, Mrs. Chadwick was dazzling Cleveland socialites with her lavish lifestyle. She spent $100,000 for a single dinner party, and that much again for a diamond necklace. She installed an organ made of gold in her living room. Her wardrobe expanded to fill 30 closets.

It seemed the bubble would never burst. Finally, though, a Boston bank got nervous about the awesome sums that Mrs. Chadwick had managed to borrow and decided to call in a loan of $190,000. Cassie politely informed them that she didn't have the cash. Word quickly spread to other financial institutions and widespread panic ensued. The Citizens' National Bank of Oberlin, Ohio, which had trusted her for $200,000, suffered a run on its deposits and went bankrupt overnight. Other houses teetered on the verge of failure. Everyone was speculating whether Cassie's bachelor father would come to her rescue. Then the coup de grâce. A spokesman for the multi-millionaire declared: "Mr. Carnegie does not know Mrs. Chadwick of Cleveland. . . . Mr. Carnegie has not signed a note for more than thirty years."

The truth came out at the trial. An ex-convict, ex-clairvoyant, and ex-prostitute, Cassie, née Elizabeth Bigley, had met the gullible Dr. Leroy Chadwick in a low-class whorehouse off Euclid Avenue and somehow managed to persuade him that she was only there to instruct the girls in etiquette. As for the trip to the Carnegie mansion, she had merely conned her way inside with a lie about wanting to consult with the housekeeper about the credentials of a maid she was thinking of employing. And what about that friendly wave to the well-dressed man at the window? "It was the butler," Cassie admitted. That blabbermouth Dillon fell for the trick and did all the rest by spreading her story far and wide.

"Cleveland's headache," as the newspapers called her, was sentenced in 1904 to ten years in prison for perpetrating the most romantic fraud of all time. She died behind bars three years later.

EMMA EDMONDS   Having passed her mandatory phrenological examination *(See also:* Orson Fowler), Emma Edmonds was engaged as a spy for the Union Army, instructed to wear a wig and stain her skin with walnut juice, and sent south to pose as a young, black, male laborer. At Yorktown, Virginia, where she wielded a pick and shovel to help build fortifications around the town, Miss Edmonds was able to sketch a detailed map of Confederate troop deployment and artillery emplacements. She then hid the map in the bottom of her shoe and hiked back to the Union lines. It was one of ten missions she served before receiving an honorable discharge and returning to her New England home.

KATE and MARGARET FOX   John Fox was a level-headed Methodist who wasn't afraid of ghosts. Over the objections of his superstitious wife, he jumped at the chance to rent a little farmhouse near Rochester, New York, even though the neighbors warned him the place was haunted by the restless spirit of a peddler murdered on the premises years before. Because of its dark history the house was a rare bargain.

Or so it seemed until late one night in March of 1848 when the family was awakened by mysterious rappings in the bedroom occupied by the Foxes' two daughters Kate and Margaret, ages twelve and nine. Mrs. Fox watched as Kate snapped her fingers three times. As if in reply, three sharp knocks came from the nearby wall. The neighbors were summoned to witness the uncanny goings-on, and everyone agreed that the noises must be "spirit rappings"—communications from the dead. An alphabetical code was devised, which the spirits quickly mastered, and soon they were tapping out long, highly personal messages. Poltergeist phenomena were also observed: tables rose into the air; crockery shattered for no apparent reason; mirrors broke in half.

Within a matter of months the Fox sisters were a national sensation. Millions believed that their unaccountable experiences proved the existence of an afterlife, and spiritual circles grew up all over the country. The girls consented to give a series of public demonstrations; prominent figures like James Fenimore Cooper, William Cullen Bryant, and Mrs. Franklin Pierce, the president's wife, came away convinced of the Foxes' supernatural abilities and absolute integrity. Governor N. P. Tallmadge of Wisconsin, a convert to the new Spiritualist religion, spoke with the ghosts of John C. Calhoun and Benjamin Franklin with the sisters serving as intermediaries. Horace Greeley backed them editorially in the *New York Tribune:* "We believe ... that these singular sounds and seeming manifestations are not produced by Mrs. Fox and her daughters nor by any human connected with them."

Under the guardianship of their older sister Leah, the girls moved to New York City where they conducted professional seances for $100 and up. Astonishing new effects were achieved. Members of the charmed circle heard musical instruments and creaking ships, saw uncanny faces and strange lights, and watched as Kate jotted down "spirit letters," written left-handed and backward at an amazing speed. For a long time business was very good, particularly during the Civil War when thousands of grieving parents paid the Foxes to establish contact with sons who had "passed over." Kate was warmly received on a British tour, where she met and married Dr. Henry Jencken, an internationally respected lawyer and legal scholar. Their first child purportedly exhibited awesome mediumistic powers at the tender age of three months and wrote automatic messages in Greek before he could talk.

Then things began to fall apart. Kate's marriage broke up. Both sisters became chronic alcoholics. Criticism from clergymen and scientists mounted. Finally, in 1888, after 40 years of persistent rappings, Margaret confessed that her entire career had been a fraud, an elaborate scheme to outfox the public. "I do not give a fig for spiritualism," she told an audience of believers and nonbelievers at the New York Academy of Music. "Spiritualism is an absolute falsehood from beginning to end." Margaret explained that she and Kate had originally begun the rappings to tease their gullible mother. Then, she poised herself on a pine table with nothing on her feet but stockings and played an eerie percussion by cracking her phalangeal joints. The next day, the *New York Herald* headlined: "HER BIG TOE DID IT ALL."

OSCAR MERRIL HARTZELL Beginning in 1913, an Iowa farmer named Oscar Merril Hartzell got seventy thousand people named Drake to invest $2 million in a campaign to force the British Crown to surrender to them their rightful shares in the long-withheld estate of their celebrated forbear, Sir Francis Drake, who had died in 1596. Of course Britain never budged an inch and Hartzell was ultimately found out and hauled off to federal prison, but his accomplishment remains impressive to this day.

It took some doing. Before he'd conned a single Drake, Hartzell spent long, dreary days in the Sioux City Public Library reading everything he could find about Sir Francis, as well as about Queen Elizabeth I and others who had figured importantly in his life. Gleefully, he discovered that although Sir Francis's fortunes were vast, the will he left behind was so muddled, such a frightful snarl of indecipherable clauses, stipulations, and conditions, that by 1913 it had yet to go to probate. He drooled in anticipation. First he formed the Francis Drake Association, the official legal arm of his campaign. He printed a letterhead, established a mailing address—for years his faithful, most of whom never met Hartzell, assumed him to work out of an elaborately staffed and appointed office when all he had was a post-office box which he visited daily to remove the money—and then assembled a mailing list of twenty thousand Drakes from Seattle to Fall River. The estate of Sir Francis, he told them, was worth some $22 billion, but to underwrite the long, costly, legal struggle to pluck the money out of the Royal strongbox, he would need generous contributions. Of course, he made clear, it paid to give generously, for contributors would share in the settlement proportionate to their investment.

They gave. Checks, money orders, and cold cash poured in daily, via the mails, telegraph, and American Express. People mortgaged their homes, sold family businesses, withdrew their life's savings to get in on the once-in-a-lifetime opportunity. By return mail Hartzell sent a note of thanks, along with a guaranteed-authentic copy of Sir Francis' birth certificate, documents relating to the case, and newspaper cuttings about the noble campaign he was waging.

Some of his supporters appointed themselves lieutenants in the cause and were a great help in mustering up more support and getting the funds to Hartzell. Others organized group meetings to discuss the campaign. Hartzell kept them interested and involved with a regular newsletter; clergymen railed weekly from their pulpits against the ungodly miserliness of the British crown. But nobody ever saw so much as a picture of their tireless defender.

Over the next few years Hartzell made repeated trips to England to prosecute his case, or so he reported to his faithful. In fact he had no business whatsoever with lawyers, probate officers, or the British crown, and did nothing but raise hell on the money that kept pouring in. He returned from one such journey to inform his contributors that he had erred in his original estimate of Sir Francis's wealth: it was *$400* billion, not 22. But more money than ever before was needed, he said, for Britain had brought its most dazzlingly competent attorneys in on the case. The money came in waves.

Though most of his contributors knew that these things take time, that fortunes are not made overnight, a few grumblings of impatience were heard in the land. There were intimations of fraud. Finally, someone had the idea to examine Sir Francis' will. With the assistance of a British Elizabethan scholar the document was read and interpreted and, wonder of wonders, it was discovered that the estate *had* been settled three centuries before. Sir Francis's wife and brother had shared in the bounty between them; there were no living heirs. Hartzell was decried a fraud and unceremoniously deported from England. Back in the United States, he was tried in federal court on charges of postal fraud. Again, incredibly, Hartzell was able to lure scores of unseen believers into underwriting his legal expenses, raging that his trial was merely part of a transatlantic conspiracy to keep him fettered and the estate locked up.

Despite psychiatric testimony that he was mentally unsound, Hartzell was convicted in federal court in St. Louis in 1934 and remanded to the Medical Center for Federal Prisoners in Springfield. He remained there till his death in 1943.

DR. WALTER J. LEVY, JR.   Is a chicken embryo snug in its shell capable of eggstrasensory powers? The man who first posed this pregnant question was Dr. Walter J. Levy, Jr., who at age 26 was appointed director of Dr. J. B. Rhine's famed Institute for Parapsychology in Durham, North Carolina, a leading center for the scientific study of the supernatural.

Dr. Levy's particular specialty was psychokinesis (PK), the supposed ability to influence the motion of physical objects by using the force of thought or will power. In 1974 he caused something of a sensation by publishing a scholarly article entitled "Possible PK by Chicken Embryo" in *The Journal of Parapsychology*. The article detailed an experiment in which he had placed fertilized chicken eggs in an incubator that was turned on and off at irregular intervals by a randomizing device. The laws of probability held that the heat in the incubator would be on exactly half the time. But the computer records showed that the incubator's heating unit was operating 52 percent of the time. Dr. Levy's conclusion: The unborn chicks were *willing* the machine to stay on and keep them warm. Just to be on the safe side, Levy performed a control experiment, placing hard-boiled eggs inside the incubator; under these conditions no evidence of PK was observed. Levy was the toast of the parapsychological profession. His results promised to revolutionize the way we look at our breakfast omelets. But some of his senior colleagues suspected fowl play.

Dr. Levy's next history-making experiment entailed implanting electrodes in the brains of laboratory rats. Again a randomizing device was hooked up, this time to give the rats pleasurable shocks 50 percent of the time. Miraculously, however, Levy found that the rats were using their PK powers to keep the agreeable current flowing about 32.5 minutes out of every hour. Further experiments showed that gerbils and hamsters used psychokinesis to avoid unpleasant shocks.

Then scandal. One of Levy's suspicious co-workers saw him repeatedly pulling a plug from a recording instrument, causing it to register only "hits"—only data tending to confirm the PK effect. A second set of instruments was installed to monitor the rat experiments without Dr. Levy's knowledge, and it recorded a less than uncanny score of 50 percent. Confronted with the evidence, Levy admitted his deception, saying that he had been egged on by professional pressure to get positive results. The young parapsychologist resigned and hasn't been heard of since.

RICHARD ADAMS LOCKE The headlines trumpeted: "Great Astronomical Discoveries Lately Made by Sir John Herschel at the Cape of Good Hope." And right there in black-and-white it said that England's most respected astronomer had built a seven-ton telescope through which he had plainly observed plants and animals on the moon. No fewer than 14 species of lunar fauna had been identified, including goats with a single horn, "a strange amphibious creature of a spherical form," and a race of superior biped beavers from whose houses smoke could be seen issuing.

The source of these amazing revelations was a series of four exclusive articles in the *New York Sun*, a struggling four-page penny newspaper. They ran in August 1835 under the by-line Richard Adams Locke, but most of the information was quoted directly from the *Edinburgh Journal of Science*. The sober tone and sprinkling of scientific terms gave the reports an air of unquestionable authenticity. A women's club in Springfield, Massachusetts hastily began collecting money to send a team of missionaries to the moon. "Not one person in ten discredited it," according to one skeptic—Edgar Allan Poe. The *New York Times* called the articles "probable and convincing." *The New Yorker* said the findings heralded "a new era in astronomy and science generally." In Paris, London, and other world capitals, newspapers reprinted the accounts verbatim.

With each issue the lunar news became more and more fantastic. Sir John had discerned pyramid-shaped mountains of solid amethyst. Sir John had counted 38 species of trees on the moon. Ultimately, Sir John had seen four flocks of winged humanoids with faces like orangutans. Overnight the *Sun's* circulation soared from a piddling 2,500 to over 19,000, making it the most popular daily of the time.

At this juncture, Yale College sent down a delegation of professors to see the original journal from which Locke quoted. It had mysteriously disappeared. Soon the scientists discovered the *Edinburgh Journal of Science* had ceased publication several years earlier. The hoax was exposed.

Who was the science fiction writer who concocted this wild circulation-building yarn? A New Yorker by birth. A graduate of Cambridge. A general reporter grinding out copy for $12 a week. Poe said his forehead was "truly beautiful in its intellectuality. I am acquainted with no person possessing so fine a forehead as Mr. Locke." In 1836 Locke resigned from the *Sun* and started his own penny daily, the *New Era*. He fabricated another hoax, "The Lost Manuscript of Mungo Park," a Robinson Crusoe-style adventure yarn. By this time, however, readers were wise to Locke's chicanery and he could never fool all of the people again.

LOZIER and DeVOE   In the summer of 1824, a couple of hoaxers named Lozier and DeVoe somehow got several hundred New Yorkers to believe that the southern end of Manhattan—where all the big office buildings were—was in imminent danger of sinking into the harbor. But the calamity could be averted, the two men reassured their horrified listeners, by sawing Manhattan from the mainland—never mind that Manhattan is an island—and turning it around.

After announcing that they'd secured the mayor's official go-ahead on the project, Lozier and DeVoe established a starting date, purchased a huge anchor that would keep Manhattan from floating out to sea like an errant beachball, and signed up scores of willing workmen. They also handed out contracts for supplies, excavation equipment, and refreshment concessions. On the first day of Project Cut-off, hundreds of would-be participants showed up at Manhattan's northern tip to await instructions from Lozier and DeVoe. But they never appeared—nor were they ever heard from again.

BARBARA ANN MALPASS   Police gave Charles Richard Williams a thorough frisking when they arrested him for vagrancy in 1959, then hustled him off to the Jefferson County, New York, jail. Shortly after his release in November, Williams's cover was blown—he turned out to be a *girl* by the name of Barbara Ann Malpass. Miss Malpass had run away from home four months earlier and, theorizing that a runaway male would seem less suspicious than a runaway female, decided to pass as a boy. Neither the arresting officer, the jail warden, nor her jailmates had so much as an inkling.

PATRICK McDERMIT   Patrick McDermit should have accepted the bet: when the 20-year-old Californian claimed that he could assume a new name, forge a new identity for himself as a high-school whiz-kid and self-made boy millionaire who spoke six languages and owned a hotel—and on that basis get admitted to Yale—a friend offered to bet $1,000 that it couldn't be done. "I thought I had no chance of winning," he later rued.

McDermit, a refurbisher of houses, who had graduated from high school with only a middling record, was able to fabricate a high-school transcript and authentic-looking letters of recommendation, and then cook up a believable if astounding story of his successes as a speculator. He told the Yale admissions office that his name was Andreas Alvea.

"The story was absolutely ridiculous," he said, "but they fell for it." McDermit was admitted, "did no work whatsoever, had a good time and met some interesting people." He dropped out in January, just before his first paper was due.

Predictably, the Yale fathers were angered and red-faced when McDermit announced he was withdrawing and blew his own cover. The dean of admissions said he was "alarmed, distressed, and surprised," but attributed the university's failure to sniff out the hoax on its own to the impossibility of screening its ten thousand new applicants each year.

"I had done this sort of thing before on a small scale," McDermit said later, "passing myself off as a businessman or newspaper reporter in bars and at parties. But this was the biggest. I'll probably do something like it again soon."

LORETA JANETA VELAZQUEZ Loreta Janeta Velazquez was so caught up by the war fever that swept the South in 1860 that she left her husband and joined the Confederate Army as "Harry T. Burford." She served with distinction in many important battles, including Bull Run, and was praised by General Stonewall Jackson, who never found out she was a woman.

EDWARD WATTERS Driving his truck along Route 78 near Austell, Georgia, one summer's night in 1953, Edward

Watters fatally ran down a 21-inch space creature. "It was a little after eleven o'clock and we were travelling about sixty miles per hour when we topped a small hill," the 28-year-old otherwise undistinguished barber explained. "One of the boys yelled stop, and then we could see a glowing thing settle down, covering half the highway. I hit the brakes and saw three or four little manlike objects run toward the thing. Two or three of the little creatures made it, jumped on top, and sunk out of sight. I hit this one at the end of a seventy-foot skid." Never one to hit-and-run, Watters dutifully retrieved the body and brought it home to the boarding house where he lived, stowing the body in his landlady's ice-box. ("Turned me sick, if you want to know the truth," she said repeatedly.)

That night and the following morning, a procession of army and police investigators, radio, TV, and newspaper reporters arrived to gape in wonder at the hairless four-pound victim of history's first intergalactic automobile accident.

It was a pair of Emory University scientists who ruined Watters' fun. His spaceman, they said, was a baby rhesus monkey. With that, the state's medical examiners arrived, elbowing Watters aside, and hustled back to their laboratories with the body, there to prove that it was indeed a young capuchin monkey minus its hair and tail.

A hoax? Certainly—but whose? Interviewing Watters, a reporter from the *Atlanta Journal* suggested it would be a shame if the author of so ingenious a prank went uncredited. Watters bit: "If anybody could shave a monkey that good," he said, "he'd have to be a pretty good barber." Then followed the confession. Accepting a bet that he couldn't get his picture in the newspapers within a fortnight, Watters bought the monkey, paying his supplier an extra two dollars not to talk, shaved it close, chloroformed it, lopped off the tail, and then bashed in its head with a bottle of soda pop before "running it down" on Highway 78. And, of course, winning his bet.

Evildoers

LOUIS ALTERIE   Before he arrived in Chicago in the 1920s Louis Alterie had been a law-fearing rancher in Colorado. But he shed his honest ways when he got to the big city and took to a life of crime in the service of gang leader Dion O'Bannion. His specialty was hijacking beer trucks, but he first made headlines by murdering the rented stable horse that had thrown Samuel J. "Nails" Morton—a close friend of Alterie's—to his death on a Lincoln Park bridle path the day before. "We taught that goddamn horse of yours a lesson," he told the stable owner shortly after the shooting. "If you want the saddle, go and get it."

Alterie, dubbed "Two-Guns" for his habit of carrying a pair of cowboy guns on his hips, wept unabashedly at the funeral of boss O'Bannion, who was gunned down in 1924. "I have no idea who killed Deanie," he told reporters covering the funeral, "but I would die smiling if only I had a chance to meet the guys who did—any time, any place." So rash was his invitation to O'Bannion's assassins to shoot it out with him at the corner of Madison and State Street in downtown Chicago at noon that even Crime Boss Bugsy Moran told him to shut up, lest he give bootlegging a bad name. With that, Alterie left Chicago to return to his ranch in Colorado, never to be heard from again.

STEPHEN ARNOLD   A Cooperstown, New York, schoolteacher known for his wild rages at pupils' errors, Arnold clubbed his six-year-old niece, Betsy Van Amburgh, to death in 1805 for misspelling the word "gig."

He fled Cooperstown and wound up in Pittsburgh where

50

he was tracked down and arrested. Handed over to the Cooperstown courts, this sultan of swat was tried quickly and sentenced to the hangman's noose.

The locals turned out by the thousands to witness his execution, an event no less festive than a presidential inauguration or a royal wedding. Bands played and children shouted as the condemned man was led to the gallows. The rope was placed around his neck, last rites were administered and then, seconds before the trap would be sprung, the sheriff stepped forward to hand the executioner a reprieve from the governor. He had received the document early that morning, he announced, but withheld it until the last possible moment both to punish the murderer and excite the crowd. They were not amused.

Arnold was forthwith returned to his jail cell and ultimately pardoned on grounds of temporary insanity.

JOHN BANKS John Banks should have known better than to demand *Godey's Ladies Book* fastidiousness from his wife Margaret. She was a known alcoholic whose ineptness at cooking and keeping house was an ill-kept secret in the New York City neighborhood where the couple lived in the early years of the nineteenth century. But when Banks asked Margaret for a cup of coffee one summer's morning and she handed him a glass of "pot-liquor" instead, he decided the time had come for sternness: seizing a coal shovel he bashed the woman senseless, then cut her throat with a knife.

At his trial, Banks protested that while the coffee affair alone was grounds for homicide, on another occasion he had brought some peanuts home and ordered her to brown them, "and that when he returned home with some eggs, found that she had done nothing." However, the court held otherwise, and Banks was hanged on July 11, 1806.

FITZHUGH COYLE GOLDSBOROUGH Fitzhugh Goldsborough's only love was his addlepated spinster sister, a star of Philadelphia society around the turn of the century. He indulged her every wish, flattered her with little gifts, and flew into a blinding rage whenever anyone, including their father, took her to task.

But Goldsborough himself, even though his family had money, was not much of a social gadabout. Thin-blooded and listless in a Proustian sort of way, he took his greatest pleasure, save for pampering his sister, by lying in bed for days at a time, reading romantic novels.

One of those books was *The Fashionable Adventures of Joshua Craig,* by the best-selling novelist David Graham Philips. A spoiled, narcissistic young socialite figured importantly in the story and Goldsborough paranoiacally figured her to be a deliberate caricature of his sister. Philips, in fact, had never met the woman nor heard talk of her.

On the morning of January 23, 1911, as the elegantly-dressed Philips ambled through New York's Gramercy Park, Goldsborough accosted him, drew a pistol, and shot him several times. Even as passersby stared in horror, he screamed, "Here you go!" and shot himself in the head. The murderer died instantly, his victim a few days later.

THOMAS HICKEY Benedict Arnold became a household word for merely planning to hand over West Point to the British during the Revolutionary War, whereas Thomas Hickey, guilty of far bolder treachery, has long since been forgotten. As a member of George Washington's personal bodyguard, he plotted with others, whom he paid a dollar apiece "by way of encouragement," to capture the father of our country, just a few short days before the country was fathered, and deliver him to Sir William Howe. The plan was uncovered when Hickey and a coconspirator were arrested on an unrelated charge of attempting to pass counterfeit currency. He was tried in military court, convicted, and sentenced to die. On June 27, 1776, at Bowery Lane in New York City he was hanged in the presence of twenty thousand gleeful spectators; it was the first execution carried out by the American Army.

AL JENNINGS The life of Al Jennings (1863-1948), the West's most awkward outlaw, is proof that nothing recedes like success. Few men have set their sights lower, but as a badman he was no damn good.

It was 1885 when Jennings and his three dimwit brothers—Frank, Ed, and John—tried to rob their first train in the Oklahoma Territory. Al stood in the middle of the tracks and attempted to flag down the oncoming locomotive; the engineer blithely ignored him and Jennings was nearly crushed beneath the wheels. The gang fared no better on their second foray. Jennings and his brothers galloped alongside a speeding train for nearly half a mile firing their pistols into the air as a way of signaling the engineer to stop. But the engineer misunderstood. Thinking they were harmless cowboys offering a friendly salute, he waved and continued on schedule to Santa Fe without so much as slowing down.

On their third try the brothers attacked a small passenger train, which had stopped to take on water, and managed to steal all of $60 from the mail car. To throw the law off their trail the gang split up. Al and Frank were nabbed the next day by United States Marshall Bud Ledbetter, who took them without firing a shot. Ledbetter ordered the hapless bandits to surrender their weapons and tie themselves up. They did.

As for brothers Ed and John, they high-tailed it into a nearby town, went into a saloon, and unknowingly picked a fight with Temple Houston, one of the Old West's toughest lawmen. Houston shot them both. Ed died on the spot; John survived and, realizing that he was not cut out for a life of crime, went back to cattle ranching.

Al and Frank were given life sentences for their felony. Paroled after five years, Al migrated to California where, according to Sheriff Jim Herron, he spent his days "stuffing dudes with nonsense and telling them wild yarns about himself in the early days." One of his standard boasts was that he could "hit a can tossed in the air from one hundred paces without ever missing." General Roy Hoffman, a Rough

Rider and World War I commander, set the record straight: "I knew Al Jennings personally and he was one of the kind of fellows who could have qualified as the traditional bad shot who couldn't hit the side of a barn." It seems the only ones who believed Jennings' tall tales were a couple of Hollywood producers who made a movie based on his imaginary life as a desperado.

Jennings grabbed headlines again in 1948 when 101-year-old J. Frank Dalton publicly claimed to be Jesse James. Jennings, then 85, was asked by the Associated Press to verify Dalton's story. The instant Jennings laid eyes on the withered imposter, he shouted "It's him! It's Jesse! There isn't a bit of doubt on earth." The next day a picture of the two old bandits, with pistols drawn, appeared in newspapers all over the country. Later it came out that Jennings could never have met Jesse James. It was also pointed out that if Dalton was Jesse he must have undergone a finger transplant. The real Jesse James accidentally blew off the tip of his left middle finger while cleaning a gun. Dalton's finger was intact.

WILLIAM KEMMLER   While hacking his sweetheart to ribbons with a woodman's axe on a cold morning in Buffalo in 1889, fruit-and-vegetable merchant William Kemmler was doubtless unaware that his own inevitable death would rate a lot more newspaper space and be a lot ghastlier than poor Matilda's. For, 17 months hence, after a long trial, countless appeals and stays of execution, Kemmler would become the first convicted murderer to die in the world's first electric chair.

The shocking event took place on August 6, 1890, at New York's Auburn State Penitentiary, where Kemmler had waited patiently since his conviction while the comparative merits of the newfangled electrocution process and the hangman's noose were debated *ad nauseam*. Kemmler was unshaven and appeared ill-rested at 6:20 that morning as Warden Charles Durston and two armed guards marched him into the execution chamber. Gathered behind barricades a safe distance from the chair were 21 invited guests, including lawyers, judges, and physicians who had figured in the Kemmler affair. There had been talk of allowing them a decent night's rest and holding the execution later in the morning. Then someone pointed out the possibility of a prison riot should the Auburn power system suddenly go dead as the inmates labored in the machine shops.

"Gentlemen, this is Mr. Kemmler," Durston announced. Kemmler bowed, as if he were about to begin a piano recital. For the occasion he wore a coat and matching vest and a checked bow-tie. His audience was visibly tense; so were the guards who strapped him into the massive oak chair, slit his trousers, and attached the electrodes to his temple and spine. Oddly, only the condemned man himself seemed at ease.

"Don't get excited," he cautioned the guards. "I want you to make a good job of this." Kemmler was nothing if not cooperative. He strained against the straps to test them, advising the guards that the band girdling his forehead needed tightening. With everything in place, Warden Durston opened the door to the adjoining control room where Edwin Davis stood posed at the control panel.

"Goodbye, William," Durston said. That was the signal: Davis threw the switch and 1,600 volts of alternating current slashed through Kemmler's body, which stiffened, turned white, and strained violently against the leather straps. After 17 seconds the current was turned off. Durston undid the straps. Kemmler lay limp and quite dead. Or so it seemed.

"He's alive!" someone screamed. And he was—Kemmler's chest was twitching, albeit almost imperceptibly. Dr. E. C. Spitzka, one of two supervising physicians, shouted, "Turn on the current instantly, you fools! This man is not dead!" Pandemonium filled the room, spectators scurrying for safety behind the barricades as Durston frantically refastened the restraining thongs. Now he signaled Davis again. This time there would be no chances taken: Davis kept the juice flowing a full 70 seconds. When he turned it off, William Kemmler was not merely dead, he was incinerated. Smoke curled up from the base of his spine and the smell of roasting flesh filled the air. His brain itself was baked hard, and his blood had turned into something black and brittle. Those who were there claimed the United Press reporter fainted, and the Erie County district attorney, who had prosecuted the dead man, ran screaming from the room.

JAMES LANDIS In these years of parental permissiveness and plummeting moral standards, the half-century-old crime of James Landis still seems unthinkable. Landis stole from the United States Mint.

He also got away with it—almost.

Born and educated in Milwaukee, Landis came to Washington in 1923, married a schoolteacher, raised two children, participated in admirable civic pursuits and was active in churchwork. He was accounted by all who knew him a quiet-spoken yet high-minded man who respected both God's law and man's.

Landis worked at the Federal Bureau of Printing and Engraving, carrying paper currency from the vaults to the packing machines, where twenty-dollar bills were done up in bundles of 4,000, bound with a pair of tight-fitting steel bands and wrapped in heavy brown paper that would be affixed with a United States Treasury Seal, serial numbers, an inspector's signature, and miscellaneous stamps and signets. Landis studied the money bricks as they passed before his bulging eyes, and decided to fashion a dummy, using discarded wrapping materials retrieved from the treasury trash bins. Then, when no one was watching, he would deftly switch it with a real bundle which he'd smuggle past the building guards.

It wasn't easy. It was three months before Landis had crafted two perfect copies, which he handily secreted from the gate guards next morning and stored in a wastepaper basket in the employees' men's room. By midmorning he'd made the switch. He stored the two real bricks, worth $80,000 apiece, in the basket, and replaced them with the fakes, secure in the knowledge that they would be moved to a vault in the mint for two months and thence to one of a dozen

Federal Reserve Banks scattered throughout the nation, where they would repose for months more before being moved again to local banks. It was so easy that he repeated the theft many times in the weeks to come. His plan was to steal $100,000 a week for a year, and then retire.

Of course, Landis knew that the cash was as easily traceable as a rotting smelt on a crowded bus, so he diligently changed every bill he stole by spending it on small purchases, like shaving soap and newspapers. But somehow he wasn't pulling in the profits as fast as he had planned. An idea: enlist a confederate who would help him with the "brick" counterfeiting and smuggling and could be trusted not to rat. The ideal choice was co-worker Claude Armstrong, but even a conspiracy of two proved too small, and the cabal grew to six. Inevitably, Landis forfeited in secrecy what he gained in increased burgling strength: a federal agent, nagged by a feeling that some of the currency bricks seemed lighter in weight than they should be, ripped one of the dummies open and discovered the ruse.

The serial numbers of the missing bills were distributed to local merchants, the Secret Service joined the case, and within days, God-fearing James Landis and his associates were arrested on charges of stealing over one million dollars from the U.S. Mint. Tried and convicted, they were sentenced to ten-year terms at Alcatraz.

HENRY LAURENS In 1770 Henry Laurens became the first American to be imprisoned in the Tower of London. He was jailed there on charges of treason and required to pay for his room and board. Twelve years later he became the first person to be cremated in the United States. A Revolutionary War patriot of much-heralded zeal, Laurens included these instructions in his will: "I solemnly enjoin it upon my son as an indispensable duty that, as soon as he conveniently can after my decease, he cause my body to be wrapped in twelve yards of tow cloth, and burnt until it is entirely consumed, and then, collecting my ashes, deposit them wherever he may see proper." What Laurens had against a proper burial, or how he settled on twelve yards of cloth as an appropriate amount to be burned in, is unknown today. But you can check what details are available in Cobb's handy *Quarter Century of Cremation in North America.*

PETER LAZAROS The meal you cannot make at home: An itinerant swindler named Peter Lazaros checked into New York City's posh Pierre Hotel and telephoned the Bulgari jewel company to say that he was in a shopping mood and would like to look over their wares. A sampling of Burgari's finest was delivered to Lazaros' room. He examined them, found nothing to his liking, and the sales representative gathered up his merchandise and left. Bulgari later found that a $35,000 four-carat diamond-and-platinum ring had not been returned. Lazaros was not happy to be cross-examined by Bulgari as to the ring's whereabouts and threatened a lawsuit. The case was dropped, Bulgari accepted a $17,000 insurance settlement from Lloyd's of London, and Lazaros disappeared from New York only to be convicted of unrelated fraud charges a year later.

Lazaros died in jail a few months after that, and when physicians cut into his stomach during the autopsy they came up with the missing ring. The most plausible explanation police offered was that Lazaros had popped the ring in his mouth for safekeeping the day he went to jail, excreted it within a couple of days, swallowed it again, and so forth.

ADOLPH LOUIS LUETGERT German-born Adolph Louis Luetgert, the obese, sex-crazed president of a Chicago sausage company, was arrested in 1898 on charges of silencing his jealous wife forever by dropping her into a chemical bath in the basement of his factory and boiling her down to sludge. Some of the late Mrs. Luetgert turned up as a sticky residue on the basement floor; less fluid chunks of her were fished out of the bath by Leutgert's unknowing employees and flushed down sewers.

At his trial, the prosecution brought forth several of

58

Luetgert's mistresses who turned against him venomously on the witness stand. One testified that the Sausage King had told her he despised his wife and that "I could take her and crush her." Another produced embarassingly maudlin love-letters. Luetgert railed pathetically against their charges, once rising from his courtroom chair to cry, "I am as innocent as the southern skies!" But the discovery of Mrs. Luetgert's teeth, shards of her bones, and an engraved friendship ring in the bath of potash that was her grave, led to his conviction. Sentenced to life imprisonment, Luetgert died in 1911.

FILBERT MAESTAS Filbert Maestas was arrested for breaking into a Denver meat-packing warehouse in 1977 and pilfering twelve hundred beef rectums.

WILLIAM D'ALTON MANN Most journalists are paid—not very well—for what they publish. Colonel William D'Alton Mann, the jovial, unscrupulous editor of *Town Topics,* was a notable exception to the rule. The articles that made him fat and wealthy were the ones that never appeared in print.

Employing a motley staff of private detectives, butlers, maids, valets, bellhops, and other informers, he carefully raked the preeminent muck, collecting a never-ending supply of sordid details about the private lives of the rich and famous. Nothing escaped his notice: bastard births, husbands who strayed, gambling debts, upper-class orgies, Society girls who "did," starched-collar crime, liaisons with call girls, and sundry other goings on. When Mann came up with an exceptionally shocking story, he made a point of reserving a table at the subject's favorite restaurant. Then, during the dessert course, the maitre d'hotel would pass along the proofs to the lady or gentleman in question. Usually the matter could be settled discreetly, then and there, with an ample check or promissory note. In this fashion Mann received $25,000 from William K. Vanderbilt, $10,000 from

William C. Whitney, $5,000 from Collis P. Huntington, $2,500 from J. P. Morgan, and similar sums from other persons of note.

Driven to desperate measures, Society families sometimes tested the loyalty of their servants by allowing them to overhear false information; if the story was retold in *Town Topics* the servant was immediately dismissed. There was another way to ensure that family secrets did not become front-page headlines. Mann also published a sumptuous leather-bound volume entitled *Fads and Fancies of Representative Americans,* which sold for a scant $1,500 per copy. Those who purchased this magnificent edition were spared embarrassment—for a while.

ELMER McCURDY TV's "The Six Million Dollar Man" was shooting on location at the Nu-Pike Amusement Park in Long Beach, California and a technical crew was setting up the Laff in the Dark funhouse for some background shots. Accidentally, one of the crew members pulled the arm off a fluorescent mummy while moving it out of the way. He was about to ask an assistant to glue the appendage back on when the words stuck in his throat: a real shoulder bone was protruding from the socket.

Indeed, it was Elmer J. McCurdy's arm the technician had pulled off, and not some plaster-of-paris funhouse novelty's. A turn-of-the-century wild west outlaw, McCurdy had taken a bullet in the chest during a barnyard shoot-out with Oklahoma lawmen in 1911. He was given a proper embalming and then, instead of being buried, was purchased by a sideshow operator who showed him off at fairgrounds in Oklahoma and elsewhere, much as the jellied corpses of other bandits of the day were exhibited. In 1968 the Hollywood Wax Museum received custody of McCurdy, and billed him as "The 5,000-year-old-Man." When the museum went bust in 1971, Elmer was moved to the Long Beach funhouse. After the unintended amputation, it took the Los Angeles coroner's office four months' lab work to make an identification.

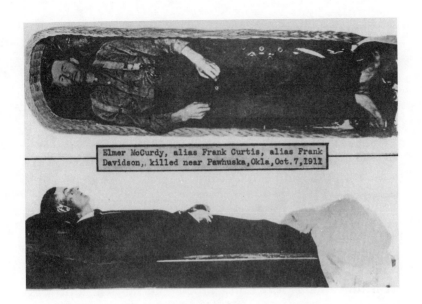

Elmer McCurdy in his casket, and later as a funhouse attraction
(Western History Collections, University of Oklahoma Library)

The postscript: old Elmer McCurdy was returned to Guthrie, Oklahoma for burial in an old territorial cemetery with fellow badmen. "He was sidetracked for a long time," said Fred Olds of the Oklahoma Historical Society, "but we feel he's part of our history."

FRED PALM It was Fred Palm's misfortune to be nabbed by police in Lansing, Michigan, during the Prohibition years with a pint of gin concealed in his pocket. He drew a life sentence.

CHARLOTTE and KATHERINE POILLON The only legitimate enterprise Charlotte Poillon ever involved herself in was prizefighting. A hard-bellied 210-pounder, she once went four rounds with Jim Corbett. But her real forte was honeying up wealthy old men, then taking them for all they had. By the time Charlotte and her sister Katherine, an absolute ox of a woman, vanished from public view in the 1920s, they had amassed a small fortune in this way. In 1903, for example, still new at the game, they sued the wealthy William G. Brokaw for $250,000 and came away with a cool out-of-court $17,500 which Brokaw paid gladly to stay out of the papers.

Not that they always came out ahead. In 1907, for instance, the girls kicked a hotel manager down the stairs when he asked them to pay their bill; they paid a ten-dollar fine. In 1909 they raised a row at New York's Hotel Willard and six men had to carry them out bodily, although not before Charlotte had beaten up three bellhops. When she was similarly ejected from Charles Rector's, a posh New York restaurant, in 1912, Charlotte sued for $25,000—and lost. Rector's maitre d' testified that Charlotte had come to the restaurant dressed as a man and that no one bothered her until she knocked two waiters to the floor as she made her way to a table reserved for other patrons. In 1923 the sisters were sued for $3,000 by an elderly laundry-chain proprietor named Charles Dusenbury who charged them with fraud. In court the girls refused to enter a plea, scissored paper dolls from newspapers, and railed anti-Semitically at their Jewish lawyer. Reprimanded by Judge McIntyre, Charlotte hammered the defense table with her fist. "Please remember that you are a woman," the judge warned, "or I may forget that you are." Later, on the witness stand, Dusenbury broke down and admitted that the $3,000 settlement he sought was precisely the amount he had paid Katherine for her favors. The case was dropped.

Other love-nest cases involving the titanic Poillons abounded until the 1920s, when the two vanished. Charlotte hit the headlines in 1929, however: a crowd had collected to watch a prizefighter working out with a punching bag in front of New York City department store. From out of the crowd, she roared, "You stink!" After exchanging unkind words with the boxer, she elbowed him aside and was hired to take his place. She remained there three weeks then disappeared.

BOSTON RASPBERRY   While playing in a sandlot baseball game in Bonifay, Florida, an unemployed steamfitter named Boston Raspberry clubbed the opposing shortstop to death with a bat following an argument over a called third strike. Raspberry was arrested, tried, found guilty of murder, and sentenced to life imprisonment, only to be pardoned by Governor Millard Caldwell, who announced that "anybody with a name like 'Boston Raspberry' should have a full pardon."

EDWARD H. RULOFF   For reasons unknown, Edward Ruloff of Ithaca, New York, slew his wife and young child in 1846, and then dumped their bodies into scenic Lake Cayuga. The police closed in on Ruloff almost at once and he was packed off to prison on a kidnapping conviction. In his cell Ruloff devoted himself to reading the classics and learning foreign languages. A decade after his conviction the state tried him anew on charges of murder, found him guilty, and sentenced him to death. Ruloff escaped. Affecting learned ways, he posed as a college professor and toured the college campuses of New York state earning good money as a guest lecturer. Tiring of that, he shed his academic robes and returned to a life of crime, rifling shops and offices, assisted by two confederates.

On one such outing in Binghamton, Ruloff and company wound up killing a store clerk, then scampered away for safety, taking refuge in the Chenago River. The two assistants promptly drowned, but their leader himself swam to safety. He was arrested several days later, however, while disguised as a hobo: someone noticed that his right foot lacked a big toe. (Ruloff was known to suffer from that deformity.) He was tried again, sentenced, and hanged, and his brain put on display at the Cornell Medical School. Physicians there said it most closely resembled the brain of Daniel Webster.

PHILIP SPENCER Midshipman Philip Spencer, serving aboard the United States brig-of-war *Somers,* was an undisciplined and high-spirited 18-year-old who liked to drink, brag, and smoke good cigars. He won many friends among the crew with his trick of dislocating his jaw and by "contact of the bones" producing melodies "with accuracy and elegance." Then one evening off the coast of Africa, when the young cadet was in his cups, he was overheard "conspiring" with several of his mates to commandeer the ship at gunpoint and take up piracy. Word of the plot got back to Captain Alexander Slidell Mackenzie who promptly arrested Spencer and charged him with mutiny, the first and only such incident in American naval history. On December 1, 1842, in accordance with the verdict of a hastily-convened board of inquiry, Spencer and two others were hanged from a yardarm while 117 men and boys, many of them in tears, looked on.

There the matter might have ended except for one small complication: Spencer's father happened to be the secretary of war at the time. When the *Somers* dropped anchor in New York Harbor, Captain Mackenzie was himself taken into custody and court martialed on three counts of murder and two counts of oppression, illegal punishment, and conduct unbecoming an officer. Although a great deal of damaging testimony against Mackenzie came out at the trial, he was ultimately acquitted of any wrong-doing. But not everyone was convinced that justice had been done. Three days after Mackenzie was released, Richard Leecock, the surgeon on the *Somers* who had reluctantly joined with his fellow officers in condemning Spencer, committed suicide. Lieutenant Guert Gansevoort, another member of the board of inquiry, was so conscience-stricken by his part in the affair that he became an alcoholic. He later recounted the story of the *Somers* mutiny to his distant cousin, Herman Melville, who used the events as a model for his novel *Billy Budd.*

To this day, members of Chi Psi, a national fraternity, regard Philip Spencer as a hero and a martyr. They insist that Spencer, who helped to found the fraternity when he briefly attended Union College, was not hanged for mutiny at all, but rather for refusing to divulge Chi Psi secrets. They say a list of names in Greek (introduced at Spencer's trial as a roster of coconspirators) was actually a confidential Chi Psi document. And, quaffing toasts in Spencer's honor, they sing a century-old song that goes:

> O here's to Philip Spencer
> Who when about to die
> When sinking down beneath the waves
> Loud shouted out Chi Psi!
>
> So, fill your glasses to the brim,
> And drink with manly pride
> Humanity received a blow
> When Philip Spencer died.

ARTHUR WAITE Dr. Arthur Waite brought years of solid medical experience to the job of poisoning his father-in-law, John Peck, in 1916, but he had not been prepared for the contempt Peck's gastrointestinal system would show for modern bacteriological theory. Waite first tried slipping a dose of diphtheria toxin into Peck's dinner, but the old man scarcely flinched. He then tried a nasal spray spiked with tuberculosis germs, and that too failed. Waite next brought out the heavy guns: a draught of calomel, then typhoid bacteria, and next influenza. Peck still survived. Ultimately Waite dropped his bacteriological pretenses and finished Peck off with arsenic. He was found guilty later that year of premeditated murder and sentenced to life imprisonment.

TIMOTHY WAYNE Timothy Wayne, age 31, was al-legedly ambling nude through New York City's Greenwich Village one March morning when a pair of police officers spotted him from their squad car. Leaping to the pavement, the patrolmen stopped Mr. Wayne and ordered him into the back seat. The suspect obeyed, immediately clambering into the driver's seat, where he seized the wheel and sped away, leaving his apprehenders behind.

A posse of police cars pursued the man, his strong, fine body glistening in the harsh March sun, north through mid-town Manhattan, and into Central Park, finally chasing him down on the banks of the Hudson River, where he leaped from the vehicle into a nearby bush. He was arrested and brought to trial in Manhattan Criminal Court on a charge of grand larceny. For the occasion he wore a raincoat and pants, although he remained shoeless. Said police captain Edward Walsh of the affair, "We do not view it as humorous."

Food Faddists
and Gourmands

G. H. BIGELOW   Perhaps the most effective after-dinner speaker of all time is Dr. G. H. Bigelow, formerly the Massachusetts State Health Commissioner, who was invited to address a faculty-student gathering at Harvard Medical School in 1932. Dr. Bigelow chose "Food Poisoning," for his topic and immediately thereafter some 50 of his audience became violently ill.

C. K. G. BILLINGS   C. K. G. Billings (1861–1937) enjoyed life's little pleasures. He was fond of sailing, for example, and happily his position as chairman of the board at Union Carbide gave him a certain amount of discretionary income, a small part of which he used to purchase a 240-foot yacht christened the *Venadis*. The operating costs alone ran $250,000 a year.

But, sad to say, for all his wealth Billings was never very successful in high society. Although his consumption was conspicuous enough, he seemed to have a regrettable penchant for the grotesque. The famous "Horseback Dinner" Billings gave at Louis Sherry's restaurant was a case in point. Guests dined in the saddle at an estimated $250 a plate. Society page writers deemed it the most uncomfortable event of the season and complained that the mounts soiled the banquet room in unappetizing fashion.

CLARENCE BIRDSEYE   To finance his college education, Clarence "Bob" Birdseye (1886–1956) used to trap black rats

C. K. G. Billings's horseback dinner at Sherry's *(Byron Collection, Museum of the City of New York)*

and sell them to biology researchers at Columbia University. Likewise, he made the rounds of the pollywog ponds in Brooklyn, capturing live frogs which he marketed to the Bronx Zoo as reptile food.

The secret of success, he once asserted, was to "go around asking a lot of damnfool questions and taking chances." His own fortune came as a direct result of his curiosity about the eating habits of Eskimos, an interest he developed while engaged in a United States government survey of fish and wildlife in Labrador between 1912 and 1915. "That first winter," he wrote, "I saw natives catching fish in fifty below zero weather, which froze stiff as soon as they were taken out of the water. Months later when they were thawed out, some of these fish were still alive." The Eskimos also taught Birdseye to enjoy frozen cabbages and caribou meat.

After returning from the Arctic, Birdseye spent seven dollars on brine, ice, and an electric fan so he could continue his experiments with quick freezing. When he exposed fresh foods to a circulating mist of brine at forty-five degrees

68

below zero, he found that the tissues would freeze almost instantly without the formation of ice crystals that would burst the cell walls. Thawed, the foods retained most of their original flavor and texture.

He took out a patent on the fast-freezing process and established the General Seafoods Corporation at Gloucester, Massachusetts, in 1924. He froze peas, spinach, raspberries, loganberries, cherries, and various meats as well as flounder and sole. "Bob would eat *anything*," an associate recalled. "Trawlers would bring in all sorts of unusual catches to the wharf—small whales, sharks, porpoises—once even an alligator—and Bob would freeze and try them all."

Finally, in 1929, he sold his patents and plant for $22 million to the Postum Corporation. His name, split into two words, was adopted as a brand name. Birdseye continued to be one of the country's most productive inventors for many years, taking out over 250 patents for inventions ranging from infrared heating to a recoilless harpoon gun for whaling to a process for converting Peruvian sugar cane into paper pulp.

Clarence Birdseye, father of frozen food *(General Foods Corp.)*

JOE CANNON   Washington lawmakers remember Nebraska's Joe Cannon, the turn-of-the-century House Speaker for his courageous stand in favor of Yankee Bean Soup.

In 1904, the story goes, Cannon settled down to lunch in the House restaurant to be told that there was no Yankee Bean Soup on the menu. "But I had my mouth set for Yankee Bean Soup," he told the waitress. "From now on, hot or cold, rain or snow or shine, I want Yankee Bean Soup on the menu every day."

The House introduced Yankee Bean Soup the following day and the Senate three years later and neither restaurant has missed a day ever since.

ALICE CHASE   Dr. Alice Chase was the author of *Nutrition for Health* and other books on the science of proper eating. She died in 1974 of malnutrition.

CLARENCE A. CRANE   Since Clarence A. Crane, a Cleveland confectioner, introduced Life Savers in 1912 over 25 billion rolls have been sold. Were all these candies stacked end to end they would form a tube 1,124,500 miles long or over four times the distance to the moon. Company officials

Clarence Crane's original Life Savers pack *(Life Savers, Inc.)*

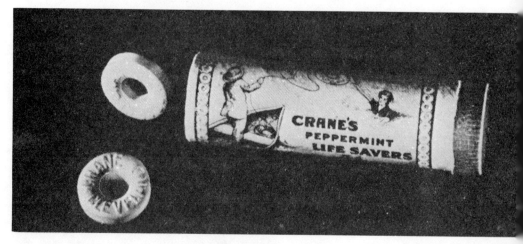

attribute this amazing success not so much to what's in a Life Saver as to what isn't in it.

The candy with the million dollar hole was a serendipitous discovery. Clarence Crane's principal business was chocolate, but during the hot summer months the bars and bon bons melted and sales fell off. To compensate for this loss in volume, Crane developed a summertime specialty of hard mints. To press the mints into shape he employed a local pill manufacturer. There was trouble with the machinery and, instead of the plain round discs Crane had envisioned, the press stamped out little peppermint rings. Crane knew immediately that he had a product with mystery, sex appeal, and sales potential. Moreover, it fairly cried out for its famous name and he registered the Life Savers trademark that year.

A footnote: By far the most sensational flavor of Life Savers is Wint-O-Green, although taste, per se, has nothing to do with that judgment. Wint-O-Green sometimes produces a strange variety of chemical fireworks, scientifically known as triboluminescence, which results from the rapid break-down of sugar crystals and the effect of the released energy on the flavoring. Thus, in a darkened room under the proper conditions, the candy literally throws off sparks as you chew it.

DR. JAMES C. CROW "Too much of anything is bad," Mark Twain once cautioned, "but too much good whiskey is barely enough." If any one man can take the credit for perfecting bourbon whiskey, for making it smooth and distinctive, that man is Dr. James C. Crow, a Scottish physician and chemist, who immigrated to Kentucky in 1823. Crow was the originator of the sour mash process, which gives good bourbon its character and uniformity. He also introduced the saccharometer, the thermometer, and the standards of cleanliness which ensure a quality product. While other distillers were stretching the mash to get the highest return, Crow would distill only two-and-a-half gallons of whiskey from each bushel of grain.

One of the most famous anecdotes of the Civil War concerns the time when Henry T. Blow, a congressman from Missouri, went to Abraham Lincoln to complain that General Grant was drunk during the Battle of Shiloh. Lincoln replied: "I wish I knew what brand of whiskey he drinks. I would send a barrel to all my other generals." Sedulous historians have since determined that Old Crow was Grant's brand; it was also the preferred refreshment of Henry Clay, Daniel Webster, Andrew Jackson, John Calhoun, and William Henry Harrison.

Dr. Crow died in 1856, but the firm of W. A. Gaines & Company carried on his name and method. The last known store of whiskey personally distilled by Crow was used by Joseph C. C. Blackburn of Versailles, Kentucky, during an 1875 congressional campaign. His opponent, Ed Marshall, seemed sure to win. With his political career on the line, Blackburn was driven to the desperate measure of tapping a ten-gallon cask of Old Crow, which he had been storing in his cellar for decades, and decanting the treasured liquid into scores of tiny cruets. Blackburn then buttonholed every die-hard Marshall supporter he could find, praised the virtues of Dr. Crow's elixir, and "poured the liquor into his soul."

"As you drink that, sir," Blackburn would say, "I want you to remember that you are helping to destroy the most precious heirloom of my family. It is the last bit of genuine Crow whiskey in the world. Observe, sir, that you do not need to gulp down a tumbler of water after swallowing the liquor to keep it from burning your gullet. On the contrary, you know instinctively that to drink water with it would be a crime. All I ask of you is to remember that you are getting something in this liquor that all the money of an Indian prince cannot buy. Drink it, sir, and give your soul up to the Lord. Then if you can vote for Ed Marshall I cannot complain, because it will be the Lord's act!"

Blackburn won in a landslide.

CHIEF GEORGE CRUM At long last let's give the man his due: it was George Crum, an Adirondack Indian chief, who chipped the first potato in a fit of rage. Crum (his real

George Crum, shown here with his spouse, invented the original potato chips *(Potato Chip/Snack Food Association)*

name was Speck, but he changed it because "a Crum is larger") was employed as head chef at Moon's Lake Lodge, a posh resort in Saratoga Springs, New York. One evening in 1853 a particularly fussy guest at the lodge kept returning his french fries to the kitchen because they were "too thick." The gentleman had just returned from Paris where ultra-thin *pommes frites* were in fashion, and the coarser "steak house potatoes" preferred in this country disgusted him. Grudgingly George Crum ad libbed his own version of shoe-string potatoes and sent them out to the dining room. Moments later, the waiter came back with a full plate on his tray and said, "He wants them even thinner."

In a fury, Crum grabbed a vicious-looking kitchen knife and stropped it with a vengeance. There was some concern in the kitchen that the chief might be planning to scalp the malcontent. Instead he grabbed a Maine potato, sliced it into pieces as thin as newsprint, and plunged the slices into boiling fat. Then he personally served the golden, curling chips to the stubborn diner.

Whether it was the chips themselves or the murderous look in the chief's eye that made the difference, the customer proclaimed the potatoes delicious. The next day Moon's Lodge featured a new dish on its menu, Chief George Crum's "Saratoga Chips." Eventually Crum left the lodge and set up his own restaurant down the road, where notables like Cornelius Vanderbilt and Jay Gould waited in line for the specialty of the house.

They were know as "Saratoga Chips" until the turn of the century, thereafter simply potato chips. Gradually but steadily they grew in popularity and today the average American consumes over 13 pounds of chips each year. (We trust you eat your patriotic share.)

JUNE deSPAIN   Miss deSpain is the author of *The Little Cyanide Cook-Book,* a hot item at the 1977 Cancer Victory Convention in Washington. (Another big seller was *Thank God I Have Cancer,* by Reverend Clifford Oden.)

THEODORE B. DUFUR   Keeping astronauts well-fed on long space journeys could be a very difficult problem. According to the British weekly, *New Scientist,* the Japan Livestock Institute, working with the National Aeronautics and Space Administration, has come up with one possible solution: they are hybridizing a breed of very small pigs to take along on the trip. An equally novel plan was advanced by Theodore B. Dufur of the United States back in 1955. He suggested that spaceships be constructed of edible substances such as cheese or frozen margarine. When the interplanetary explorers land on Mars, Dufur explained, they could simply nibble away at the craft until the next expedition arrives.

KAREN DWYER and PATRIKA BROWN   Anatomically honest gingerbread men and women are a specialty at the Erotic Baker, Inc., owned and operated by Karen Dwyer and Patrika Brown of New York City. Other piping hot goodies for sale include cakes, cookies, and breads shaped and decorated to resemble mammaries and genitalia.

The vice president of the 83d Street Block Association has declared the x-rated bakery "shouldn't be in a residential neighborhood." He is determined to see that the two women get their just desserts, like all the other pornographic entrepreneurs.

"We're bakers, not censors," Ms. Brown remarked, but in an effort to conform to community standards she and her partner have put a curtain over the store window to prevent children from peeping in, and have hung a sign on the door that reads: "A BAKERY FOR GROWNUPS."

ANTOINE FEUCHTWANGER   That the name of Antoine Feuchtwanger should languish in obscurity proves that fame is fickle. John Montagu attained immortality when he spent twenty-four hours at the gaming table without any other refreshment than some slices of beef between two pieces of toast; he was the Fourth earl of Sandwich. Sylvester Graham (q.v.) lives on eponymously in the cracker he invented. By all rights, then, the favorite food at baseball games should be *feuchtwangers* with mustard.

Feuchtwanger, a Bavarian immigrant, introduced the frankfurter sausage to America in the 1880s from his small stand in St. Louis. Initially, however, there was a major handling problem to overcome. Feuchtwanger could not afford to serve his franks on china plates with silverware; on the other hand, his customers could hardly be expected to eat piping-hot sausages with their bare fingers. After long thought, his first brainstorm was to issue a pair of protective gloves along with each frankfurter; but too many people walked off without returning their gloves, and, besides, the laundry bills were prohibitive. Then Feuchtwanger came up with the inspiration of a lifetime—cradling his wurst in a long sliced roll. The rest, as they say, is history.

An etymological note for frankophiles: On a cold April day in 1900, Harry Stevens, who ran the concessions at the old New York Polo Grounds, instructed his vendors to yell out the slogan "They're red hot. Get your dachshund sausages while they're red hot." Sitting in the press box that day was Hearst newspaper cartoonist Tad Dorgan, who, inspired by the vendors' cries, set to work on a cartoon depicting dachshund sausages cuddled in rolls barking at each other. Dorgan, according to his fellow journalists, was a miserable speller. So instead of attempting to write "hot dachshunds" below his sketch, he simply jotted "hot dogs," the first recorded use of that term.

Not everybody was happy with Dorgan's pet phrase. Coney Island vendors felt it implied that their sausages contained dog meat, or worse, and in 1913 the Chamber of Commerce banned the mention of "hot dogs" there, substituting the term "Coney." This year alone, Americans will consume over 16 billion frankfurters (or hot dogs, or conies, or weiners, if you prefer). That works out to roughly 80 franks for every man, woman, and child.

ALBERT FISH In 1934 Albert Fish, a New York City housepainter of nondescript visage, was charged with murdering and eating 15 schoolchildren, including a 10-year-old girl whom he cooked in a stew with carrots and onions. (The dish fed him for over a week.) Fish was convicted of his excesses and died in the electric chair.

BETSY FLANNAGAN The cocktail made its world debut at Halls Corners, a small tavern at Dobbs Ferry in Westchester County, New York. Historians say the credit for making alcohol even more enjoyable belongs to Betsy Flannagan, a patriotic barmaid who decorated the taproom with brightly colored plumes picked from the rump of a Tory neighbor's rooster. One day in 1777 a group of revolutionary officers were seated at the bar, swilling tall drinks made of rum, rye, and fruit juices. A Frenchman in the group asked Betsy to insert a rooster tail in each glass, either for use as a swizzle stick or to make the drink more festive. He proposed a toast to the maiden's health, then followed with another in franglais: "Vive le coq's tail!" And that, according to a number of sober etymologists, is how the mixed drink got its name.

76

HORACE FLETCHER   While they had little else in common, John D. Rockefeller, Upton Sinclair, and William Gladstone all shared one distinctive habit: at breakfast, lunch, and dinner they chewed every morsel of food a minimum of 32 times, once for each tooth.

The man who instructed them in this time-consuming practice was Horace Fletcher (1849–1919), whose philosophy of life is epitomized in the slogan he composed, "Nature will castigate those who don't masticate." Fletcher believed that unless food is chewed into a liquid state, one cannot possibly derive from it it's full nutritional value. Even soup and milk should be sloshed around in the mouth a full 15 or 20 seconds to give the saliva ample time to do its work. Although it made for tedious meals and tired jaws, thousands of people here and in Europe swallowed this dubious theory of digestion, and in the 1890s mothers dutifully exhorted their children to "fletcherize" every bite on their plates.

"Horace Fletcher saved my life," crowed novelist Henry James. "And, what is more, he improved my disposition." Fletcherism also worked wonders for Fletcher. In 1903, testing his legs on the Yale University ergometer, he raised 350 pounds, double the record of the school's most powerful athlete; and to celebrate his fiftieth birthday Fletcher bicycled an incredible two hundred miles in one day. His meals, consisting principally of milk, prepared cereals, and maple sugar, cost an average of 11 cents a day, and once as an experiment he subsisted on potatoes alone for two months. Every aspect of digestion engaged his interest. During one memorable period of his life, he arranged to send periodic samples of his feces to the United States Department of Agriculture for testing and analysis.

EDWARD GEIN   To label Ed Gein a cannibal and leave it at that is to rob him of his due. Gein, who has been confined since 1957 to Wisconsin's Central State Hospital for the Criminally Insane, did not merely feast on the flesh of at least 15 of his female neighbors. He *wallowed* in it, dressing himself in the skins, fashioning souvenir-store ashtrays and curios from the bones, and growing intoxicated on the sheer touch, taste, and smell of human meat. He was in all ways an American Original.

Gein first dallied in fleshly pursuits in the early 1950s. He was living alone then, a quiet-spoken, somewhat reclusive Plainfield, Wisconsin, farmer and handyman who turned to the study of female anatomy when a government subsidy program made it worth his while to leave his land untended and take it easy. Bored with his medical texts, he took to robbing graves, hauling his booty back to his farmhouse by night, where he flayed each body and paraded around the kitchen garbed in the skins. The internal organs and the bones appealed to Gein the most, and those he kept; the rest he incinerated.

But grave-robbing too began to pall, so Gein walked into a tavern in nearby Pine Grove one winter's day in 1954 and shot 51-year-old Mary Hogan and hauled her home on a sled. The murder went unsolved until 1957 when Gein shot and killed a Plainfield hardware store owner named Bernice Worden. He carried off not only her body, but her cash register as well.

It was not a well-planned caper. Gein left a pool of Mrs. Worden's blood on the floor behind the counter where he had drilled her, along with a receipt for the half-gallon can of antifreeze he had earlier that week told Frank Worden he planned to buy. Frank Worden was Bernice's son. He was also Plainfield's deputy sheriff.

Gein was arrested for the murder of Mrs. Worden but it wasn't till after he was locked up that the enormity of his crime became apparent. Checking his home for clues, young Worden and the town's sheriff found more than fingerprints and a smoking gun. They found a vase full of human noses on the kitchen table, a drum made from skins stretched tight over a coffee can, a soup bowl fashioned from a skull, several bracelets, a pair of leggings, a vest, and a purse made from human skin, assorted bones, skulls, and organs festooning the walls, a pair of lips on a string hanging from the window, and a heart in a frying-pan atop the stove. Gein's refrigerator freezer held a nice assortment of fresh organs on ice.

Although coroners sorted out the remains of at least 15 women in his kitchen, Gein swore he could remember murdering only 2. He owned up to swiping Bernice Worden's cash register, but bristled at implications that he was a thief.

"I'm no robber," he protested. "I took the money and the cash register because I wanted to see how it worked."

SYLVESTER GRAHAM The Reverend Sylvester W. Graham was America's first home-grown vegetarian apostle and champion of bowel regularity. A Presbyterian preacher by trade, he traveled throughout the country in the 1840s delivering fire-and-brimstone sermons on the evils of white bread, flesh-eating, and rum, while stressing the importance of moving the bowels once a day. The newspapers promptly dubbed him "the Peristaltic Persuader."

"Meat," he warned, "is a powerful constipator which stimulates sexual excess." Condiments, like mustard, vinegar, and pepper, excite the system, causing depression and insanity. Chicken pie induces *cholera morbus*. And so, thousands of fanatical Grahamites—including Horace Greeley, Thomas Edison, and J.H. Kellogg (the cornflake king)—sat down three times a day to tables heaped high with fresh fruits and vegetables. To top off each meal they greedily devoured special whole-wheat wafers invented by their leader—the original Graham crackers.

In 1841 Graham infuriated Boston bakers with charges that they adulterated white bread with chalk, pipe clay, and plaster of Paris. In retaliation, a lynch mob surrounded the Marlborough Hotel, where the "mad enthusiast" was scheduled to speak. The crowd burst through the police barriers and it looked like Graham would be strung up like the sides of prime beef he found so distasteful. At the last moment, a brigade of loyal supporters, stationed by the second-story windows of the Marlborough, shoveled clouds of slaked lime onto the attackers. The air was filled with choking, burning powder, the "eyes" had it, and the rabble retired.

Graham survived to espouse other visionary reforms, such as sleeping with the windows open and an end to tight lacing of corsets. According to his calculations, "folly in dress" killed over eighty thousand Americans in 1835. Masturbation was another dread killer. Graham helped to formulate the "Hands-Off Policy" and recommended cold showers as an effective prophylactic against self-abuse. He advised parents and teachers to be on the lookout for the telltale signs of chronic onanism—"the characteristic languor of the student's gait, his haggard countenance, his failing memory."

HANSON CROCKETT GREGORY   Shocking as it seems, the original American doughnut had no hole. Where the hole should have been there was a nut; hence, of course, the name. But there was no convenient handle for dunking, nothing to peep through, no mystery at all. In fact, it is impossible to imagine the doughnut attaining its current fame and favor had it not been for the experimental genius of one man, Captain Hanson Crockett Gregory, the inventor of the hole.

Born at Clam Cove, Maine, in 1832, Hanson Gregory is still remembered as a brave and able captain of Yankee merchant vessels. Several apocryphal stories maintain that the captain made his vacuous discovery while at sea. According to one account, six sailors on Gregory's ship fell overboard soon after eating a prodigious number of fried cakes (as doughnuts were sometimes called in pre-hole days). The sheer weight of the doughnuts (sinkers, presumably) sent the sailors plummeting to the bottom of the ocean, whence the bodies were never recovered. For a long time Captain Gregory brooded over the tragic loss of his men and he resolved to find a way to make the doughnut less ponderous. Then it came to him! Inspired by the design of the life preserver, he grabbed a belaying pin and punched a hole through every doughnut on board.

Another version has it that Captain Gregory was at the wheel of his ship eating a fried cake when a squall blew up. The wheel lurched suddenly, sending a spoke through the center of the cake and creating the first doughnut hole. Both versions seem highly improbable, considering that Gregory was only 15 years old in 1847 when the hole was born.

To get the true story, we contacted Fred Crockett, a great-grand-nephew of the captain. "The invention of the doughnut occurred on dry land," Crockett insists, "at the stove of the old Gregory homestead in Clam Cove. Hanson was watching his mother cook up a bunch of fried cakes when he noticed that the centers didn't get quite done. 'They never do,' his mother said. And so Hanson got a fork and poked it through the center of the fried cake and the doughnut hole was born."

It was so simple! So brilliant!

"The Doughnut Corporation of America, Dunkin' Donuts, and Mister Donut have all acknowledged Captain Gregory as the 'Father of the Doughnut Hole,' " Mr. Crockett says. And the whole question was settled once and for all at the Great Doughnut Debate, sponsored by the National Dunking Association on October 27, 1941. Fred Crockett was there with a pile of documentation. In opposition was Chief High Eagle, a member of the Wampanoag tribe from Mashpee, Massachusetts. "The chief said that the doughnut hole was invented on Cape Cod by a distant ancestor of his," Crockett recalls. "He said that a Pilgrim housewife was cooking fried cakes when the Indian, a member of the Yarmouth tribe, shot an arrow into the air meaning to kill her. The arrow went astray and pierced the center of the fried cake, creating the first doughnut hole in history."

We asked Fred Crockett whether he gave any credence to the chief's claim. "Of course not," he answered, "the story was full of holes." A panel of impartial judges—among them Clifton Fadiman, Franklin P. Adams, Elsa Maxwell, and Dr. Funk of the *Funk & Wagnalls Dictionary*—decided unanimously in favor of Captain Gregory, and a straw poll of the audience showed that they supported the Yankee captain over the Indian by a three-to-one majority.

During the doughnut hole centennial celebration, a bronze plaque was placed on the Gregory home, which still stands in

Clam Cove (now Glen Cove). And sculptor Victor Cahill of Portland, Maine, envisioned an even more ambitious memorial. In 1939 he carved a life-size statue of the captain, doughnut in hand, which was to serve as the model for a 300-foot colossus to be erected on the summit of Mount Battie on the Maine coast. Cahill planned to illuminate the monument with powerful floodlights so it could be seen 50 miles out to sea on fogless nights.

With a note of disappointment in his voice, Fred Crockett reports: "It never got that far."

ERNEST A. HAMWI   A lesser intellect might have thought of an ice cream cylinder, an ice cream pyramid, or conceivably even an ice cream duodecahedron. Ernest A. Hamwi intuitively recognized the folly of such configurations. He was the brains behind the cone.

In 1904 the Damascus-born pastry vendor obtained a permit to sell zalabia (a wafer-thin Persian waffle, served with sugar or jam) on the grounds of the St. Louis World's Fair. Just a few steps away from his concession stood one of the 50 ice cream stands that dotted the fairgrounds, dispensing five and ten cent scoops in small dishes. One infernal summer's day, Hamwi couldn't give away a hot zalabia. The ice cream man, in contrast, was overwhelmed with customers and soon ran out of dishes. Hamwi saw his chance. He grabbed a zalabia, formed it into a cornucopia, let it cool, and plopped a scoop of ice cream on top. Fairgoers liked the idea and the "World's Fair Cornucopia" was an immediate success. After the fair was over, Hamwi went on to establish the Cornucopia Waffle Company and later founded the Missouri Cone Company.

His claim to fame has been recognized by the International Association of Ice Cream Manufacturers, the National Geographic Society, and a gaggle of frozen dessert historians. In the interest of fairness, however, we should also mention the competing assertion made by Charles E. Menches, who sold ice cream sandwiches at the fair. Menches, so the story goes, gave an ice cream sandwich and a bouquet of flowers to a girl he was courting. Lacking a vessel in which to hold her posies, the girl took one layer of the sandwich and wrapped it around the flower stems as a makeshift vase. The remaining layer was rolled into a similar shape and the ice cream put on top—the prototype of the modern cone. It all sounds rather messy and improbable, but that's the version credited by *Kane's Famous First Facts*.

DEBI HORN Debi Horn, a 229-pound housewife from Gibraltar, Michigan, was the first overweight American to slim down by having her jaws wired together by an oral surgeon. By the summer of 1974, just seven months after her last solid meal, the tight-lipped Ms. Horn had shed 73 pounds and the man with the wirecutters, Dr. Daniel M. Laskin, D.D.S., had gone into the mouth-shutting business whole hog, so to speak, locking up an additional 100 mouths. In an interview, Dr. Laskin cautioned overeaters about opting too quickly for the mouth-wiring method. Insisting that it was gimmicky, he noted that he had turned down many applicants for the procedure.

ROBERT GIBBON JOHNSON During the early decades of the nineteenth century, the tomato, or "love apple," was considered pretty poison. This recent South American import was widely admired as an exotic ornamental shrub, but the luscious red fruit was considered lethal to eat.

Almost single-handedly, Robert Gibbon Johnson of Salem County, New Jersey, rehabilitated the tomato's reputation. Johnson was a wealthy and well-traveled man who had sampled the pulpy viscera of the love apple on a trip through southern Spain. In August, 1820, he returned to New Jersey and announced his intention to eat the deadly fruit in public on the Salem courthouse steps. This he did with juicy pleasure while a horrified crowd looked on, expecting at any moment to see him drop to the ground in fatal convulsions.

Johnson survived, of course, and from that day on the tomato became increasingly acceptable in the nation's salads. Moreover, Johnson put his money where his mouth was, founding county fairs throughout the Mid-Atlantic region and offering cash prizes for the finest tomatoes in the land.

JOHN JOHNSTON John was his given name, but his friends and followers knew him as Liver-Eating. Liver-Eating Johnston of New Jersey, a lawman, '49er, and soldier of fortune, roamed the badlands in the 1850s nourishing his six-foot, 260-pound frame principally on the livers of nearly 250 Crow Indians.

Born in Newark in 1822, Johnston went west with the Gold Rush, then retired to Wyoming where he took an Indian bride and lived quietly as woodsman and hunter. But the Crows came one night to capture and slay Johnston's wife, six months pregnant, and the tragedy sent him off the deep end. For the next few years he cultivated his appetite for the internal organs of the Crows, ultimately making his peace with the tribe and becoming a blood brother to their chief.

In the 1860s Liver-Eating fought with the Union in the War Between the States and was also a sheriff. He died destitute in Santa Monica in 1900 and was buried in Sawtelle Veterans Cemetery.

The story doesn't end there. It wasn't Johnston's idea to be buried in Sawtelle. He had made abundantly clear to his friends his desire to return to the Northwest, the land of the Crows. In 1968, as his bones mouldered in the subtropic climes of greater Los Angeles, a group of seventh-graders in nearby Lancaster, California, organized "The Committee for the Reburial of Liver-Eating Johnston" and campaigned vigorously to have their hero properly relocated. In 1969 the federal government okayed the removal of old Liver-Eating to a grave on the banks of the Shoshone River, in Wyoming. The Veterans of Foreign Wars were outraged and stormed that "no veteran remains safe in his grave," but Liver-Eating Johnston was happy at last.

THOMAS LaBOTT LaBott was known in health-food circles as the man who ate nothing but sand. When he died in

Chicago in 1972, physicians agreed that his singular dietary preferences were *not* a factor in his death.

KONSTANTINOS LOGGINOS More amazing than the better-than-adequate four-course meals Konstantinos Logginos was serving for 69 cents in his Springfield, Ohio, restaurant in 1977 was the fact that within three months of its opening, attendance had fallen to barely a third of what it had been just after the place opened. It certainly wasn't the quality or even the quantity of the food that kept customers away. According to the *Wall Street Journal,* "Most people who have been to Dino's," as the establishment was known, "say the food is fine. The dinner begins with soup and a tossed salad. The main course one recent night was shrimp scampi, pepper steak or sweetbreads with mushrooms. The vegetable was peas. Dessert was cake or pie. Frank Case, a broker ... in Dayton, 30 miles away, says he and some friends have been 'delighted with not only the quantity but the quality of the food.' "

Then why the flagging attendance? For one thing, reservations were impossible, a result not of restaurant policy but rather the lack of a telephone. In its palmier days, patrons would crowd into the place and wait on line to be seated, only to be told that the chef had run out of food. In Mr. Logginos's words, "When that happens, I have to push them out and tell them, 'No more.' " Too, the restaurant's ambience, noted the *Journal,* "is just a cut above an Army chow line's." Such necessaries as tomato catsup and crackers were unavailable, and water was priced at 25 cents the glass.

Logginos was born in Greece and learned from his restaurateur father the ins and outs of running a dining establishment. He migrated to the United States in 1963 and worked in miscellaneous kitchens and hashhouses till he opened Dino's 1 in 1976. He now has dreams of opening a Dino's No. 3 elsewhere in Springfield: "There is no Dino's No. 2; we're skipping the even numbers."

KATHRYN NILES Mrs. Kathryn Niles spent 28 years developing over ten thousand new and original recipes using eggs, chicken, and turkey. She is one of the immortals enshrined in The Poultry Hall of Fame (yes, it really does exist) in Beltsville, Maryland. If chickens could vote, she probably would have been blackballed.

ALFERD PACKER It was unpardonable what Alferd Packer did in the winter of 1874: On a grueling trek across the Rockies he ate most of the Democratic party of Hinsdale County, Colorado. For that unconscionable breach of good taste, Packer was hustled off to Gunnison State Jail later that year, the only person in American history ever to be convicted of cannibalism.

In all fairness to Packer, who was roundly reviled as a "mad hyena," a "voracious, man-eating son of a bitch," and "the Colorado Cannibal," his gourmandism was no mere dietary caprice. It happened this way. On February 9, 1874, he set out on the 75-mile hike across the Rockies with five mining companions, good Democrats all. (There were said to be only two others throughout the rest of the county.) Sixty

Alferd Packer—cannibal and his fare *(Colorado Historical Society)*

86

days later, Packer arrived alone at his destination, the Los Piños Ute Agency, bearded, filthy, and missing his right thumb, but otherwise in improbably robust health for a man who had just weathered two hellish months in the mountains, where food was scarce and the mercury often dipped to 50 below.

"Where are your companions?" the Los Piños regulars asked. Packer avoided their questions and their stares. Finally he confessed that fellow traveler Shannon Wilson Bell had slain the others in the party and that he in turn killed Bell in self-defense. Then, to stay alive, he roasted and devoured the flesh of his dead companions. "It tasted like jerked beef," he said.

Packer served 17 years in the Gunnison jail, a model prisoner in all ways who spent his idle moments tending his beloved plants and shrubs and weaving horsehair belts. He died a free man at age 65 in 1907.

MELVIN PAGE   Florida dentist Melvin Page thinks milk is bad for you and he's given the best years of his life to helping Americans resist the temptations of the dairy. "As far as I know," he wrote in *Degeneration-Regeneration* in 1949, "man and a certain species of ant are the only ones who use an animal secretion after the age of weaning." Newborn babies do well enough on mother's milk, Dr. Page admits, but drink it as an adult and you're courting colds, colitis, cancer, and certain death. The proof, he offers, is that the state with the highest per capita rate of cancer is Wisconsin.

PHILIP SYNG PHYSICK   Next time you knock back a Coca-Cola or a glass of Moxie, drink a toast to Dr. Philip Syng Physick, the Philadelphia physician who in 1807 commissioned chemist Townsend Speakman to invent carbonated water. It was Dr. Physick's thought that the carbonation would prove health-giving for his patients, although it remained to Speakman to make the beverage more tolerable by mixing in fruit juices.

But soda pop is not Dr. Physick's sole claim to fame. In an

operation in 1831 he removed one thousand stones from the bladder of Chief Justice John Marshall of the United States Supreme Court.

FRANK REESE While serving a term in Collin County Jail, Texas, Frank Reese, age 44, took to unscrewing light-bulbs from their sockets and eating them. Local TV news-men did a story on Reese who smiled into the cameras and then wolfed down 14 fresh bulbs and the sheriff's sunglasses.

J. I. RODALE Appearing on the Dick Cavett Show in 1971, nutrition expert J. I. Rodale declared, "I'm so healthy that I expect to live on and on." Moments later, as Cavett and guest Pete Hamill looked on in stunned disbelief, Rodale suffered a fatal heart attack on camera. The pretaped show was never aired, sparing viewers a late-night first. *(See also:* Chris Chubbuck.)

DR. J. WATERMAN ROSE Back in 1945 Dr. J. Water-man Rose summarized the advantages of a herbivorous diet for the edification of a *New York Times* reporter: "Vege-tarians have less gout, cancer, tuberculosis, and rheumatism than non-vegetarians. They live longer. They smell better. Their skins are clearer. Their teeth are better." A naturopath, or nuts-and-berries healer, by profession, he went on to pro-claim: "What's wrong with modern doctors is that they only cure the symptoms instead of going to the cause of the disease—meat!"

George Bernard Shaw once observed that flesh-eating was "cannibalism with its heroic dish omitted." Dr. Rose could not have agreed more. For many years he was the director of the Bronx Vegetarian Center, but he is probably best remem-bered for his well-manicured goatee and for proposing the establishment of a new vegetarian city, where it would be illegal for the residents to eat meat. There, practicing vege-tarians might bring up their children on a healthy diet of kale, black bread, carrots, and soy cutlets, in the illustrious tradition of Buddha, Socrates, Pythagoras, and John D.

Rockefeller. A site near Middletown, Connecticut, was chosen, and there was animated debate on whether to call the settlement Vegetonia or Vegetaria. A flag was designed. An anthem was composed:

> Eat no flesh at all.
> Eat no flesh at all.
> Peace will come when man has learned
> To eat no flesh at all.

Then, for reasons that remain obscure, the project withered and died like a blighted pear.

LOTHROP WITHINGTON, JR. The goldfish-swallowing craze, with its nationwide intestinal reverberations, began innocently enough in the ivy-covered dining halls of Harvard College. Lothrop Withington, Jr., a 21-year-old biology major, was eating dinner with two classmates, Harry Newman and John Lacey, when he happened to mention that he used to swallow live goldfish as a kid. His companions didn't believe a word of it and were willing to wager five dollars, then and there, that Withington wouldn't dare devour a squirming fantail in public view at the Harvard Union. It was "mind over matter," he explained years later. "I didn't mind and the goldfish didn't matter."

The tradition-setting epicurean never had a moment's doubt that he could do it. Back in 1928, his parents had taken him on a vacation to Hawaii, where he had watched a native capture goldfish at the beach and down them whole with no apparent side effects. After that, he performed the same feat several times himself, to the consternation of his parents. But Withington was surprised and even a little embarrassed by all the media attention the stunt attracted. On the appointed day, March 3, 1939, reporters from all the wire services and major Boston newspapers were on hand to watch as he caught a lively four-inch specimen by the tail and dropped it into his wide-open mouth.

"Waves of perplexity passed over Withington's face once

the fish had disappeared," according to the *Boston Globe*. "There seemed to be some difficulty at first—some internal struggle—but after a brief moment of confusion the fisheater swallowed and all was well." He gulped down a few draughts of water then announced, "That's good. Just like chowder."

The ensuing publicity launched a new era in intercollegiate competition as undergraduates everywhere vied with one another for the goldfish-swallowing championship of the world. The standard rose progressively from one, to five, to twenty-eight, to forty-two. The species was being devastated, and Robert F. Sellar, for one, was livid: "Nobody knows how a goldfish feels," the director of the Boston Animal Rescue League declared. "We cannot sidestep this issue." Sellar called for strict new legislation to stop the slaughter.

Defying rising opposition from pisciphiles, Howard Francis of Kutztown State Teachers College in Reading, Pennsylvania, ingurgitated 43 goldfish in 54 minutes; he was immediately suspended from school for "conduct unbecoming a student in a professional course." Then, Gordon Southworth, a pre-veterinary student with a stomach of iron, established a mark that would stand for 28 years, consuming 67 fish in just 14 minutes and washing down the meal with milk and a peanut butter sandwich. When the president of Middlesex College was asked whether he would take disciplinary action against Southworth, he replied, "Nope." Inquisitive biochemists subsequently performed a fractional gastric analysis on Southworth and found that his digestive system functioned twice as fast as the average gut.

In the spring of 1967 Robert Auve, a junior at St. Joseph's College in Philadelphia, upped the world record to 199 live ones. And what about Lothrop Withington, who started it all? At last report, he was a successful heating oil dealer in Plymouth, Massachusetts.

Inventors and Innovators

JOHN ALBERT   John Albert may save us all from a frosty annihilation yet. A New York-based chemist with a passion for plants, Albert contrived a system for heating buildings with elephant dung laced with wholewheat flour. Zebra dung is effective too in case your elephants aren't producing, although pachyderm poop is indeed the fuel of choice. And it really works.

Albert's first and most prestigious client was his employer, the New York Botanical Gardens, which began heating one of its hothouses using weekly shipments of high-grade manure from the nearby Bronx Zoo. The manure, representing the best efforts of the zoo's five resident elephants, would arrive packed in a crate labeled "special handling." Running around 165 degrees F. on delivery, the stuff would then be stored in a vat, its vapors sucked by a fan through heating pipes into the hothouse. After cooling off, it could be used as fertilizer. Albert's dream for the future includes racetrack grandstands heated with horse manure, and chicken coops kept toasty warm with chicken excreta. Meanwhile, budgetary restrictions at the zoo forced Albert from the rolls, and he went to work as a horticulturist on an estate owned by the Rockefellers in upstate New York.

PHILIP BACHMAN   With real estate values skyrocketing, even in cemeteries, inventor Philip Bachman has patented a remarkable process that could save on costly burial plots while revolutionizing the mortuary profession. In brief, he

91

proposes to freeze dead bodies in liquid nitrogen at 150 degrees below zero and then to run them through a machine for "surface enhancement"—that is, pulverization. Next the tiny chunks are freeze-dried like instant coffee crystals before finally being deposited in a funeral urn. What would happen if boiling water were added? One shudders to think.

ALFRED ELY BEACH   On a moonless night in February, 1868, Alfred Ely Beach, publisher of *Scientific American,* stood in the ill-lit basement of Devlin's Clothing Store, beneath the corner of Broadway and Warren Street in lower Manhattan. With him were his 21-year-old son, Fred, and a team of workmen bearing picks, shovels, wheelbarrows, and a special hydraulic boring device of Beach's inventing.

"Gentlemen," he said, chalking a spot on the rear wall, "we commence here." In total secrecy, the most daring excavation project of its time was about to begin.

It was a project the great Beach had first envisioned nearly two decades earlier. "My plan," he had written in 1849, "is to

Alfred Ely Beach, the inventor of the subway *(New York Public Library Picture Collection)*

92

tunnel Broadway through its whole length with openings for stairways at every corner ... [laying down] a double track, ... the whole to be brilliantly lighted with gas. The cars ... will stop every 10 seconds at every corner." Although Beach was a highly regarded publisher and patent attorney, respectable people sneered at his "underground tunnel" and thought it the stuff of a madman's dreams.

But their scorn was unjust, for if any city in the world desperately needed a subway system, it was traffic-choked midcentury New York. Beach himself knew the situation first-hand: although his law office and apartment were scarcely two miles apart, he was nearly an hour getting home each night. Nor was he a man to be scorned. An inventor's inventor, he had created, at the age of 21, the world's first working typewriter (a "literary piano" is what he called it) and demonstrated it at the 1856 Crystal Palace Exposition. But neither his typewriter nor his other wonderful inventions provided him with much income. It was from his publishing career and law practice that he earned his living. In addition to his stewardship of *Scientific American,* Beach also ran the *New York Sun* for a while and established an additional two dozen publications, some of which still exist.

By the late 1860s, Beach realized that a *horse-drawn* subway would be dangerously impractical, and turned his thoughts to man-made locomotion. It quickly became obvious that of all the alternatives, pneumatic power was by far the most desirable. Obvious too was the need to build his experimental subway undercover, considering the public's cynicism toward his scheme. So Beach applied for no charter, asked for no assistance. The workmen who followed him to Devlin's basement that night in 1868 were sworn to absolute secrecy.

Night after night they returned to the lengthening tunnel via the basement, digging and scooping further and further into what surely must have seemed a Dantean nightmare. It took 58 nights to bore through to Murray Street, the northern terminus of the Broadway Tunnel. Assembling the 22-passenger railroad car that would shuttle its length, and outfitting the station took another two years and $350,000 of Beach's own money.

The day of the unveiling was February 26, 1870. A master of public relations, Beach invited the press, the city fathers, and a throng of VIPs to view his underground brainchild, regaling them with a sumptuous four-hour buffet lunch and, of course, test-rides on his pneumatic marvel. The visitors were as impressed with the elegance of its furnishings as with its mechanical superiority. The car itself, upholstered in dark leather and red velvet, would please a sultan. The walnut-paneled waiting room that ran half the length of the tunnel was appointed with mirrors, costly divans, paintings, a fountain and a grand piano. Even the once-cynical *New York Times* was rhapsodic. Everyone was.

Of course, Beach's experiment in below-the-ground transport was merely that—an experiment. What he really wanted was to extend the tunnel five miles north to Central Park and add several cars. Running at full throttle, he claimed, the subway would skate along the rails at a mile a minute and carry twenty thousand passengers a day.

The physical obstacles blocking Beach's way were as nothing compared to the political obstacles. In 1870 all transportation companies in New York, large and small, paid fealty to Boss William Tweed, the most powerful man in the state. When Beach took his case to the state capital at Albany, Tweed viewed it as an insurrection, and squashed it by pushing through a bill of his own that called for a public outlay of as much as $65 million to erect an elevated tramway. The public was outraged, the press blistered, Beach grew despondent, but nothing could be done. Meanwhile, he continued to operate his subway as a profitable tourist attraction at 25 cents a ride, his son Fred doubling as brakeman and conductor. Over the next few years he campaigned for the passage of his Beach Transit Bill. Finally, in 1872, with Tweed in jail and a more public-spirited governor in Albany, Beach got his go-ahead.

Now construction could proceed at last. Or could it? It was

a full three years since the inventor's initial triumph. Public enthusiasm for the subway was not what it had been. Beach himself nurtured some doubts. The panic of '69 had dried up many of the financial wellsprings from which the subway would have to be underwritten. And downtown real estate magnates like John Jacob Astor were ranting vigorously against the project, convinced that once the excavation began, Trinity Church and the surrounding towers of lower Manhattan would topple like dominoes. With the approved Beach Transit Bill in his pocket, Beach approached his wealthy friends for support only to find that no one was interested.

In the following years Beach, grown mellower and less adventurous, turned his efforts to other matters—to his publications, his philanthropic endeavors, his religion. By the time of his death in 1896 he had long since disappeared from public view.

BEN BLUMBERG   The energy crisis is over, and we have Ben Blumberg of Sunnyvale, California, to thank for it. Blumberg, a power systems engineer, proposes to supply every man, woman, and child with a stationary bicycle attached to a small electric generator. With some vigorous pedaling in our spare moments, he says, our nation could become self-sufficient in energy and a world power in bicycle racing.

"Operation of these machines for just four hours a day would save 100 million barrels of oil each year," Blumberg calculates. That's equivalent to the output of 40 nuclear power plants.

Children could pedal during gym class. Government employees could pedal while doing their paperwork. The whole family could pedal while watching TV. Soon our population will have "the strongest legs in the world."

"We waste two thirds of our present fuel when we burn it for electricity. But pedal-produced energy, which goes directly into a generator is 97 percent efficient." What's more,

95

it's clean and virtually free. The only foreseeable drawback is an awesome national perspiration problem.

Blumberg expects stubborn opposition from the oil companies, but he is confident his bicykilowatt system will prevail in the end. "Once people discover they can make their own electricity instead of buying it from someone else, they will demand their pedal machines and the Department of Energy will have to supply them."

JAMES C. BOYLE In the 1890s the etiquette of hat tipping was rigidly observed. Every gentleman was expected to hoist his headcover and discreetly remove his cigar from his mouth whenever he encountered a female acquaintance of equal or superior social standing. During the course of a leisurely Sunday stroll one might be called upon to doff one's bowler as many as a hundred times; it made for a very tiresome outing.

To the rescue came James C. Boyle of Spokane, Washington, who invented the Boyle Derby Tipper. It was a godsend for every man with genuinely nice manners. This modern labor-saving convenience comprised an elaborate series of gears and levers which automatically raised one's hat, when activated by a slight tilt of the head. With the Boyle Derby Tipper, paying one's respects to ladies, flags, cathedrals, royal visitors, and passing funeral processions was no longer the fatiguing chore it once had been. Boyle was granted Patent Number 556,248 for his device, but it never achieved commercial success.

BOB BROWN While assembling an electric guitar in the garage of his Hipass, California, home, Bob Brown crossed some wires evidently not meant to be crossed and a horde of observing rats fled for their lives, as if a million fingernails had been dragged across a million blackboards. Following his instinct, Mr. Brown shelved his unfinished guitar and built a "rat repellent box" instead. That was in 1971, when the wheelchair-bound Mr. Brown, a victim of polio, was living on social security. Today he is the owner of the Amigo Ecology Corporation, the sole manufacturers of the box, whose net profits in 1977 were $800,000. Mr. Brown himself is a millionaire.

Over a period of six years, Mr. Brown sold some 18,000 rat repellent boxes to farmers in the San Joaquin Valley and the governments of South American nations. A poultry breeder whose hens were harassed nightly by 10,000 mice "cleared his place in four or five days" with the box, according to its inventor. The Venezuelan government ordered 300 to exterminate cockroaches in food stores in Caracas; Spain ordered 1,000 for its granaries. The University of Georgia took 200. Over a three-year test period, all but one worked.

While the box's signals, pitched at a million cycles per second, are far beyond the range of human hearing, rats go absolutely ape and cockroaches fall on their backs, totally devoid of balance. "We're jamming the sensory systems of rats, cockroaches and even ants like a foreign broadcaster jams our radio," Mr. Brown explains.

CHARLES BURTON   Burton invented the baby carriage in 1848 and instantly incurred the wrath of New York City pedestrians who viewed his brainchild as just another hostile vehicle to dodge. An epidemic of collisions and barked shins sent Burton fleeing to England, where he opened a factory, called his carriages perambulators, and numbered Queen Victoria, Queen Isabella of Spain, and the Pasha of Egypt among his customers.

DAVID BUSHNELL   "I then thought, and still think, that it was an effort of genius," wrote George Washington. He was referring to David Bushnell's *American Turtle,* the world's first operational submarine, which, under Washington's orders carried out one of the boldest and most ineffectual missions of the Revolutionary War.

Bushnell was a frail and nervous young farmer from Saybrook, Connecticut, who loved to blow things up. In his

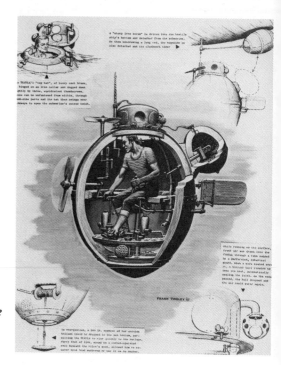

David Bushnell's
American Turtle,
the first submarine *(Submarine*
Force Library and Museum,
Groton, Connecticut)

freshman year at Yale College he demonstrated to the faculty the first underwater gunpowder explosion; it made a tremendous splash. Then, in 1775, with the clouds of war gathering, he began to work feverishly on a delivery system for his new bomb.

The ship he devised was the oddest contraption that ever went to sea. Constructed of oak frame timber "smear'd with tar," it was shaped like a hollow egg standing on its narrow end. The interior of the vessel, measuring about six feet in diameter, was so cramped with machinery that paunchy General Putnam of the Continental Army could not squeeze his way inside it on an inspection tour. To submerge, the pilot depressed a foot spring allowing water to flow into a tank underneath the belly of the boat. To resurface, the water had to be forced out with two brass handpumps. When cruising under the waves the *Turtle* contained "sufficient air to support the operator for thirty minutes," according to Bushnell. But when candles were tried for lighting, they quickly consumed so much of the oxygen that the test pilot nearly suffocated. "Two pieces of shining wood, or foxfire" were substituted. For propulsion Bushnell installed a pair of hand-operated screw propellers (another first), one controlling vertical, the other controlling horizontal motion. By turning the crank vigorously, the pilot could manage a top speed of about three miles an hour.

On September 6, 1776, after the British had forced the Americans to evacuate Long Island, Washington ordered his secret weapon into action, its objective to sink Admiral Richard Howe's 65-gun flagship, the *Eagle,* anchored off Staten Island. Bushnell expressed heartfelt regrets that ill health prevented him from manning the controls himself. Perhaps he was exercising discretionary valor; he knew full well that the slightest jolt could detonate the 150-pound box of gunpowder that the *Turtle* was carrying.

The volunteer chosen to command the *Turtle* was Sergeant Ezra Lee of Lyme, Connecticut, a true, unsung national hero. At midnight he set out from Whitehall Wharf on Manhattan's nether tip. A powerful tide quickly carried the craft out toward the open sea and when Lee surfaced he found he had overshot the British fleet by several miles. It took two and a half hours of furious cranking to maneuver the submarine back below the man-of-war. Lee then set to work boring a hole in the enemy's hull with a long screw mechanism. The plan was for Lee to string a rope through the hole and tie it on to the bomb. Luckily for two hundred British seamen, there was an unanticipated obstacle; the bottom timbers were sheathed in thick copper and the drill could not penetrate the armor.

With daylight fast approaching, the submariner decided he had better make a run for it. Cruising underwater, he again lost his bearings and surfaced just a few hundred yards from Governor's Island, in plain view of hundreds of British soldiers. A party of armed men set out from the shore in a barge to investigate the "sea monster"; Lee armed and released his bomb, closed his portholes, filled his tanks, and dove for his life. He made good his escape and cranked his way back to Manhattan where he was ultimately rescued.

Meanwhile, the bomb floated merrily in the East River for half an hour. Then, in the words of one eyewitness, "a terrible explosion shook the place. It threw into the air a prodigious column of water, resembling a great water spout, attended with a report like thunder." Only a few fish were injured.

The *Turtle* was dispatched on a second mission, this time in the Hudson River, with no better results. Undaunted, Bushnell continued to hatch explosive schemes. In the winter of 1777 he set adrift in the Delaware River dozens of kegs filled with gunpowder, hoping they would float downstream and blow up a British flotilla stationed south of Philadelphia. Some of the kegs detonated when they bumped into ice floes. One blasted a small dory to smithereens, killing its occupants. Alas, they were civilians.

ELLEN CHURCH   The person who did more than anyone else to make the much-advertised "friendly skies of United" so amiable was Ellen Church, a registered nurse from Iowa.

Ellen Church (upper left) and other original airline stewardesses *(United Airlines)*

With exceptional foresight, she wrote to airline executives in 1930, suggesting that qualified women might be employed as cabin attendants on board the new, unheated, unpressurized passenger airplanes. The company liked the idea, hired Miss Church, and assigned her to train seven other nurses for airborne duties. The flying Florence Nightingales were required to be unmarried, no more than 25 years old, no taller than five feet four inches, and no heavier than 115 pounds. They wore what were considered "chic" dark green woolen twill uniforms, with batman capes, and shower-cap style hats.

Miss Church's maiden flight, on May 15, 1930, took her from the Oakland, California, airport to Cheyenne, Wyoming, with five intermediate stops. En route, she served a prototypical airline meal consisting of fruit cocktail, unpalatable fried chicken, rolls, and coffee or tea. Most of the eleven passengers on the trip were pleased with the innovation; but not so the pilots' wives, who mounted an organized campaign to get the first stewardesses replaced by men.

A. C. ELLITHORPE   The earliest elevators, introduced to a wary public in the mid-1800s, carried passengers to their destinations with more of a bang than a whisper. It remained to Colonel Ellithorpe of Chicago to develop the first reliable air-cushion for elevators, although his first efforts were perilously imperfect.

In 1880 the lift in Boston's swanky Parker House hotel was equipped with the Ellithorpe air cushion and eight persons were recruited for the initial run. With reporters, hotel guests and assorted dignitaries watching, the volunteers walked into the lift, the cables were cut, and the car plummeted like a rock, sending up a thunderous boom that could be heard a block away. The air-cushion cushioned nothing, and the free-falling elevator landed with an explosive crash amid a litter of shattered glass and twisted steel. Its passengers were badly shaken, although none was critically injured. Colonel Ellithorpe was thoroughly embarassed.

Happily the mishap turned out to be the work of a construction error and not the Colonel's thinking, which was sound. The air reservoir at the bottom of the shaft had not been dug sufficiently deeply nor had a proper air-escape valve been provided. The Colonel returned to his drawing board and later that year a second demonstration was held, this time at the Chicago Exposition, and with astounding success. A 2,800-pound car fell 109 feet and its 20 passengers exited smiling and unruffled. In other experiments that same day, passengers made the descent carrying baskets of fresh hen eggs and glasses of ice-water filled to the brim; in no case was an egg broken or a drop spilled. The Colonel was triumphant.

DR. RICHARD GATLING   "I witnessed almost daily the departure of the wounded, sick, and dead," wrote Dr. Richard Gatling early in the Civil War. "The most of the latter lost their lives, not in battle but by sickness and exposure incident to the service. It occurred to me if I could invent a machine—a gun—which by its rapidity of fire, ena-

Dr. Richard Gatling invented the first practical machine gun
(The Smithsonian Institution)

bled one man to do as much battle duty as a hundred, that it would, to a great extent, supersede the necessity of large armies, and, consequently, exposure to battle and disease would be greatly diminished."

Out of these honestly humanitarian motives, Gatling invented the first practical machine gun, a revolving six-barrel affair that could fire two hundred shots a minute, a devastating increase in firepower over the muzzle-loading rifles then in use. President Lincoln opposed the adoption of the Gatling gun by the Union Army, not out of "charity for all," but because he suspected the North Carolina-born physician of pro-Confederate sympathies. Gatling's gun, known affectionately as the "gat," later became standard equipment for every modern army in the world. The gun and its successors have caused the death of more people than any single man-made device, exceeding even the automobile and the aerial bomb.

JOSEPH C. GAYETTY It was Joseph Gayetty of New York who, in 1857, gave the world toilet paper, marketing it as "Gayetty's Medicated Paper—a perfectly pure article for the toilet and for the prevention of piles." Fashioned from unbleached, pearl-colored, pure, manilla hemp paper, it was watermarked with the inventor's name and priced at half a dollar per hundred sheets.

SYLVAN N. GOLDMAN Imagine how bothersome grocery shopping would be if you had to carry everything—frozen orange juice, disposable diapers, a dozen cans of Mighty Dog, a 16-pound turkey, and enough eggplants to feed a growing family—in a hand-held wicker basket or your own two arms. Only a juggler under contract to Ringling Brothers could manage it. And yet that was the deplorable state of affairs prior to June 4, 1937, the day Sylvan N. Goldman of Oklahoma City put the cart before the housewife.

As the owner of two supermarket chains, Standard Food and Humpty Dumpty, Goldman was pained to see his cus-

Sylvan Goldman's shopping cart
(The Smithsonian Institution)

tomers head for the checkout counter after filling up a single hand-held basket; their consumption was limited by the size of their baskets and biceps. "On weekends," he recalls, "when a clerk would see a customer's basket practically full, he would hand her another and tell her she could find the first basket by a certain checkout stand." This simple procedure considerably increased sales volume, but Goldman was not satisfied. He dreamed of an entirely new mode of transport that would allow customers to carry away $20 worth of groceries, quite a sum in those days, in one shopping spree.

Other inventors were hard at work on the same problem. One supermarket operator laid out the shelves of his store in an M pattern with a miniature railroad track running alongside. The baskets were outfitted with grooved wheels and customers glided them along the tracks. The drawback was that everyone had to travel the entire length of the railway. The express shopper who only came in to pick up a bottle of prune juice would be caught behind the local shopper laying in supplies for an eight-course banquet.

So it remained to Sylvan Goldman to devise the first practical shopping cart. The inspiration came late one night while he was sitting in his office brooding about sluggish sales: "I had some folding chairs that salesmen used when they called on me. I thought that if I put wheels on the bottom of these chairs, raised the seats some so I could have room to put another shopping basket at the bottom, our customers could shop in ease with two baskets. Then when the carts were not in use they could be folded up for storage in the front of the store."

Goldman had a carpenter make the necessary alterations on several dozen carts, then ran an advertisement in the *Oklahoma City Times* proclaiming, "It's new ... it's sensational ... a revelation in food buying." Goldman coyly avoided any precise description of this "revelation" in hopes of attracting thousands of shoppers to his stores out of curiosity. The next day: "I went down there with great expectations. When I got there there wasn't a damn soul using a shopping cart." He asked one woman weighed down with canned goods why she eschewed this new convenience. "I've pushed my last baby buggy forever, I hope," she told him. Male customers were even less receptive to the idea. "Don't you think this arm is strong enough to carry a shopping basket?" one brawny fellow growled.

Undaunted, Goldman placed a second ad in the *Times* which said, "Shoppers came, saw, and said, 'It's a wow!' " He confesses now, "It was the biggest lie." Going one step further, he hired actors to push carts through the aisles, posing as happy, unencumbered shoppers, so that people would "get the idea." Eventually they did.

Today, next to the automobile, the shopping cart is the most widely used contraption on four wheels. Over 1.25 million are manufactured every year, and there are 20 to 25 million carts rolling around the world. In fact, the shopping cart is regarded as such an important article of Americana that the Department of Cultural History at the Smithsonian Institution has enshrined one of Sylvan Goldman's original folding chairs on wheels in its permanent collection.

During a recent interview with Mr. Goldman, CBS newsman Charles Kuralt asked, "Did the shopping cart make you rich?" To which the nearly 80-year-old inventor, sporting gold shopping cart cufflinks, replied: "It didn't make me poor."

GEORGE F. GRANT   George F. Grant achieved several notable breakthroughs during his lifetime: he was the first black graduate of Harvard College and the first black instructor at Howard Dental School. Like many of his dentist colleagues, Grant spent his Wednesday and Saturday afternoons pursuing the dimpled ball, and in 1899 he was granted patent number 638,920 for the invention of the golf tee. Duffers who wish to pay homage can visit his home at 108 Charles Street in Boston, which is now a museum.

CHESTER GREENWOOD   "When I was a child," admitted Maine State Representative Stephen R. Gould, "my ears stuck out so far I was six years old before my parents knew whether I would walk or fly." With ears like Dumbo, Gould would not have dared to venture out-of-doors during the blizzardy Maine winter without a cozy pair of earmuffs for protection. And so, in remembrance of the man who struck a mighty blow against frostbite, Gould sponsored a bill in 1977 to designate December 21, the winter solstice, *Chester Greenwood Day.*

As a boy, Chester Greenwood also possessed a pair of protruberant and sensitive auricles that turned white, then scarlet, and finally an alarming shade of blue when he stayed outside too long. Then, in 1873, 15-year-old Chester received a pair of two-dollar double bladed skates as a Christmas present. Eagerly he rushed down to the local pond to try them out; a few minutes later the frustrated skater was back in the house, his ears stinging fiercely and on the verge of falling off. The next day he wrapped a heavy woolen scarf

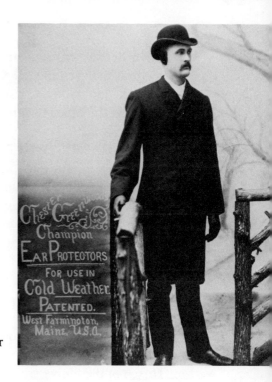

Chester Greenwood, earmuff inventor
(The Greenwood Family)

around his head before venturing out, but he never even made it to the ice. "Too itchy!" he complained. Young Chester tried and tried again until he developed the perfect arctic earware—two pieces of fur attached to an arc of wire. He tested the muffs with several hours of skating on the pond and experienced no earitation whatsoever.

Soon Chester's mother and grandmother were busily turning out earmuffs (also known as earlaps) for all of their neighbors in the little town of Farmington, Maine, and the young inventor was assigned Patent Number 188,292 for "Greenwood's Champion Ear Protectors." Orders started pouring in from out of state; the Greenwoods hired on extra workers; construction was begun on a factory. Before long, Farmington became the undisputed "Earmuff Capital of the World," and Chester Greenwood became a millionaire.

Not everyone in Maine is an ardent Greenwood admirer. Governor James B. Longley balked at the legislation honoring the Earmuff King and griped about "a proliferation of these days." (His mother probably made him wear a hat

107

when he was growing up.) But Longley was pragmatic; he realized that vetoing the Greenwood bill would be political suicide, and today Chester Greenwood Day is an annual event on the official Maine state calendar.

MARY HARRIMAN The Junior League was formed in 1900 when pretty debutante Mary Harriman suffered conscience pangs because she received an excess of bouquets from young male admirers. Instead of allowing her flowers to wilt unappreciated in her living room she decided to distribute them among patients in local hospitals. She persuaded other popular young girls to do the same, and from this frivolous beginning the league grew into an important service organization supported by the upper crust.

ERIC D. HIRSCH Grown weary of traditional methods of grading term papers and final exams, Professor Eric D. Hirsch of the University of Virginia English Department won a $137,935 grant from the National Endowment for the Humanities to work out a new-and-improved system for assessing the "relative readability" of classroom prose. His plan: enlist 11 bright graduate students to read and rewrite several hundred typically stodgy student papers over the course of a year, then hand the "before" papers to one test group of undergraduates, the "afters" to another group, and see which versions are read faster. As the professor explained it, "If it takes two minutes to read the good version, and 2.3 minutes to read the original student version, that gives you a proportion of 87 percent, meaning the student's paper is 87 percent effective."

Professor Hirsch admitted that his plan might be too cumbersome to work, but he seemed unruffled by the risk of failure. "If it doesn't work in practice," he said, "I guess I will have wasted a lot of time and some graduate students will have gotten paid for a year's work."

JAMES WRIGHT and PETER HODGSON In 1945 research engineer James Wright was attempting to develop a new form of synthetic rubber to aid the American war effort when he accidentally spilled some boric acid into a test tube containing silicone oil. The resulting blob-like substance behaved like a cross between a liquid and a solid. Tests conducted at the New Haven research center of the General Electric Corporation demonstrated that one could snap it, stretch it, or roll it into a ball with a 75 percent bounce-back capability (half again as resilient as an ordinary rubber ball). It was also inadvertently discovered that one could flatten it and take an impression from a page of newsprint. Its elastic properties were truly astonishing, but notwithstanding thousands of man hours of study no one could figure out any earthly use for the stuff.

What a leap of genius it took for marketing executive Peter Hodgson to conceive of the goo as "a toy with one moving part!" Packaging one-ounce dabs in plastic eggs (so it could be shipped in inexpensive cartons obtained from the Connecticut Cooperative Poultry Association), he distributed it to toy stores under the trademark Silly Putty. At last someone had determined what the ooze was good for. About $6.5 million in sales per year.

NELSON HOWER According to *Billboard,* tights made their debut in the circus arena in 1828 when Nelson Hower's usual outfit, consisting of a jacket, knickers, and long stockings, failed to arrive on time from the cleaners. The show had to go on, and for lack of anything else the bareback rider with the Buckley and Wicks troupe performed in his long underwear. Later, the celebrated French aerialist Jules Leotard would affect the same brief costume by reason of vanity. "Do you want to be adored by the ladies?" he asked rhetorically in his *Memoirs.* "(Then) put on a more natural garb, which does not hide your best features."

WALTER HUNT Anyone who's ever diapered an infant or in an emergency fastened a pair of snapless trousers with a safety pin owes a debt of gratitude to Walter Hunt, mid-nineteenth-century draftsman, inventor, practicing Quaker, and study in nose-to-the-grindstone resourcefulness. Broke, yet obliged to pay back a $15 debt immediately, Hunt took three hours to hammer out the design for the world's first safety pin, fashion a working model out of a single length of wire, and sell the rights for $100. This was in 1849 and while America's safety pin manufacturers went on to make millions, Hunt earned not a single cent beyond that original sale.

Hunt's lack of business sense hurt him in other ways too. In the early 1830s he devised the world's first lock-stitch sewing machine but held off patenting it at the urging of his daughter, who feared it would spell economic doom for the nation's seamstresses. In 1854 Hunt had second thoughts and sought a patent, to be turned down summarily: Elias Howe had been granted a patent for a lock-stitch machine eight years earlier.

ROBERT A. ILG   In the Chicago suburb of Niles, Illinois, millionaire industrialist Robert A. Ilg built a half-scale replica of the Leaning Tower of Pisa in 1932. He lived on an 11 degree angle for 17 summers before moving to a level residence in California.

MARY PHELPS JACOB   In 1914, Mary Phelps Jacob (later known as Caresse Crosby) was a dazzling and unconventional debutante of 19, the star of the New York social season. To all appearances, she had everything. Beauty. Beaus. Fabulous wealth. But like so many well-endowed young women of her day, she yearned for freedom—freedom from the stays and tight laces of her whalebone corset.

One Saturday evening in November, while dressing for a swank country-club dance, she committed an act of dainty rebellion. With the connivance of her French maid, Marie, she stitched together two lace handkerchiefs and a saucy pink ribbon, creating a garment that was to play a major supporting role in the twentieth century; the first modern brassiere.

Robert Ilg's half-scale leaning
tower of Pisa in Niles, Illinois
*(Bob Riemer, Chicago Historical
Society)*

That starlit night marked the beginning of the end for
whalebone and the wasp-waisted style. Mary disturbed and
excited the young men from Yale and Princeton with the
unconfined symmetry of her god-given shape, and soon her
envious friends were begging her to sew bras for them, too.
When a total stranger wrote to ask for a sample of her
"contraption," enclosing a dollar, she realized the tremendous commercial potential of her design, and applied for a
patent.

Creative genius ran in her family. Robert Fulton was her
great-grandfather, as she noted proudly in her autobiography, *The Passionate Years.* "I believe my ardour for invention springs from his loins," she declared.

After an unsuccessful attempt to produce and market the
"Backless Brassiere" on her own (with the loyal Marie doing
all the sewing), she sold her patent to the Warner Brothers
Corset Company for $15,000. She was gypped. Over the next
two decades, Mary Jacob's bra earned Warner Brothers over
$20 million.

111

ANNA M. JARVIS   "A mother never gets hit with a custard pie," movie director Mack Sennett once declared. "Mothers-in-law—yes. But mothers—never."

Although nearly everyone has a soft spot in his heart for mom, it took Anna M. Jarvis (1864–1948) to institutionalize the sentiment. A devoted daughter—devoted to the point of obsession—she was heartbroken when her own mother died in 1905. In her grief she conceived the idea of a special holiday to honor mothers everywhere. There were a lot of ungrateful or indifferent offspring to persuade, but Miss Jarvis was willing to sacrifice all her time and money for the great cause. She wrote thousands of letters to influential people, enlisted the support of millionaire businessman John Wanamaker (who knew a good sales gimmick when he heard one), and on May 10, 1908, arranged simultaneous Mother's Day Services at churches in Philadelphia and Grafton, West Virginia, her old home town. Not coincidentally, the date chosen was the anniversary of her mother's death; further-more, Miss Jarvis personally initiated the tradition of wear-ing and giving carnations on the day because they were her mother's favorite flower.

The idea caught on. Several states proclaimed official Mother's Day celebrations. Then on May 7, 1914, a group of devoted sons introduced a bill in Congress to set aside the second Sunday in each May as national Mother's Day: "Whereas the service rendered by the American mothers is the greatest source of the country's strength and inspiration ...," it began. The legislation was passed without a single dissenting vote (who would dare?) and President Wilson signed the proclamation, urging that the Stars and Stripes be flown.

Miss Jarvis later came to deplore the growing commercial-ism of the holiday as greeting card companies, candy makers, florists, and department stores advertised the importance of giving presents. Bitterly, she withdrew from public life and became a virtual recluse. Though attractive and intelligent, she never married; she was always her mother's daughter, never a mother herself. In her efforts to promote Mother's

Day and in a series of bad investments, she managed to fritter away a $700,000 fortune, only to die blind and penniless in a West Chester, Pennsylvania, sanitarium.

Today there are two stained glass windows, one of Anna and one of her mother, in the Andrews Methodist Church at Grafton where the holiday began. There is also a small museum where they sell Mother's Day cards the year around.

CARL LEFLER Edwin Lowe, a struggling toy salesman during the Depression, became intrigued with a game called "Beano" as he watched it being played one night at a little tent carnival outside of Atlanta. On an impulse, he purchased some of the hand-printed cards and a cigar-box full of wooden numbered discs, and brought them home for his family and friends to enjoy. Soon the entire neighborhood was hopelessly addicted. One evening Lowe was calling out the numbers and he watched with fascination as a young woman grew more and more excited during a game. Finally, she filled in the last bean in a row, jumped to her feet almost speechless in ecstasy, and instead of screaming out "Beano" she sputtered "B-B-B-BINGO!"

Said Lowe: "I cannot describe the strange sense of elation which that girl's shriek brought to me. All I could think of was that I was going to come out with this game—and it was going to be called 'Bingo!' "

Within a matter of weeks, Lowe was manufacturing and distributing a simple 24-card Bingo kit which retailed for two dollars. All went well for about a month until he received a telephone call from a priest in Wilkes Barre, Pennsylvania. To raise money for the parish, the clergyman had sponsored a church "Bingo Night"—probably the first in the nation—awarding prizes to the winners. The problem: with just 24 cards there were sometimes as many as ten winners in a single game; the parish lost money on the operation. "Clearly," the priest suggested, "more numerical combinations are needed."

Thinking up patterns of numbers that didn't repeat was a

mind-boggling task and Lowe was forced to hire an expert mathematician for the job, Professor Carl Lefler of Columbia University. Lefler was commissioned to think up six thousand completely different cards. With each card the calculations became a little more difficult, and the mental effort began to take its toll on the aging scholar. "We were driving him," Lowe admits regretfully, "offering him as much as a hundred dollars a combination toward the last. It was a terribly tough job. I was going daffy myself checking those cards." Stubborn as the Rocky Mountains, Lefler persisted until all six thousand cards were done. But the labor left him insane.

THADDEUS SOBIESKI COULINCOURT LOWE

Thaddeus Lowe dreamed that someday soon passenger balloons would waft from America to Europe on a regular schedule. On April 20, 1861, at Cincinnati, Ohio, Lowe ascended into the wild, blue yonder, cradled beneath a balloon filled with coal gas, to study the strong west-to-east winds of the upper atmosphere that could make possible transoceanic flights. Nine hours later, thoroughly lost, he descended through the clouds and landed near Pea Ridge on the border of North and South Carolina, some nine hundred miles from his starting point.

His timing couldn't have been worse. That very day Union and Confederate soldiers were slaughtering each other at Bull Run in the first major battle of the Civil War. When the misguided balloonist touched down, rebel militiamen arrested him at once and, ignoring his protests that he was on a purely scientific expedition, made hasty preparations to hang him as a Yankee spy. Lowe was the South's first prisoner of war and he might have earned the dubious distinction of being the first aeronaut ever executed, except for a bit of good luck. At the last moment, a local farmer, who had seen him go aloft at Charleston a year earlier, came forward and vouched for his status as a harmless civilian. Lowe was returned North, but his airbag was impounded.

This narrow escape influenced him to do what he had been

Dr. Thaddeus Lowe inflating a war balloon *(New York Public Library, Picture Collection)*

mistakenly accused of doing; he volunteered to make military reconnaissance flights over northern Virginia in a balloon. On June 18 he arranged a tethered ascent at the Washington Mall to demonstrate the feasibility of aerial espionage, during which he sent President Lincoln the first telegraph message from a balloon. "The city, with its girdle of encampments, presents a superb scene," he tapped out in Morse code. The army was delighted and commissioned him chief and first member of the United States Air Corps. Soon, with five balloons and 50 men under his command, he was sailing above the rebel lines, just out of rifle range, snapping the first aerial photographs of troop emplacements, and directing artillery fire at enemy targets.

Fifteen years earlier, John Wise of Philadelphia, the "Patriarch of American Aeronauts," had offered to serve as a balloon observer during the Mexican War. He went on to propose an aerial bombardment of the castle at San Juan de Ullos, considered the key to the defense of Vera Cruz. William L. Marcy, the amused but skeptical secretary of war,

115

vetoed the plan as impractical. This time around, however, the press and high officials could scarcely contain their enthusiasm for airpower. They predicted that Lowe's weapon would put an early end to the war. Every move the rebels made could be spotted from above. A flotilla of balloons could launch an airborne raid on Richmond and Atlanta and lay them in ruins. As it turned out, balloons were never used offensively by either side, but Lowe's high altitude observation greatly aided the Union cause. He was elected an honorary member of the Loyal Legion. And Confederate General Jubal Early, for one, declared that the spy-in-the-sky should have been strung up at Pea Ridge, after all.

S. R. MATHEWSON The horses that powered Boston's streetcars in the 1870s did not take kindly to their electric and steam-driven horseless counterparts. Chroniclers of the day report that whenever one of the newfangled trolleys moved into view, cart horses would panic and go wild with fright, often causing nightmarish traffic snarls, collisions and injuries to passengers. S. R. Mathewson, a Boston engineer, seemed to have the answer. He designed and built a gas-driven street car that looked like a horse. Several of the cars actually were put into use, but the scheme was quickly abandoned and inventor Mathewson died destitute.

MICHAEL McCORMICK After countless hours of research and experimentation, Michael McCormick invented a device that strictly enforced the maxim "Waste not, want not." In 1896 he applied for and received a United States government patent for the first electrical male chastity belt which delivered painful sensations to the wearer when, "through forgetfulness or any other cause his thoughts should be running in lascivious channels. Voluntary self-abuse [a Victorian euphemism for masturbation] will be checked, presuming the wearer be desirous of benefit, as he will not take the trouble to relieve himself of the appliance, and cannot continue the practice without removing it." The belt, advertised as the "modern protection against insanity,"

116

could be worn beneath clothing without telltale wires or bulges.

FRANK McGURRIN   It was a classic confrontation reminiscent of John Henry and the steam hammer. The odds-on favorite in the competition, staged at Cincinnati on July 25, 1888, was Louis Taub, the fastest four-finger typist the world has ever known; his fingers moved as swiftly as hummingbird wings over the keyboard of his late-model Calligraph machine. The lightly-regarded challenger was Frank McGurrin, the official stenographer for the Salt Lake City Federal Court, who purportedly used all ten fingers to operate his Remington and never bothered to look at the keys. From the outset, McGurrin surprised almost everyone. Taub, the master hunt-and-pecker, fell a little further behind everytime he had to glance down at his hands. McGurrin won the national speed typing championship and $500 that day. He also established once and for all the superiority of his novel "touch typing system," which would become the standard training method for secretaries everywhere.

JAMES HENRY McLEAN   On the steamy, midsummer day in 1849 that James McLean arrived in St. Louis to open a medical practice, that city was wracked by a cholera epidemic that left hundreds dying and dead but evidently made little impression on the young medic. No sooner had he dropped his bags at his hotel than he went out in search of real estate bargains, buying and reselling a choice piece of acreage before nightfall.

Fueled by such resourcefulness, Dr. McLean earned a small fortune in real estate in the coming years, and by hawking such-tried-and-true nostrums as McLean's Volcanic Oil Liniment, McLean's Strengthening Cordial and Blood Purifier, Mexican Mustang Liniment, and Indian Queen Vegetable Anti-Bilious Pills. He became a respected presence in St. Louis, editing his own newspaper, *The Spirit of the Times,* serving the First Methodist Church in numerous capacities, and making himself miscellaneously useful.

But his principal contribution to society was his authorship of *Dr. J. H. McLean's Peace Makers,* a 200-page catalogue of firearms, artillery, and instruments of torture and mutilation of his own inventing, all of them so hideous and swiftly lethal as to frighten mankind into eternal world peace. He called himself a "savior and liberator of his race," a man "whose name will soon be heralded from one end of the earth to the other."

McLean's Devil Fish Torpedo, for example, was equipped with powerful magnets whereby it would attach itself leech-like to a targeted vessel, detonating by a pre-set timer. A machine gun of unparalleled destructiveness was capable of firing 33 shots a second and mowing down advancing soldiers like duckpins. The good doctor called it the Lady McLean, naming it fondly for his wife. Equally efficient were his "monster breech-loading cannon," "Annihilator," and "General Grant Pulverizer." Then there was Dr. McLean's Wonderful Hydrophone. Affixed to the bows of ships at sea, it was sensitive enough to detect a porpoise's mutterings or the muffled crunch of an approaching iceberg.

Dr. McLean also offered diagrams for an "Impenetrable Fortress," such as might have helped France stave off Germany's successful storming of Paris in 1871. By Dr. McLean's figuring, that routing cost the French over $15 billion, of which $5 billion was for "national humiliation."

McLean, who elsewhere in his book proposed the formation of a "colossal" Peace-Maker Manufacturing Corporation, underwritten to the tune of $20 million ("Fortunes to be made everywhere!"), insisted that his impregnable fortresses be made available to all the nations of the world. He sent particulars to all the European monarchs; none were impressed except for the Sultan of Turkey, who put in his order for two pistols, two larger guns, and a supply of cartridges.

The Sultan also invited Dr. McLean to become director of the Turkish artillery works. The doctor turned him down, assuring the leader he was "deeply sensible of the honor." By the time of his death in 1886, virtually none of the Peace-Makers he had designed had been manufactured.

Morris Michtom's original teddy bear
(Ideal Toy Corporation)

MORRIS MICHTOM   When President Theodore Roosevelt went to Mississippi in November of 1902 to help settle that state's running border dispute with Louisiana, he took the opportunity to get in a little bear hunting. The end result was a historic encounter with a little bear. As reporters told it, a frisky cub wandered into the president's rifle sights, but, out of sportsmanship, he refused to shoot it. The incident inspired a newspaper cartoon called "Drawing the Line in Mississippi" by Clifford Berryman, which appeared in the *Washington Evening Star* and many other newspapers around the country. Morris Michtom, the owner of a candy store in Brooklyn, saw the cartoon and conceived the idea of creating a toy animal made of brown plush with movable limbs and button eyes. He put the finished plaything in the candy store window along with a copy of the cartoon and a sign reading "Teddy's Bear."

Michtom, having recently immigrated from Russia, was uncertain whether naming a toy after a president was proper or even legal, and so he wrote to the White House asking Mr. Roosevelt for permission to use "Teddy" as a trademark. In a handwritten note the president replied: "I don't think my name is worth much in the toy bear cub business, but you are welcome to use it."

By 1906 Michtom's Teddy Bear was the nation's best-selling toy and the design was being pirated by dozens of manufacturers. In fact, the craze reached such proportions that a Michigan priest worried aloud whether the Teddy would interfere with children's natural bond to their mothers and in the end threaten the survival of the human species. Somehow the race endured. As for Michtom, he went on to found the Ideal Toy Corporation, now the world's largest doll manufacturer.

CECIL NIXON   In 1940, a Californian with the improbable name of Nixon designed and built a zither-playing robot with a repertoire of 3,000 songs. Dubbed "Isis," after the Egyptian goddess she was built to resemble, the robot reclined languorously on a divan, her instrument in her lap, and plucked out tunes as soon as anyone asked her to, provided the request came from within a radius of 12 feet. Nixon designed 1,187 wheels, 370 electromagnets, and assorted hardware into Isis, whose mechanism was sensitive to heat as well as to sound. On a warm day, she would take off her veil.

JOSEPH OPPENHEIM   "What has broad stripes, bright stars, and flies?" The answer, according to the editors of

Joseph Oppenheim, inventor of the original manure spreader and his brainchild *(AVCO New Idea Farm Equipment Division)*

120

American Heritage, is a red, white, and blue Bicentennial manure spreader.

In 1976 the New Idea Farm Equipment Company of Coldwater, Ohio, decorated a Model No. 224, ten-ton manure spreader with hand-painted stars and stripes, and a banner reading "Proud to be a part of America's agricultural heritage." New Idea executives described the spangled machine as a tribute to our nation's two-hundredth birthday and to company founder Joseph Oppenheim, who—lest we forget—invented the manure spreader in 1899.

JONATHAN SCOBIE Jonathan Scobie, an American Baptist minister, invented the rickshaw. You can look it up. Living in Yokohama, Japan, in the 1860s, Scobie devised the two-wheel carriage for the benefit of his physically handicapped wife, who would otherwise have been housebound. When his parishioners saw him dutifully shlepping her through the streets they went wild over the idea and copied it.

WILLIAM J. SIMMONS Thirty-six "splendid citizens of Georgia" joined together in a "patriotic, secret, social, benevolent order." From the sound of it, William J. Simmons could have been describing a newly-formed Elks chapter or even a Bible study group; in fact, he was referring to the modern Ku Klux Klan, founded in 1915 at Stone Mountain.

The Klan had been out of action for decades and it might have stayed that way if Simmons, a pseudo-colonel and redneck preacher, hadn't paid ten cents to see D. W. Griffith's racist classic *The Birth of a Nation* at a local movie theater. Shortly afterward, while staring at his bedroom wall, he saw in a "vision" the Klansmen of yore riding in their Inquisition-style white robes. Well, Colonel Simmons got right down on his knees and swore to the Almighty that he would resurrect that gallant old fraternity, or die trying. At least that's the way he liked to tell it.

Historians who have studied the Klan paint a somewhat different picture, concluding that Simmons was inspired mainly by the profit motive. Previously he had earned a precarious living as a commissioned recruiter for the Woodmen of the World, an innocuous rural lodge. The money-making potential would be far greater, he reasoned, if only he could get in on the management end of the business. The Klan was duly incorporated and members were allowed to take out group-rate life insurance through the organization. There was a ten dollar initiation fee and the official white robes sold at a whopping mark-up. When things got going good Simmons was netting at least $40,000 a month, more than enough to finance a fine old Southern mansion in Atlanta called the Klankrest.

Simmons seems to have taken childish delight in making up alliterative titles for every Klan officer and function. When a *konklave* (meeting) was convened at a *klavern* (meeting place), the opening prayer was offered by a *kludd* (chaplain), whereafter a *kleagle* (minor leader) took over the proceedings. A few of the higher echelon officials somehow escaped the obligatory "kl" formation. A state leader was a Grand Dragon; a regional leader was addressed as Grand Goblin; and Simmons dubbed himself Imperial Wizard. But the Halloween costumes and the cutesy terminology in no way disguised or mitigated the Klan's fundamental purpose—to keep down blacks (as well as Catholics and Jews), through an organized campaign of intimidation and violence.

When Simmons felt Klan membership was about to peak, he sold his interest to a Texas dentist for $90,000 plus a monthly living allowance. It was a disastrous miscalculation. Simmons's successors built the Klan into a nationwide society of hate with an estimated membership of nearly four million; the Klan became so powerful that it was able to elect candidates to political office in Texas, Oklahoma, Indiana, Oregon, and Maine as well as the Deep South states. Simmons could have kicked himself. In his frustration Simmons lapsed into messianic delusions: "I am the door of Klankraft," he proclaimed, "no man may enter therein but by ME. ... I am the way, the truth and the life in the kingdom of Klankraft. . . . Come unto ME all you who yearn and labor after Klankraft." A fitting klimax to a malodorous kareer.

LUCY STONE The wedding of suffragist Lucy Stone to Henry Blackwell in 1855 is intriguing as a footnote event in American social history and because it set the pattern for feminist nuptials even to this day. The marriage was preceded by the signing of a carefully-worded legal agreement between Lucy and her fiancé specifying the rights and responsibilities of each spouse. ("While we acknowledge our mutual affection, . . ." the unromantic document began.) The ceremony itself, described by the presiding minister T. W. Higginson as the "most beautiful bridal I ever attended," pointedly omitted the word "obey" from the bride's vows. But the most radical departure from convention came when Lucy announced her intention of keeping her own name after marriage, merely substituting the title Mrs. for Miss. Historians who have studied the women's movement say it

Lucy Stone, the first woman to keep her maiden name after marriage *(New York Public Library, Picture Collection)*

was the first such protest against what Mrs. Stone regarded as the "symbolic loss of individuality" that occurs when a woman is compelled to take her husband's name. In spite of all its political trappings, though, the Stone-Blackwell union was apparently a genuine love-match, and when the knot was tied Lucy broke down and wept "like any village bride."

Other woman's rights advocates imitated Mrs. Stone's independent gesture and kept their maiden names, thus giving the American language a new noun, "lucy stoner," defined in *Webster's Dictionary* as "a married woman who uses her maiden name as a surname."

FRANKLIN TEMEL In 1974, after spending eight years and $110,000 on research and development, inventor Franklin Temel of Miami patented a flush toilet for cats and dogs. The potty is encased in a stall, to provide poochie with the utmost in canine privacy, and serviced by spray nozzles and a water tank beneath the stainless steel floor. Although the unit he installed in his own home set him back $10,000, Temel says that the device could be mass-produced for $250.

GEORGE THOMAS Chemical engineer George Thomas had a vision of a Better America, a nation of 400 million armpits redolent of flowers and perfume. True, underarm deodorants had been on the market for many years, but they cried out for an easier, more streamlined method of application. Using the ball-point pen as his model, Thomas experimented with 450 combinations of plastic, glass, metal, and other materials to fashion the world's first roll-on deodorant applicator—a milestone in the history of personal intimacy.

CHARLES N. VAN CLEAVE A man who struck paydirt in the lower intestine: Charles N. Van Cleave invented the coin-operated lock in 1910, the basis of the pay toilet.

HOMAN WALSH Workmen preparing in 1847 to build the first railway suspension bridge connecting the United States and Canada were stymied by the problem of how to get the first cable across the steep gorge at Niagara Falls. At wit's end, the chief engineer offered ten dollars to anyone who could come up with a solution. The reward was claimed by a 13-year-old boy named Homan Walsh, who fastened a light line to a kite and flew it from the American to the Canadian shore. Progressively heavier lines were attached to this initial line and pulled across the chasm, until the cable itself could be strung into place.

ROSS WILLIAMS Without his daily bath Ross Williams wasn't good for much. Unfortunately, a water shortage aboard the ship he served on during World War II deprived Williams of his customary ablutions, and made it impossible for him to fall asleep at night. After the war he addressed himself to inventing the closest thing to a portable, emergency bathtub, and in 1953 created Wash-'n-Dry, a paper towel soaked in a soapy solution and sealed in foil. A single Wash-'n-Dry does the work of a quart of water, ending forever the scourge of enforced bathlessness. And now Ross Williams sleeps at night.

JOHN L. WRIGHT The inventor of Lincoln Logs, the children's log cabin building kit, was John L. Wright, son of famed architect Frank Lloyd Wright.

ARTHUR WYNNE Amid tasteless ethnic jokes and naughty verses about newlyweds, the crossword puzzle made its obscure debut on December 21, 1913, in *Fun* magazine, a Sunday supplement of the *New York World*. The perpetrator was Arthur Wynne, the Engish-born editor of the "tricks and games department." In his never ending quest for new amusements, Wynne recalled how his grandfather had entertained him as a child in Liverpool with a Victorian parlor game called "Magic Square" or "Double Crostic." The black squares and numbered clues were Wynne's own brainchildren. For lexiphiles the puzzle was as irresistible as gravity. And F. Scott Fitzgerald noted that "By 1927 a widespread neurosis began to be evident, faintly signalled, like a nervous beating of the feet, by the popularity of crossword puzzles."

Another hero in the crossword puzzle hall of fame is Robert M. Stilgenbauer of Los Angeles, who between 1938 and 1949 composed the longest crossword puzzle ever published, comprising 2,008 vertical clues and 2,007 horizontal clues. Over 125,000 copies have been distributed and, to date, no one has ever fully solved it, although Robert Vizet of Bayside, New York, has reportedly completed 93.5 percent of the squares.

Lawmakers, Plaintiffs, and Defendants

CHESTER ASHLEY Ashley, who served as United States Senator from Arkansas from 1844–48, is forgotten today except for his unique inability to agree with his counterpart, Senator Ambrose Sevier, on the proper pronunciation of the territory they represented.

Sevier, a native of those parts, referred to "Ark-en-saw" in all his public and private utterances. But Ashley insisted on the ear-jangling "Ar-Kansas." While Ashley was born a New Englander and simply may not have known any better, he stood by his pronunciation militantly, refusing to answer roll calls unless addressed as "The Senator from Ar-Kansas." Several decades later, the Arkansas State Legislature adopted "Ark-en-saw" as the official pronunciation.

DAVID RICE ATCHISON Forget what the history books say. The twelfth president of the United States was David Rice Atchison, a man so obscure that Chester A. Arthur seems a household word by comparison.

At exactly 12:00 noon on March 4, 1849, Zachary Taylor was scheduled to suceed James Polk as chief executive. But March 4 was a Sunday and Taylor, a devout old general, refused to violate the Sabbath by taking the oath of office. Thus, under the Succession Act of 1792, Missouri Senator David Rice Atchison, as President Pro Tempore of the Senate, automatically became president of the United States.

Atchison is said to have taken the awesome responsibilities of his high office very much in stride. Tongue in cheek, he appointed a number of his cronies to high cabinet positions, then he had a few drinks, and went to bed to sleep out the remainder of his brief, uneventful administration. On Monday at noon Taylor took over the reins of government, but the nation can look back fondly on the Atchison presidency as a peaceful one, untainted by even a hint of corruption.

GASTON AYOTTE, JR.   Casting its vote for sexual equality, the Woonsocket, Rhode Island, City Council unanimously approved a personnel ordinance amendment changing such time-worn usages as "utility man" to "utility person" and renaming manholes "personholes." But two weeks after the 1978 vote, the Council decided "personholes" was going too far. "We are sick and tired of the adverse publicity we were getting," Council President Ayotte confessed. "All over the United States people were laughing at Woonsocket personholes." He said he'd been particularly hurt by the gibes of a Washington columnist who'd telephoned to interview him about the personhole vote. "He kind of made fun of me," Ayotte said.

NAN BRITTON   "If you were a girl, Warren, you'd be in the family way all the time. You can't say No." Those words, spoken by Dr. George Tryon Harding to his son, proved to be all too accurate. Subsequent history confirmed that Warren Harding, as the twenty-ninth president of the United States, was not unduly resistant to temptation in any form, be it whiskey, public funds, or the nubile charms of Nan Britton.

Miss Britton was a pretty blonde from Marion, Ohio, who attended secretarial school in New York City, where she developed good skills. After graduation, she wrote to then Senator Harding, whom she had known since high school, and asked him for a job. With eager cordiality Harding replied that he would soon be coming to New York and would interview her then. The meeting took place in the bridal suite of the Manhattan Hotel, and Nan later described the business they transacted in palpitating detail:

> We had scarcely closed the door behind us when we shared our first kiss ... I shall never, never forget how Mr. Harding kept saying, after each kiss, 'God, God, Nan!' in high diminuendo, nor how he pleaded in his tense voice, 'Oh, dearie, tell me it isn't hateful to you to have me kiss you.' ... Mr. Harding tucked $30 into my brand new silk stockings and was sorry he had no more time to give me.

The romance was fraught with political hazards; after all, Harding was a married man. The two lovers were forever trying to duck reporters and find themselves a private place to enjoy adulterous good times. Once they were interrupted *in flagrante delicto* by two hotel detectives who entered their room with a pass key. "Get dressed," they ordered. "There's a paddy wagon waiting outside." As Harding was fumbling with his socks, one of the men picked up a hat and noticed the senator's name embossed in gold on the sweatband. Suddenly the detectives lost their zeal for justice; they respectfully helped the couple to pack, escorted them to a side entrance, and received twenty dollars for their tactfulness. "Gee, Nan," Harding said once they were safely installed in a taxi, "I thought I wouldn't get out of that for under a thousand dollars."

Nan received $150 every week to care for their illegitimate daughter, Elizabeth Ann, who was conceived on a black leather couch in the Senate Office Building. Then when Harding moved into the White House, a Secret Service agent was entrusted to carry letters and money from the president to his mistress. As often as possible, the two would arrange a rendezvous in a White House coat closet not more than five feet square.

In 1923 the newspapers began uncovering the corrupt dealings culminating in the Teapot Dome scandal, and Harding found it expedient to take a trip to Alaska, where he dined on king crab, contracted food poisoning, and conveniently died. (There were those who said his wife had murdered him.) Following the funeral, Nan contacted Warren's father and requested a tenth of Harding's $500,000 estate to provide for Elizabeth Ann. When the family stubbornly refused any settlement, she wrote and published *The President's Daughter* in which she "told all." It was one of Gertrude Stein's favorite books. Reviewers called it "torrid," and it earned well over $100,000, a portion going to establish the Elizabeth Ann Guild, an organization to assist young girls "in trouble." Plans to make the book into a movie were vetoed by "Czar" Will Hays, who administered the motion picture industry's censorship board. Perhaps it was only a coincidence that Hays had been Harding's postmaster general.

A few years later, Miss Britton and her daughter dropped out of sight.

ISABELLA W. CANNON Styling herself "the little old lady in tennis shoes," Isabella W. Cannon, age 74, ran as a Democratic candidate for mayor of Raleigh, North Carolina, in 1976. She wore sneakers to all of her campaign appearances as a trademark, and was elected by a large majority. She now wears sneakers to the office.

ZACHARIAH CHAFEE Zachariah Chafee, a Harvard University law professor, authored the Federal Interpleader Act, an abstruse procedural statute governing the way disputed sums of money are handled by the courts. So proud was he of this obscure achievement that he had the entire text of the Interpleader Act carved into his tombstone.

LYMAN A. CUTLER One of the longest and least celebrated conflicts in American history was the War of Griffin's Pig, a testy border dispute on San Juan Island near Vancouver. The trouble grew out of some vague wording in the Treaty of 1846, which established the boundary between the United States and British Columbia, but left the ownership of San Juan in doubt. Both British and American nationals settled the tiny parcel of land and coexisted uneasily for a time.

Then on June 15, 1859, an incident occurred which threatened to escalate into an all-out war between the two nations. Lyman A. Cutler, an American citizen, discovered a black boar, owned by British subject Charles Griffin, rooting in his potato patch. As Cutler later explained, "Upon the impulse of the moment [I] seized my rifle and shot the hog." Griffin called it nothing short of murder. Cutler countered by charging that the British-operated Hudson Bay Company had trained the clever porker to sabotage his garden. Also at issue was who should get the hams.

British authorities in Victoria dispatched the war ship *Satellite* and a contingent of soldiers to arrest Cutler and bring him to trial. Reluctant to face a British judge on charges of massacring a British pig, Cutler sought out the protection of Brigadier General W. S. Harney, the hotheaded American commander in the area. Harney landed nine infantry companies on the island, supported by eight pieces of artillery. The British responded with 2,140 infantrymen, including 600 Royal Marines. Offshore five dreadnoughts, armed with 167 guns, put on a show of force.

If General Winfield Scott had not arrived on the scene and relieved Harney of command, it is quite possible that Lyman A. Cutler's itchy trigger finger might have precipitated yet another British-American War, the third in 100 years. As it was, the events leading up to the Civil War distracted the jingoists in Washington, and local tempers had time to cool. For the next 12 years the opposing camps vied with each other in an exchange of complimentary banquets. Finally, Kaiser Wilhelm I of Germany agreed to arbitrate the dispute and, in 1872, San Juan Island was awarded to the United States.

JIMMY DILLIO   By all rights Jimmy Dillio doesn't belong in this book; nor did he belong in the Tombs Police Court in New York City. To understand Dillio's plight you have to realize that not so long ago all animals were equal before the law; a potato beetle or a cocker spaniel accused of some offense against the public morals was subject to arrest, trial, and punishment like any human malefactor. Cotton Mather mentions in his journals that a "wretch, one Potter by name" was executed in New Haven for sodomy; to compound the punishment the authorities first dispatched the lascivious pig while Potter was forced to watch. Similarly, in his *History of New England from 1630 to 1649,* John Winthrop describes how one Hackett, a servant in Salem ... "was found in buggery with a cow upon the Lord's day." Hackett and his bovine partner in sin were both tried, convicted, and stoned to death. It is not known whether such harsh sentences served to deter other animals from yielding to improper advances.

Which brings us to the *cause célèbre* of Jimmy Dillio. On November 28, 1877, Mary Shea of Mulberry Street appeared in Tombs Court, demanding that the magistrate throw the book at an organ grinder's capuchin monkey which had bit her. Regardless of the legal precedents, the magistrate was well aware that "this is 1877." Not wishing to look like a fool in the morning papers, he informed Mrs. Shea that it was no longer the practice in the United States to lock up animals. Her finger still wrapped in a bloody handkerchief, Mrs. Shea let out a shriek of righteous indignation. "This is a nice country for justice," she exclaimed, then stormed out of the courtroom. The monkey, dressed in a scarlet coat and velvet cap trimmed with gilt lace, was understandably pleased at his exoneration; according to the *New York Herald,* he scrambled up onto the magistrate's desk, wrapped his tail around the gas lighting fixture, and tried to shake hands with His Honor. On the official police blotter the court clerk entered the following data: *"Name:* Jimmy Dillio. *Occupation:* Monkey. *Disposition:* Discharged."

CLEVELAND H. DOWNS There were 56 giant green turtles aboard the cargo ship *Saratoga* when it steamed into New York Harbor on October 18, 1911, and they clearly

132

weren't traveling first class. To keep them from wandering about, Captain Downs had punched holes in their flippers, then looped them together like keys on a chain. Lawyers for the newly-formed A.S.P.C.A. spotted the suffering reptiles as they were unloaded and immediately filed charges against the captain, who was thenceforth held in $500 bail.

In court Downs admitted the flipper-piercing had been his doing, but his lawyer argued that cruelty to animals was hardly in question since turtles were not animals under the law. In a decision that would change the lives of amphibians everywhere, Magistrate Freschi ruled that turtles were indeed animals and entitled to all the rights, and privileges accruing therefrom. The malevolent Captain Downs was found guilty as charged.

JOHN ESPOSITO Let no man question John Esposito's commitment to the sanctity of the marriage vows, whether among humans or insects. In February, 1977, as the New York State Assembly was about to designate the praying mantis as the official state insect, Assemblyman Esposito's was a solitary voice of reason and morality. It would be wrong, he cautioned, to thus honor an insect that eats its mate.

To be sure, the lawmaker who had sung most loudly the virtues of the praying mantis, Assemblyman Eugene Levy, proved himself a man of reason as well by offering to table the bill and allow a statewide referendum of schoolchildren instead to decide whether the mantis or some other insect should be honored. (It was precisely in that manner that the state had settled upon the rose as its official flower in 1923, and on the sugar maple as the state tree, in 1897.) Still, Assemblyman Levy was at pains to point out that the praying mantis was a creature of many charms. For one, "It can turn its head around just like a man."

DAVID FULLER No history of civil disobedience and man's quest for dignity and justice would be complete without mention of David Fuller, a horse-drawn carriage operator in Charleston, South Carolina, who proudly defied a local statute requiring horses to wear diapers. The law took effect on December 1, 1975, and Fuller was handed a traffic summons and banned from the streets that very day. No matter, he said: he and his horse would return on the morrow and neither would be wearing diapers. The happy postscript: Charleston lawmakers gave in to the protests of Fuller and other horsemen and dropped the ordinance within weeks.

SYMON GOULD　One day in 1909 Symon Gould, the son of an immigrant tailor, threw a textbook at a teacher at Townsend Harris High School in New York City. His formal education ended then and there, but the incident, he later said, "launched me on a career as a Bohemian." His activities as a poet, socialist, and operator of New York's foremost art cinema spanned many decades. As a publisher, he brought out Emile Coué's bestseller, *Self Mastery Through Conscious Auto-Suggestion,* which had millions of Americans repeating "Day by day in every way I am getting better and better." In 1960 he became the first presidential candidate nominated by the Vegetarian party; his platform called for outlawing the consumption of all meat. A carnivore candidate by the name of John Fitzgerald Kennedy won the election.

LARRY HAND　*Ms.* magazine recently reported that Larry Hand, a convicted rapist serving time in San Quentin, filed suit to remove two women prison guards because "their presence constituted cruel and unusual punishment."

THOMAS HANSEN　How sharper than a serpent's tooth department: in 1978 Thomas Hansen of Boulder, Colorado, sued his parents, Richard and Shirley Hansen, for $350,000 on grounds of "malpractice of parenting." Mom and dad had botched his upbringing so badly, young Hansen charged in his suit, that he would need years of costly psychiatric treatment.

LARRY HERMONE "I'm proud to be paying taxes in the United States," Arthur Godfrey once declared. "The only thing is—I could be just as proud for half the money." That sums up how a lot of taxpayers feel, including Larry Hermone of San Jose, California.

Several years ago, when he fell behind in his tax payments, Hermone asked the Internal Revenue Service to allow him to settle his liability in regular monthly installments. He wasn't looking for special favors; the IRS often permits such arrangements. But for reasons of their own the tax collectors denied Hermone's request. Infuriated, Hermone went straight to the San Francisco Federal Reserve Bank where he obtained 250,000 pennies, the exact amount he owed the government. Then he rented a truck to deliver the mountain of coins to the local IRS office. After a lengthy discussion, a bewildered revenue agent finally agreed to accept the remittance which weighed just over one ton.

In 1977 when Jean Reymann, a supermarket checker in Rocklin, California, received a bill for $566 in back taxes, she was furious. "They took the shirt off my back, so I decided they might as well take it all," she declared, then wrote out a draft for the full amount on a pair of "dusty rose" panties. The IRS forwarded the panties to the Bank of America for collection, which honored the check.

TOM HORSELY Tom Horsely arrived at a San Francisco bar in 1978 to meet Alyn Chesselet for an evening on the town, and found her there with another man. Now Horsely had just motored 50 miles from Campbell, California, and did not take well to Miss Chesselet's explanation that her escort was an old flame who had popped into town at the last minute and asked her out, and that she had tried several times to telephone Horsely to cancel. As he saw it, he'd endured one broken date too many, and billed her for his expenses—$15 for fuel and wear-and-tear on his car (15 cents a mile) plus $17 in professional fees. (A Certified Public Accountant, Horsely sets his fees at $8.50 an hour and up.)

Miss Chesselet refused to pay and Horsely took her to court, the first man ever to sue a woman for standing him up. He lost.

EDWARD HYDE   From 1702 to 1708 Edward Hyde, Lord Cornbury, was the colonial governor of New York and New Jersey, the highest political office in this country ever attained by an overt transvestite. Hyde frequently appeared in public wearing women's clothes, and went so far as to pose for his official portrait in a low-cut evening gown and a lacy kerchief. He raised eyebrows, and questions about his sanity, by imposing a tax on males wearing wigs and by charging admission to his private dinners. On at least one occasion he was arrested on a morals charge; officially, however, he was dismissed from office for taking bribes.

RICHARD M. JOHNSON   In the presidential election of 1836, Martin Van Buren won a comfortable electoral college victory. But, incredibly, his running mate, Congressman

Richard M. Johnson, sometime Vice President *(New York Public Library, Picture Collection)*

Richard M. Johnson of Kentucky, did not. Southern electors, scandalized by Johnson's notorious sexual affairs with slave women, refused to cast their votes the way their states had voted, throwing the vice presidential contest into the Senate, the first and only time this has ever occurred. There the hard-drinking Johnson was finally elected by a vote of 33–16.

If we may believe John Nance Garner, the number two spot "isn't worth a pitcher of warm spit," and the principal challenge of the job is devising ways to fill the idle hours. At this Johnson proved unusually resourceful. More than any other man he put the vice back into the vice presidency. He antagonized Capitol Hill by having sexual congress with the wives of at least four prominent legislators. Then in 1839, during the midst of a depression and the Aroostock War, he took a nine-month paid "leave of absence," and returned to his home in White Sulphur Springs, Kentucky, to manage a profitable hotel and tavern business. One guest at the popular spa reported that "Colonel Johnson gives his personal superintendence to the watermelon selling department."

The indignity of it was too much for the Democrats to bear, and in 1840 the party's convention declined to endorse Johnson or any other vice-presidential candidate. Van Buren was renominated *without a running mate.* Undaunted, Johnson ran as an independent.

Throughout the wild, hard-fought campaign of 1840, Whig crowds chanted "Tippecanoe and Tyler, too," in an effort to capitalize on General William Henry Harrison's distinguished war record. Johnson's supporters countered by ballyhooing the heroism of their favorite, who claimed—fraudulently, it seems—to have killed the fearless Shawnee chief Tecumseh at the Battle of the Thames. To celebrate this questionable achievement, an unknown political poet composed the couplet: "Rumpsey dumpsey, rumpsey dumpsey/ Colonel Johnson killed Tecumseh," a slogan never surpassed for electioneering imbecility.

WAYNE KIDWELL Can one state sue another for ripping off its clouds? If a legal precedent is ever established, credit the groundwork to Idaho Attorney General Wayne Kidwell. In the wake of a killing drought in the Pacific Northwest in the late 1970s, Kidwell charged neighboring Washington State with seeding east-moving clouds clearly earmarked for Idaho. Washington Governor John Evans dismissed the threatened lawsuit as so much grandstanding, but Kidwell was dead serious. Since the adjoining states have agreements for sharing rivers that straddle their common boundary, he contended, similar agreements should be worked out for sharing wind currents that whisk rain-bearing clouds across interstate lines.

EARL LANDGREBE   If you live in northwestern Indiana, Earl Landgrebe may be a famous American you *do* know exists: in 1972 the Republican congressman did his constituents proud by becoming the first elected United States official to be arrested for selling Bibles in Moscow. He smuggled the books—all 100 pounds of them—into the Soviet Union while on an official visit there, hoping to slip them to eager Christians. But police trailed him to a movie house and put the nab on him when several volumes concealed under his topcoat slipped to the floor.

Back in Washington Landgrebe rallied America's pro-cancer factions with his lone stand against a House bill to fund cancer research. The appropriation was much too generous, he argued, and even if it weren't, curing cancer "would only change which way you're going to go." According to the *Wall Street Journal,* "once he even voted 'no' on a quorum call; he says he had a good reason but he can't remember exactly what it was." *New Times* magazine voted Landgrebe one of "the ten dumbest Congressmen" and he earned a spot on a Washington environmentalist group's "Dirty Dozen" list three years' running.

But Landgrebe's finest hour was Richard Nixon's last: in the closing days of the Nixon administration, even as the beleaguered chief executive was no doubt drafting his resignation speech, Republican Landgrebe mysteriously announced that the balance of congressional support seemed to

138

be shifting in Nixon's favor. Of course, Landgrebe had defended his president all along, once exclaiming that if Nixon had "lied to a few congressmen, so what?" Another time he'd sputtered, "Don't confuse me with facts; I've got a closed mind."

DIXON HALL LEWIS Lewis, who represented Alabama in the House of Representatives, from 1829–44, weighed over 500 pounds, more than any other United States congressman before or since. Shortly after he began his first term in office the House voted to provide him with extra-large chairs for use during roll calls and other congressional business.

MATT LYON Matt Lyon got himself arrested in 1800 for seditious writings, but the Vermont electorate made him their congressman anyway, and the first person to be elected to federal office while serving a jail term. Lyon also became the first brawler in the history of the House of Representatives, when he tussled with a fellow lawmaker whose face he had spat upon.

GEORGE MALEDON "I never hanged a man who came back to have the job done over," boasted George Maledon, the Fort Smith, Arkansas, executioner who turned hangmanship into High Art. More a craftsman than a fiend—or so his admirers claimed—Maledon fashioned his own hanging ropes from costly Kentucky hemp and kept them oiled and supple. During his tenure at Fort Smith he sprung the trap door on 60 convicted criminals, collecting a fee of $100 for each execution.

JOHN A. MARKEY "It's tragic," New Bedford, Massachusetts, Mayor John A. Markey told a live, prime-time TV audience, "to have to do things like this to get a point across." With that, he stripped down to his socks and undies, as the ruthless gaze of the TV cameras held firm. But Markey's brief exercise in mayoral ecdysiastics was not the sign of a brain gone haywire. He did it, he said, to illustrate the "stripping away of the city's budget base," by an arbitration panel's decision to grant an $800,000 pay hike to the city's fire department. But even as he inveighed against fiscal waste, Mayor Markey had a decidedly unmayoral afterthought. "Wait till my wife sees me," he said.

BETTY McALPIN   Betty McAlpin ordered a bottle of beer at the Tiara Club, near Eudora, Arkansas, drank half of it, and discovered a dead mouse on the bottom. With that, she became "violently ill," and was subsequently unable to work for several weeks thereafter. (She was, irony of ironies, a waitress at that very same establishment.) Sufficiently recovered to pursue her rights, she sued Anheuser-Busch Inc. for $100,000, claiming that she had endured "pain, suffering and mental anguish, past, present and future."

The court awarded Ms. McAlpin one-tenth that amount, and she walked away a happy woman. But the story doesn't end there. Stung to the quick, Anheuser-Busch appealed the decision on the grounds that it "was obviously based on passion and prejudice of the jury when there were no medical bills," and the Arkansas Supreme Court dropped the settlement to a mousy $3,000.

EMIL MATALIK   Emil Matalik—farmer, Air Force officer, and ex-Boy Scout—was probably the most ecumenically-minded third-party presidential candidate in United States history. "Actually, I'm really interested in being president of the *world,*" he said when he announced his candidacy for the nation's highest office in 1975. "The problems around the world are building up to an explosive point. The only solution is a world president."

Among those problems, Matalik explained, was "an excess of animals and plant life. Especially trees." Under his administration each family would be permitted a maximum of one child, one animal, and one tree. Matalik prosecuted a spirited campaign from his farm in Bennet, Wisconsin—which, he promised, would become the world capital upon his election. He has since disappeared from public view.

MARSHALL McCOMB After a lengthy investigation, Justice Marshall McComb of the California Supreme Court was forced to retire from the bench at the age of 83. A spokesman for the California Commission on Judicial Performance alleged, "He fell asleep during hearings and once wore a Shirley Temple wig. In court, and also in conferences, he would run through a set of eye exercises and also fitness exercises."

JOHN MONKS Whenever John Monks makes a speech on the floor of the Oklahoma State House of Representatives a number of his fellow legislators pull out miniature American flags and wave them enthusiastically. It is a tribute to Representative Monks's most memorable legislative achievement: getting anti-cockfight legislation killed by arguing that it was Communist-inspired. Quoth Monks: "In every country where the Communists have taken over, the first thing they do is outlaw cockfighting."

GEORGE NEWETT "Roosevelt gets drunk," Michigan newspaper editor George Newett wrote in his *Ishpeming Iron Ore* in 1912. "And not infrequently—and all his intimates know it." That was Teddy Roosevelt he was thus defaming, twenty-sixth president of the United States and at the time campaigning for reelection. After the contest, which Roosevelt lost, he initiated a lawsuit against Newett, and the case came to trial on May 26, 1913, in Marquette, Michigan. By that time, Roosevelt and his attorneys had assembled an imposing group of witnesses, including cabinet officers, generals, and clergy who would swear to the ex-chief executive's uncompromising sobriety.

Newett, one of the most powerful small-town editors in the Midwest, knew he was licked, and on the sixth day of the trial he took the witness stand himself and admitted that he had been "unable to find in any section of this country any individual witness who is willing to state that he has personally seen Mr. Roosevelt drink to excess."

Teddy beamed triumphantly and asked the judge to award

him only nominal damages. Nominal is what he got: the court commanded Newett to pay TR a settlement of six cents, the minimum then allowable under Michigan law.

FRANCIS O'DONNELL What a trooper! Francis O'Donnell was reelected to the Philadelphia City Council in 1975 even though he had died of a heart attack a week earlier.

HAZEN S. PINGREE Although it isn't likely that he needed the extra paycheck, Hazen Pingree moonlighted as Mayor of Detroit while he was Governor of Michigan. He was also the guiding force behind the Potato Patch mania that swept the United States at the turn of the century, turning countless thousands of acres of unbuilt-upon urban lots into vegetable gardens.

To be sure, Potato Pingree, as he came to be known, was no faddist. There were a lot of out-of-work immigrants in Detroit during his term of office and it seemed sensible to him to turn over unused land to them for raising produce. Other cities picked up on the idea, including New York, where in 1907, a promised building boom had fizzled dismally, leaving numerous investment and real estate firms holding newly-purchased lots in the city with no wherewithal to build. The Pingree plan was adopted, a "back-to-the-farm" movement materialized, and in their first year the vacant lot farmers of New York harvested over $15 million in crops.

Hazen "Potato" Pingree (with beard) served simultaneously as Mayor of Detroit and Governor of Michigan. *(Michigan Department of State)*

MARIO RIVAS Waiter Mario Rivas's story is that he delivered a basket of fruit to the room of an Arab sheik at the Century Plaza Hotel in Los Angeles and was slapped smartly in his face for his trouble because the delivery was two hours late. But the sheik said poppycock: "I would never order a basket of fruit. I am a diabetic and do not eat sweets or fruit." The sheik's protests notwithstanding, Rivas claimed his ear, right cheek, and feelings had been injured in the assault and sued for two million dollars.

RICHARD SAKS and THOMAS GEORGE Aficionados regard the July 1977 action by Richard Saks and Thomas George of New York City as the most unusual protest demonstration since the Yippies threw wads of dollar bills onto the floor of the New York Stock Exchange. Occupying seats in the visitors gallery of the House of Representatives, the two men suddenly screamed out "You cockroaches!" then hurled a paperbag filled with six-legged vermin down among the legislators. The roaches quickly found their way into the cracks and corners of the Capitol, while Saks and George soon found themselves in court charged with disrupting Congress while in session. For the record, they were protesting the lawmakers' failure to pass a bill boosting the minimum wage and making foodstamps available to strikers.

SUSANNA MEDORA SALTER When 27-year-old Susanna Medora Salter went to the polls on April 4, 1887, to vote for mayor of Argonia, Kansas, she was astonished to see her own name on the ballot. The local chapter of the Women's Christian Temperance Union had nominated her as their candidate, but had somehow neglected to inform her of the decision. Her failure to campaign proved to be no handicap. By a two-thirds majority she was elected the first woman mayor in the United States and served for one year at a salary of one dollar.

ABBY and JULIA SMITH In November of 1873 the town tax collector of Glastonbury, Connecticut, called at the home

Susanna Medora Salter, the first woman mayor *(The Kansas State Historical Society, Topeka)*

of Julia and Abby Smith to inform them that their property taxes would be going up by $100. A seemingly trivial incident. But before the matter was resolved, freedom, due process, women's rights, and the fate of seven cows would hang in the balance.

The injustice couldn't have been more blatant. Only two parcels of land in all of Glastonbury had been reassessed—the Smiths' and a house owned by two elderly widows—whereas the property taxes owed by the voting males of Glastonbury had not been raised a single penny. It was a clear-cut case of taxation without representation. Abby, age 82, was incensed. She sat down and composed a blistering oration, which her younger sister Julia, 77, agreed to deliver at the next town meeting. "All we ask of the town," they said, "is not to rule over them as they rule over us, but to be on an equality with them." The menfolk received the speech with stony silence.

A few days later the collector attached seven of the Smith

144

cows for unpaid taxes and impounded them in a neighbor's barn to await public auction. The homesick bovines responded with a stubborn campaign of civil disobedience. They lowed plaintively day and night, disturbing the entire village. They refused to be milked until Abby and Julia came and stood beside them.

Then on January 8, 1874, the cows went up for sale. Bargain hunters were disappointed to discover that while the sisters were unwilling to pay a $101.39 tax bill, they were prepared to outbid all comers to ransom their pets. The Smiths managed to buy back four—Jessie, Daisy, Whitey, and Minnie—before their money ran out. The other three, sadly, were sold into bondage.

A writer from *Harper's Weekly* picked up the story and referred to Abby Smith as "Samuel Adams redivivius." Almost overnight the plight of the Glastonbury Seven became the focus of national attention. A Smith sisters defense fund was formed. A Chicago group wove hairs clipped from the cows' tails into flowers, tied ribbons around them, and sold them to raise cash for Abby and Julia. Lucy Stone (q.v.), one of America's leading feminists, journeyed to Glastonbury and declared, "Here some day, as to Bunker Hill now, will come men and women who are reverent of the great principle of the consent of the governed." And Abby, despite her years, went on a speaking tour throughout the Northeast declaring in a high, quavering voice: "They can't shut us up as they did our cows, and what is worse still they cannot shut our mouths!"

Meanwhile the unrelenting tax collector again assessed the elderly ladies for nonpayment, this time announcing the sale of 15 acres of prime Smith pasture land. At the last moment the location of the sale was shifted to prevent the sisters from attending, and an unscrupulous neighbor, who had been trying to get hold of the property for years, purchased the lot worth nearly $2,000 for just $78.35. Abby and Julia hired a lawyer and sued the tax collector. The litigation dragged on for years, going through a whole series of appeals, until a final verdict was rendered in their favor a few months before Abby's death. The cows were never returned, but feminists across the nation rejoiced.

"Abby Smith and her cows are marching on like John Brown's soul," said Isabella Beecher Hooker after the funeral. She went on to suggest that the cow be adopted as the emblem for "our peaceful suffrage banner." As for Julia, the press coverage brought her a proposal through the mail from a widowed New Hampshire judge. The fiery spinster was married in her living room at the age of 86. Later she called it the biggest mistake of her life and asked to be buried next to her sister with only her maiden name on the tombstone.

SALLY STANFORD   When citizens of Sausalito, California, address Sally Stanford as Madame Mayor, they know whereof they speak. In her 1974 campaign, the septuagenarian politician made no secret of the fact that she had operated one of San Francisco's most notorious whorehouses during the 1930s and 1940s. Her former career neither helped nor hindered her politically, she says. "People voted for me because I've got common sense."

FRANK D. STEMBERK   No one knew what to do about the rats that were overrunning Chicago's west side in 1977, nipping children as they slept, ravaging vegetable gardens, helping themselves to unguarded kitchen stores. Alderman Frank "Bring Me the Tail and Ears!" Stemberk had the solution: offer a bounty of a dollar a rat and watch the buggers scatter.

Soliciting local merchants for contributions and adding dollars from the ward coffers, Stemberk put together a $720 rat bounty fund which prompted a massive rat-hunt reminiscent of the Holy Crusades. Besieged west-siders ferreted out the infidels with flashlights, then battered them senseless with baseball bats and Budweiser empties. One particularly zealous family averaged 20 hits a night. Result: the fund ran out in less than a week, whereupon Stemberk appealed to Washington for federal aid.

GLORIA SYKES   When 25-year-old Gloria Sykes was hit by a cable car in San Francisco, it appeared on first examination that she had only suffered a few minor cuts and bruises. Only later did she discover that the accident had caused psychological and neurological damage of the most remarkable sort.

Ms. Sykes filed suit, claiming that because of her run-in with the cable car she had become a nymphomaniac, engaging in sexual relations with nearly 100 men. The court found in her favor and awarded her $50,000 in damages.

Ms. Sykes's lawyer, Marvin Lewis, has become something of a specialist in lusty torts. In 1974 he took the case of a 47-year-old mother of seven from Santa Ana, California, who was suing a health club for $1 million. The woman charged that she was trapped in a sweltering sauna for 90 minutes, a traumatic experience which compelled her to pick up 24 men in singles' bars. The case was eventually settled out of court.

GEORGE and SUSAN TEEBAY   Clyde comes from a broken home.

When George Teebay and his wife Susan were divorced, she was awarded custody of Clyde, but Mr. Teebay was allowed "reasonable visitation" rights. But as so often happens when families break up, the problems did not end there. In 1978, Mr. Teebay filed suit in the Oakland, California, Supreme Court, alleging that his ex-wife had prevented him from seeing Clyde, a large male golden retriever, and had neglected to care properly for the dog. An insulted Mrs. Teebay told the judge that she had, in fact, been taking excellent good care of Clyde. (He was in good coat; his nose was wet.) Furthermore, she needed Clyde at home for protection. The judge, himself the proud owner of two golden retrievers, issued a landmark ruling in the case: "George shall have visitation of the family dog, Clyde, on the second and fourth weekends of each and every month from Friday at 7 P.M. until Sunday at 4 P.M., commencing forthwith. It is expected that the parties will cooperate with one another to effect the intent of this order."

GARY S. THOMAS   Judge Gary S. Thomas, who presides over the Municipal Court of San Rafael, California, believes in teaching law-breakers a lesson. Since 1975 he has been sentencing petty offenders to write "I will not steal" and "I will not appear in court" as many as 2,000 to 3,000 times. "It's as good a deterrent as any," he reports.

JOHN M. TODD   There was no way to spend half an hour in John Todd's barber chair without feeling close to the ribline of American history. After all, he was the most influential barber the nation has ever known. He cut hair for 62 years in Portland, Maine, during the 1800s, and for 26 of those years he was the town's most powerful politician. William Henry Harrison won the presidency in 1840 largely due to Todd's support. (Never mind that Harrison caught a chill on inauguration day and died a month later.) Todd, who was bald and bearded and resembled an Old Testament prophet, was an ardent foe of strong drink and labored long and hard to keep Maine a dry state; he was a Shaker, a spiritualist, and an enemy of meddling government, and he wrapped up his life's thinking in a 322-page autobiography that became something of a barber's bible. In it he established a barbers' hall of fame, peopled with such tonsorial greats as Charles C. Haskins of Bar Harbor, "The King of the Left-Handed Barbers"; J. J. Sullivan, who once shaved a man in a minute and a half flat; J. C. Morey, whose magic razor skated over some 718 miles of facial surface in 45 years; and the immortal J. Williams of Quebec, "Professor of Cranicultural Abscission and Cranilogical Tripsis, Tonsorial Artist, Physiognomical Hair Dresser, Facial Operator, Cranium Manipulator, and Capillary Abridger."

Todd was above all fiercely intellectual, and stocked back issues of the *North American Review, The Nation,* and *Scribner's* for his customers as they waited. *Police Gazette* fans took their business elsewhere.

ALICE STEBBINS WELLS   Whether she knew it or not, Angie Dickinson, the star of the long-running television se-

148

Alice Stebbins Wells was the
first policewoman *(Los Angeles
Police Department)*

ries *Police Woman,* owed a debt of gratitude to Mrs. Alice
Stebbins Wells. When she was sworn in as a full-fledged
member of the Los Angeles Police Department on September 12, 1910, Mrs. Wells, a social worker by training, became
the first woman in the country with full powers of arrest. She
was the original woman in blue.

Initially, people refused to believe that she was for real.
The skepticism of street car conductors was most aggravating
of all. At the time, members of the police force were allowed
free rides on public transportation while on duty or commuting to and from work. But whenever Mrs. Wells stepped into
a trolley, flashed her badge, and tried to take a seat, the
conductor would accuse her of unauthorized use of her husband's credentials. The problem was finally resolved when
she was issued "Police Woman's Badge No. 1" and permitted
to wear a feminine-looking but official uniform of her own
design.

To begin with, her duties were pretty tame stuff, at least
when compared with the pistol-happy, karate-chopping ex-
ploits of Miss Dickinson. She was entrusted with "the suppression of unwholesome billboard displays" and enforcement of the laws pertaining to "dance halls, skating rinks,
penny arcades, picture shows," and other similar places of
public recreation. Soon, however, the department instituted a
policy whereby "No young girl can be questioned by a male
officer. Such work is delegated solely to policewomen, who,
by their womanly sympathy and intuition, are able to gain
the confidence of their younger sisters."

149

Mrs. Wells sought to educate other police departments throughout the country regarding the important role women could play in keeping the peace. By 1916, largely as a result of her efforts and example, there were women officers in 17 United States cities.

JEROME L. WILSON   The campaign fund-raising dinner sponsored in 1964 by New York State Senator Jerome L. Wilson was no ordinary evening of "chicken and green pleas." To spare his supporters a boring evening and a case of indigestion, Wilson mailed out engraved invitations to an exclusive $25-a-plate non-banquet with no politicians, no clumsy waiters, no menu, and no one in attendance.

"The coffee won't turn cold before the introductions are finished," Wilson promised. "No endless parade of speakers ... will drone on into the night." There was a star-studded program of nonspeakers, headed by New York City Mayor Robert F. Wagner, all of whom graciously accepted the invitation not to speak.

SAMUEL WILSON   Unlikely as it seems, the original Uncle Sam was a meat packer from Troy, New York. Samuel Wilson (1766–1854) was his real name, and during the War of 1812 he provided sides of prime beef to the infantry and later served as an inspector of army supplies. Quartermasters throughout the Northeast called him "Uncle Sam" because of his beard and his avuncular appearance. Part of his job as an army inspector was to stamp meat barrels with the insignia "U.S.," and the soldiers he worked with jokingly said it stood for Uncle Sam, old Sam Wilson. Someone even came up with a slogan: "Uncle Sam—he feeds the army." Gradually Samuel Wilson's nickname came to stand for the entire United States government.

Money-Makers

JOHN ALLEN   Spunky little John Allen ran a well-known saloon on the New York City waterfront in the 1800s, where a man could drink unashamedly and ogle buxom girls in tight-fitting dresses who would alternately dance and hustle drinks.

Running such a place, and administering a resounding slap on a dancer's fanny from time to time, seemed unlikely work for Allen, who had graduated with honors from the Union Theological Seminary and numbered several clergymen among his brothers. But then those influences were not forgotten at Allen's establishment. Patrons found the tables littered with religious tracts placed there by the proprietor, and the rooms where some of Allen's saucier girls invited customers were furnished with Bibles. Once a band of evangelists raided the place, found the proprietor dead drunk, and conducted a prayer meeting that attracted so much new business that night that when Allen came to, he invited the reformers to hold nightly meetings.

J. C. BABCOCK   It seems unjust that no monument stands in either Miami Beach or the Catskills to J. C. Babcock, the man who brought mahjong to the United States in 1922. A West Coast businessman, Babcock saw the game played in the parlors and gaming dens of Shanghai by intense men who might gamble away thousands of dollars in a single evening. He carried several sets of tiles back to California with him, sold them easily, then got the idea to have additional sets shipped from China for sale in the States.

Babcock profited quickly from his scheme although com-

151

petitors, lured by the lack of copyright protection, moved in to manufacture sets of their own. Some 130,000 sets were sold in 1922, and an additional 1.5 million in 1923. Most were manufactured in China, although raw materials ran low toward the end of '23 and Babcock sent boatloads of animal bones from the Chicago stockyards to his Chinese suppliers to be made into mahjong tiles.

CHARLES CARROLL   A cat, as Ambrose Bierce defined it, is "a soft, indestructible automaton provided by nature to be kicked when things go wrong in the domestic circle." Cats, withal, have other qualities to recommend them; they can, for instance, be made into warm and elegant overcoats.

Recognizing this, Charles Carroll, the grandson of a signer of the Declaration of Independence, purchased thousands of black cats as an investment. Why black? Because the price was low, owing to the superstitious prejudice against them, and because the Chinese, great admirers of feline pulchritude, were willing to pay top dollar for fine black pelts.

In the fall of 1846 Carroll transported his clowder of cats to Poplar Island, Maryland, near the mouth of the Choptank River. There he turned them loose on an unfenced range, hoping they would breed and multiply. He looked forward to a bountiful harvest in the spring.

When two thousand black cats get together in one place, a little bad luck is to be expected. Call it coincidence if you like, but the winter of 1847 turned out to be one of the worst of the century, and the brackish water surrounding Poplar Island froze over for the first time in memory. As for Charles Carroll's cats, every last one of them pussyfooted across the ice to the mainland and escaped.

RALPH CHARELL   Nobody takes advantage of Ralph Charell anymore. Or if someone does, he ends up regretting it. The New York City media executive is generally recognized as the world's most successful complainer, the archetype of the perspicacious, hard-nosed, demanding consumer we would all like to be. Over the past decade, Charell has

152

griped about poor telephone service, utility overcharges, faulty goods, landlord policies, tardy deliveries, and much, much more. He has collected over $80,700 in settlements thus far, and he's still far from satisfied.

ROBERT AUGUSTUS CHESEBROUGH Ponce de Leon wandered for hundreds of miles through the swamps of Florida looking for the secret of long life when all he really needed was a jar of Vaseline. Or so Robert Augustus Chesebrough would have us think.

For some reason, during a visit to America's first producing oil well in Titusville, Pennsylvania, Chesebrough developed a fascination for "rod wax," a colorless residue that formed around the pump rods gumming up the mechanism. When the young chemist returned to his laboratory in Brooklyn, New York, he carried with him a large keg of the gluey stuff. Chesebrough conducted hundreds of experiments and finally evolved a process in 1859 for extracting the wax, which he called "petroleum jelly," from crude oil. Then the only problem was figuring out what to do with it. In order to test its healing powers Chesebrough inflicted horrible cuts and scratches on himself and burned his skin with matches and acid. For the rest of his life he looked as though he'd been run over by a McCormick reaper, but he succeeded in proving that virtually any wound feels better when smeared with petroleum jelly.

There was widespread sales resistance to the product at first. People were afraid it would explode. To gain acceptance for petroleum jelly, he traveled all over the Northeast in a buggy, giving out free samples to every housewife who would take one. Soon orders were pouring in.

There is a romantic, though disputed, story concerning the derivation of Chesebrough's famous brand name. It seems that during his experiments he was forever running out of beakers in which to store the massive quantities of jelly he produced. Each day his wife would bring in a bouquet of fresh cut flowers to decorate his laboratory, and each day Chesebrough would throw out the flowers and fill the vase

153

with grease. "-Line" was a common suffix for patent medicines in the nineteenth century, so when it came time to register a trademark Mrs. Chesebrough suggested Vaseline. Other authorities insist the word grew out of Chesebrough's cockamamie theory that crude oil was formed by the decomposition of water in the earth and the uniting of hydrogen with carbon. They say he merely took the German word *wasser* (water) and coupled it with the Greek word *elaion* (olive oil).

Regardless of its etymology, Vaseline has been utilized for purposes its inventor could never have anticipated. Hollywood directors have used it to simulate tears; fisherman had dabbed it on their hooks as trout bait; homemakers have discovered it removes white rings on mahogany furniture. Sales boomed in Russia in 1916 when peasants found that Vaseline added to their oil-burning lamps cut down on the smoke and unpleasant fumes. Demand soared in China during Sun Yat Sen's revolution when coolies, who shaved off their queues as a symbol of their liberation from the feudal landlords, learned that petroleum jelly soothed the pain of razor burn. There are, of course, many other lubricant and lubricious uses we need not mention.

Chesebrough himself was convinced that Vaseline was the elixir of life, the very oozings from the Fountain of Youth. Every morning he swallowed a heaping teaspoon of the goo and attributed his own longevity to this dosage. He was spry and alert until his death in 1933 at the age of 96.

GEORGE DASHNAU "Death holds a fascination for us mortals," says Philadelphia advertising executive George Dashnau. "It's a very good angle."

To capitalize on what he sees as a tremendous, untapped demand for lugubrious whatnots, Dashnau recently opened a mail-order supply house specializing in the sale of human skulls at $100 a head. The skulls are sectioned to allow viewing of the brain cavity, and the lower jaw is outfitted with springs which "permit opening and shutting of the mouth in a realistic manner," he says. The firm's advertising is aimed primarily at "business executives who want an unusual desk ornament."

"I've been looking for a way to get rich for many years," the Associated Press quotes Dashnau as saying. "I've been looking for a product that will catch the public's fancy. If this doesn't do it, nothing will."

STANLEY FOX Foxy fellow, this Stanley Fox. Having made his first million selling go-carts and snowmobiles, he retired to Miami, grew restless, and returned to his native Wisconsin, where he established a company creating fox-related novelty items for people named Fox.

"My average customer says to himself, 'When I have guests over, they knock on my fox door knocker,' " Mr. Fox said. " 'We drink out of my fox tankards. When we play cards it should be a fox deck. Meanwhile, I run around serving them in my fox costume.' " Who are his average customers? People named Fox, naturally. There are some 90,000 of them throughout the United States, and when Mr. Fox started his firm in 1974 he sent 30,000 of them catalogues; four percent replied favorably. That's a remarkably good rate, even if there was no competition to outfox.

In addition to door-knockers and beer steins, Mr. Fox's company—called Foxy, Inc., and headquartered in Janesville, Wisconsin—distributes placemats, jigsaw puzzles, rings, belts, blankets, bath towels, pen-and-pencil sets, table-cloths, backpacks, Christmas tree ornaments, and all manner of jewelry, including a foxhead brooch that is pure kitsch. The price: $545.

Mr. Fox numbers name-conscious businesses as well as individuals among his customers. Some rent fox outfits for everyone attending sales conferences. Foxy's Wheel 'n' Ski Shop in Beloit, Wisconsin, is a steady customer; so is Fox the Florist, in Richmond Heights, Ohio, whose saleswomen wear fox T-shirts.

"All those people out there named Fox are like a clan, a

fraternity of Foxes, and these things make them happy. They make me happy too," Mr. Fox admitted. "Even though my real name is Fuchs."

DARRELL GARMANN   Part-time prospector Darrell Garmann has staked out one of the richest claims in the Reno, Nevada, area since the Comstock Lode was played out back in the 1890s. Garmann was crossing the bridge over the Truckee River outside of town in 1973 when he chanced to look down. "I could see coins glimmering," he says. From folks living nearby he learned that it is considered lucky after obtaining a Reno divorce to throw your wedding ring or a coin into the troubled waters of the Truckee.

Lucky for Garmann. With an official prospecting permit in hand, he began dredging the riverbed on weekends. Thus far, he's come up with 120 pounds of pennies, 20 silver dollars, 60 pounds of silver coins (including a rare 1872 dime minted at Carson City and valued at $800), a valuable old .45-caliber pistol, a $1,200 diamond ring, and 300 gold wedding bands. He estimates the total value of his claim at more than $30,000.

HARRY GRAY   Every year *Business Week* magazine publishes the salaries of America's top executives. Harry Gray, president of United Technologies, received the highest one-year earnings recorded to date, grossing $1,662,000 in 1976.

MARTI HOUGH   After an eight-week course in self-assertiveness, previously unassertive Marti Hough found herself with more self-assertiveness than she knew what to do with. To channel it constructively, the 30-year-old Chicago housewife formed "Hough's Speak-Up Service." For $5 plus phone charges, Ms. Hough & co. will relay to the recipient of your choice any message which you are unable or uninclined to transmit yourself. Not surprisingly, three out of every four jobs handled by the service are unpleasant—bids for pay hikes, consumer complaints, dunning notices. "Most people have difficulty getting their point across on sensitive issues,"

156

says Ms. Hough. "They know what they want to say, but can't bring themselves to say it."

STAN MAZANEK Stan Mazanek knew a good deal when he saw one: While a student at the University of Arizona he took an insurance company up on its widely advertised offer of reduced premiums for undergraduates by purchasing a six-month policy on a sixty-cent guppy. The cost was one dollar. While Mazanek did not indicate the species and genus of the insured, he did supply all information requested on the application form, including the height of the insured (three centimeters) and its age (six months.)

As young Mazanek had hoped, the application sailed through the processing channels unchallenged and he was soon the owner of a bona fide insurance policy with himself named as sole benefishiary.

The guppy died within a few weeks and Mazanek put in his claim, to be turned down unceremoniously. When he threatened to sue, the insurers weakened and offered a $650 settlement.

FRIER McCOLLISTER Seventeen-year-old Frier McCollister was admitted to Columbia University but found himself stymied by an economic paradox: his family's annual income of $25,000 was enough to render him ineligible for financial aid yet not enough to handle first-year expenses of $7,000. Young McCollister's solution: begging.

Wearing a mortarboard and a sandwich sign reading, "Future Nobel Prize Winner," he spent the summer panhandling along Michigan Avenue in Chicago. One woman dropped twenty dollars into his pewter mug, but others ignored his pleas, and at least one man took a swing at him. By summer's end he had netted $330 for his troubles.

JOHN WOOD McMAHAN At the University of Illinois commencement exercises in 1939, McMahan became the first person ever to receive a Ph.D. degree in Accounting.

GEORGE A. MYERS   Living in the era of the Remington Electric, it is difficult to appreciate the special relationship that existed between a man and his barber in the heyday of the straight razor. Is there anyone alive today to compare with Junius Oliver Beebe, the Boston millionaire, who would travel anywhere in the world to receive the ministrations of an expert tonsorialist? Once Beebe heard of a legendary master in Santiago, Cuba, who could debeard a customer with five clean strokes of a well-honed Solingen blade; he immediately went out and booked passage on the next vessel bound for that distant port of call. As his brother, Lucius Beebe, recounts in *The Big Spenders,* a book about the foibles of the super-rich, "Junius returned two weeks later not quite a stretcher case, but bandaged like a Pharaoh's mummy and smelling powerfully of antiseptic. It was some days before the scars were sufficiently healed for him to talk about his experience coherently, and then all he said was, 'He did it in four.' "

Unfortunately, Beebe was born too late to sit in the well-padded chair of George A. Myers of Cleveland, Ohio, the black proprietor of what author Elbert Hubbard called "the best barber shop in America." Myers shaved no fewer than eight United States presidents and served as exclusive barber to political wheeler-dealer Mark Hanna. In the words of Dr. Harvey Cushing, a famed neurosurgeon and Pulitzer prize-winning biographer, "It was a mark of distinction to have one's insignia on a private shaving mug in George A. Myers' personal rack, and to receive his addresses, both intra- and extra-cephalic." By which the doctor meant to say, Myers could tell a dirty joke as well as give a good haircut.

OMAR THE BEGGAR   "To be successful, you have to be glib, inventive, patient, fast, and aggressive. And you have to be well-dressed, well-groomed, and well-spoken." The formula for climbing to the top of the corporate ladder? Not exactly. Actually, those are the rules for success laid down by "Omar," the pseudonymous headmaster of Omar's School for Beggars in New York's Greenwich Village. *Money* magazine dubbed it "Fagin Prep."

Omar's many students, who pay $100 for a week of night classes, are out to learn how a poor man can become a rich man through gainful employment as a beggarman. "The most effective pitches involve a medical emergency," Omar teaches. "Everyone can identify with an emergency situation, and they don't want you to die at their feet. It's a nuisance. They give you money to get you out of their lives."

One prosperous graduate patrols the area around Lincoln Center with a fake bruise on his forehead and a ketchup stain on his $20 designer shirt. Passersby automatically assume he is a mugging victim and support him to the tune of $700 a week, tax-free. A pretty *summa cum laude* from Omar's, who also graduated from Oberlin and has an M.A. in fine arts, collects $1,000 a week in Chicago's O'Hare airport. She tells travelers that she is a 14-year-old runaway trying to raise the plane fare to get back home.

JAMES J. RITTY Ritty's saloon on Main Street in Dayton, Ohio, managed to do a booming business and still not show a decent profit. Everyone knew why. Sticky-fin-

James Ritty, the inventor of the original cash register and his creation *(NCR Corporation)*

gered bartenders pocketed at least as much money as they put in the till, and short of pouring the whiskey himself there was nothing the proprietor could do to prevent it. Jake Ritty fretted about the lost income day and night until he finally worried himself sick and was ordered by his doctor to go on a long sea voyage to recuperate.

En route to Europe, Ritty made a tour of the ocean liner's engine room, where he was fascinated by a device which counted the revolutions of the propellers. Using the same mechanical principal, he reasoned, one should be able to contrive a machine for recording business transactions. The days of the larcenous bartenders were numbered, or so he thought.

Back in Dayton, Ritty collaborated with his mechanically-minded brother John to develop a metal contraption resembling a large table clock. There was a little hand which indicated dollar amounts, and a big hand for cents. Controlling these hands were two rows of keys arranged across the lower front of the machine. Each key had a number printed on it; pressing the $1 key caused the dollar hand on the dial to point to 1, and pressing the 25¢ key advanced the cents hand to 25, logically enough. When a customer paid his bill, the cashier rang up the amount on the dial where it could be seen by all. At the same time, inside the machine two adding disks (which could not be tampered with) kept a running total of the sales rung up on the register.

The brothers patented their invention on November 4, 1879, and dubbed a later model "Ritty's Incorruptible Cashier." Pilferage was reduced, though hardly eliminated. Ritty was never able to perfect the bartender.

DR. WILLIAM SCHOLL Yes, Virginia, there is a Dr. Scholl. Drawing on the anatomy he learned while attending two medical schools simultaneously, the shoemaker turned foot doctor designed his first arch support, the "Foot Eazer," in 1904 when he was 22 years old. He scrupulously adhered to his personal credo, "Early to bed, early to rise, work like

160

hell, and advertise," walking ten hours a day from shoe store to shoe store marketing his wares. His favorite attention-getting device was to approach the store manager, pull a skeleton of a human foot out of his briefcase, and throw it on the table. To increase national foot awareness, he sponsored walking contests and, in 1916, a "Cinderella Foot" contest. In the latter event women were urged to go to the nearest Dr. Scholl's store and have their footprints taken by a "Pedo-Graph," a machine designed by Scholl to measure foot imbalance. A panel of distinguished judges selected America's most perfect foot from the thousands of entries submitted, and the winner received prizes and the thrill of having her footprint displayed in newspapers all over the country.

With the millions "Billy" Scholl earned by treating painful corns, bunions, and blisters, he traveled all over the world and accumulated the world's largest antique shoe collection.

SUZI SKATES   Few people are lucky enough to be born with names containing both a subject and a predicate. Evidently, though, 19-year-old Susan Johnson of San Francisco changed her named to Suzi Skates for professional rather than grammatical reasons. Suzi makes her living on roller skates, going wherever she is paid to go, delivering flowers to hospital patients, greeting people at airports, and distributing advertising leaflets. Her standard fee is five dollars an hour with a surcharge for extra mileage.

LAWRENCE SPERRY   To demonstrate the practicability of a small, inexpensive, private airplane—and promote sales—Lawrence Sperry landed his prototype on Capitol Plaza in 1922 and taxied to the steps of the Senate Wing.

FREDERIC TUDOR   Frederic Tudor (1783–1864) was an egotistical and hard-driving youth, consumed by an ambition to become "inevitably and unavoidably rich." "A man without money," he once wrote, "is like a body without a soul."

It was in the winter of his twentieth year that he conceived his fantastic and wholly original scheme to make a fortune by cutting thick blocks of blue-green ice from his father's pond in Saugus, Massachusetts, and shipping them to the tropics. All of Boston thought him mad. Stout-hearted seamen refused to make the trip with him for fear the ice would melt and swamp the ship. Oblivious to all warnings and objections, Tudor stowed 130 tons of ice into the hold of the Yankee brig *Favorite* and set sail for the Caribbean.

On March 6, 1806, he arrived in the sultry harbor at Saint-Pierre on the island of Martinique. The blazing sun was fast diminishing his frozen assets, and he realized he had little time to lose. After protracted negotiations, he convinced the proprietor of a local restaurant, the Tivoli Gardens, to serve fresh frozen ice cream on an experimental basis. Tudor concocted the sweet desserts himself and took his turn cranking the hand freezer. The ice cream was an instant success. Tivoli Gardens dished out $300 the first night. The next day there was an editorial in the local newspaper hailing "a remarkable epoch in the history of luxury and enterprise, which began when ice creams were eaten here probably for the first time since the settlement of this country lying 14 degrees north of the equator."

Promoting direct retail sales turned out to be more of a problem. The price was high—thirty cents per pound. And, as Tudor noted in a letter to a friend, the West Indians had a lot to learn about the proper care and handling of ice: "One carries it through the street to his house in the noonday, puts it on a plate before his door, and then complains, '*Il fond.*' Another puts it in a tub of water, a third by way of climax puts his in salt." When the merchandise melted into a tepid puddle, dissatisfied customers hounded the young entrepreneur for a refund. Soon he began issuing a detailed sheet of instructions with each cake of ice.

Tudor lost $3,500 on the Martinique venture, but his enthusiasm for the export business did not cool. Characteristically, on the front of his journal, the "Ice House Diary," he wrote: "He who gives back at first repulse without

Lawrence Sperry lands his plane at the Capitol steps *(The French Collection of the Library of Congress)*

Frederic Tudor harvested ice and shipped it to the tropics *(New York Public Library, Picture Collection)*

striking the second blow has never been, is not, and never will be a hero in war, love, or business."

Over the years he worked tirelessly to develop better methods of cutting, packing, transporting, and storing his product, and he devised many innovative merchandising gimmicks to increase demand. He gave away free refrigerator jars—along with a year's free supply of ice—to saloon keepers who agreed to serve iced drinks at the same prices as warm drinks. Thus in Charleston, Havana, and New Orleans he soon built up a thirsty clientele that insisted on icing their bourbon. He set up dozens of ice cream factories. He encouraged the use of carbonated water chilled with ice. In Brazil he taught physicians to use ice packs and iced drinks to control fevers.

The Tudor Ice Company was far from an overnight success. More than once his creditors lost their patience and had him arrested for debt. But when, in 1833, Tudor sent a cargo of ice to Calcutta it captured the imagination of every New Englander. (One beturbanned Parsee was said to have inquired: "How this ice grow in your country? Him grow on trees? Him grow on bush?") Historian Samuel Eliot Morison observed that "Mr. Tudor and his ice came just in time to preserve Boston's East India trade from ruin." His militant entrepreneurialism converted ice from "a Yankee liability into an asset."

Ice was Tudor's passion. He never wrote the word without capitalizing the "I." Still, he was an innovator in other fields, as well. For example, in 1830, he brought the first steam locomotive to Boston. It was a tiny, toy-like, one-half horsepower machine that ran on the sidewalk, to the distress of pedestrians, at a top speed of four miles per hour. Then, in 1859, Tudor (by then a millionaire several times over) opened America's first amusement park in Nahant, Massachusetts, where visitors up from Boston could enjoy swings, Punch and Judy shows, dancing, a wheel of fortune, and—inevitably—an ice cream parlor.

One of the last glimpses we have of the "Ice King" comes from Henry Wadsworth Longfellow. The poet thought him a

164

striking figure with his winter white hair, his scarlet cravat, and his blue overcoat with military brass buttons. "He showed me his wheat field by the sea," Longfellow recalled. "Having heard that wheat will not grow in such a place, he is determined to make it grow there."

ALVIN VERETTE   In New Roads, Louisiana, Alvin Verette owns and operates the Point Coupee Funeral Home, the nation's first and only drive-in mortuary. For the convenience of time-pressed mourners, the deceased is displayed before a five-by-seven picture window, the casket marked with a cross and a blue neon light. Friends and relatives can drive right up to the window, pay last respects, and depart, all in the twinkling of an eye.

This is not to imply that Mr. Verette does not offer more traditional arrangements, or that the interior of the establishment is other than tasteful. In fact, the Future Young Women of America have used the parlor for a wine and cheese party.

Says Mr. Verette, "We wanted something for people who didn't have time to dress."

DICK WAGNER   After he purchased a couple of power-hungry appliances, Californian Dick Wagner's electric bill shot up to $76.65. Irked by the stinging increase, but compelled to pay, he got his revenge by dumping $76.65 in pennies, weighing 52 pounds, on the floor of the gas and electric company. According to news reports, the company's manager told Wagner, "It's been a pleasure to do business with you."

Overdoers

ELEANOR BARRY Poor, literate Eleanor Barry. Living alone in her Long Island home, the 70-year-old woman surrounded herself with mountains of reading matter of every sort—books, yellowing newspapers, magazines, department store catalogues. As she lay in bed sleeping one night one pile swayed and fell, crushing her to death. The police had to be called to dig her out.

JAMES GORDON BENNETT, JR. The wealthy James Gordon Bennett, Jr., had a innate gift for scandal. He is perhaps best-remembered for the events of January 1, 1877, when, smelling of the cork, he staggered into a reception at the Fifth Avenue home of his fiancée, Caroline May. During the course of the party, he consumed an additional quantity of wine until the pressure on his bladder became uncontainable. Without so much as a "pardon me," Bennett unbuttoned his fly and micturated a long and steady stream into the blazing fireplace. The social consequences were stern and instantaneous. First, Bennett, followed by his hat and cane, was thrown into the street. Then, the following day, Caroline's brother Frederick horsewhipped him outside of the Union Club. This led, in turn, to a duel which luckily ended without bloodshed.

The doors of most respectable homes were closed to Bennett forever. To find company and ready amusement, the young playboy was compelled to spend much of the rest of his life in France, a punishment which had its compensations. Bennett loved the wine, the women (particularly if they were married), and best of all the mutton chops—especially those served at a certain Monte Carlo bistro. Arriving there one day without a reservation, he was disappointed to find all the tables occupied. Rather than wait a moment, he approached the owner and bought the establishment on the spot with $40 thousand in cash. He ordered that a table be cleared immediately and sat down to a hearty meal. After finishing his coffee, he gave his waiter the deed to the restaurant on the condition that there would always be a table reserved for him and mutton chops would be on the menu for every meal.

A lifelong collector of owl figurines, Bennett became obsessed in his declining years with the desire to be entombed in a 200-foot-high, owl-shaped colossus on New York's Washington Heights. Stanford White, the foremost American architect at the turn of the century, was commissioned to draw up the plans. Bennett proposed that the bird's eyes could serve as twin observation windows and that his coffin could dangle from a chain in the owl's head instead of being buried in the ground. But before construction could begin on the monumental eyesore, Stanford White was murdered in Madison Square Garden, and Bennett had to content himself with a less ostentatious resting place in Paris, where two granite owls guard his grave to this day.

CLYDE BOLTON The best dressed man who ever worked on an assembly line is Clyde Bolton. Those who labor next to him at Ford's Chicago plant may be content with overalls or jeans, but Bolton prefers white suits, tuxedos, and ruffled shirts with pink collars. The 30-year-old bachelor spends about $3,000 a year on his attire and somehow manages to avoid stains and grease spots as he puts the finishing touches on new Thunderbird engines. "His body doesn't touch the car," his supervisor marveled. "It's absolutely incredible." And a fellow worker commented, "On an average day he's tricked out better than the chairman of the board."

Why the fancy threads? Bolton has an elegantly simple explanation: "I feel better when I'm well dressed."

WALTER CAVANAGH Walter Cavanagh of Santa Clara, California, applied for a Newberry Department Store credit card recently only to be rejected with an admonition that he was pushing a good thing too far. In point of fact, Cavanagh is the uncontested credit card champion of the world, having amassed a total of 864 to date, with no duplicates. Cavanagh, who wears a T-shirt with the word CHARGE emblazoned across the chest, collects credit cards the way other people collect hotel towels, beer cans, or parking tickets. Not content with Visa, Master Charge, and American Express, he has established accounts with 49 separate gasoline companies and retailers in all 50 states. Cavanagh's credit has reached $750,000 and it's still growing steadily.

HENRY CHILDRY Worm fancier Henry Childry of Indianapolis showed up at the Claremont, New Hampshire, Chamber of Commerce's annual worm auction in 1978 having promised himself to spend prudently and not go hogwild over the offerings. But when five descendants of Hoopman-Page, considered by many to be the world's premier racing worm, were put up for sale, Childry lost his head and bought the lot for $2,600. "If Indianapolis has the world's fastest race cars," he told reporters as he cuddled his babies, "it might as well have the fastest worms too."

HARVEY COHEN "There's nothing Miami Beachy about this party," insisted one of the guests at 13-year-old Harvey Cohen's bar mitzvah. On the other hand, a rabbi termed the event "more bar than mitzvah." Reasonable people can disagree about matters of taste.

According to his dad, young Harvey is a rabid sports fan, "born with a ball in his hand." Thus, when Stanford Cohen, a Miami Beach lawyer, began looking around for a place to hold his son's bar mitzvah, it naturally occurred to him, "Why not rent the Orange Bowl?" As it turned out, the one-night fee for the 80,000 seat stadium was a modest $1,500. There were a lot of extras, though: the tents in case of rain, the stadium lights, the disco group, the bartenders decked out in striped referee shirts, the "Happy Birthday, Harvey" message on the scoreboard, the golf carts to transport the guests, like relief pitchers, across the Astroturf, and the entire 68-piece Hialeah Senior High School marching band with pom-pom girls. A six-course meal, including matzoh ball soup and other traditional dishes, was served by waitresses in tennis dress with a big "H" across the chest. "H" for Harvey. A *People* magazine reporter estimated the final pricetag at roughly $19,500.

"This is a tribute to a good son," Stanford Cohen said with pride. To which the lucky bar mitzvah boy responded: "I'll remember this all my life!"

CHRIS CHUBBUCK A Sarasota, Florida, newscaster named Chris Chubbuck herself became the news when she concluded a local evening news wrap-up in 1974 by denouncing station policies and shooting herself through the head with a revolver.

RICHARD DODD On December 7, 1968, Richard Dodd returned an overdue casebook on febrile diseases to the University of Cincinnati Medical Library, an incident noteworthy in the course of human events only because the volume had originally been checked out 145 years earlier by Mr. Dodd's great-grandfather. The fine, amounting to $2,646, was waived.

CURT EMERSON The management of the Bancroft House Hotel, in Saginaw, Michigan, showed poor judgment when they failed to invite local tycoon Curt Emerson to their gala opening banquet in 1879. As most of Saginaw's elite feasted on such delicacies as terrapin à la Maryland, the snubbed Emerson swept into the room screaming like a banshee. He clambered atop the dais, hounding the diners from their place settings, and destroyed over $2,000 worth of crockery and glassware. He sent the hotel a check for that amount the following day.

169

MAMIE STUYVESANT FISH   At the turn of the century Mrs. Stuyvesant Fish was noted for staging entertainments both lavish and outrageous. Once she engaged the entire sideshow of the Barnum and Bailey Circus—midgets, Siamese twins, bearded ladies, and the rest—to perform at a private party. On another occasion she gave a ball at which the guests were required to talk baby talk. Her husband, the director of the Illinois Central Railroad, could easily afford a few extravagances if only to please Mamie. Their house on East 78th Street was designed by Stanford White in the style of a doge's place; their villa in Newport, the *Crossways,* is now a museum.

When it came to excess Mrs. Fish was determined never to be outdone. On hearing that Thomas W. Lawson, the Massachusetts financier, had paid $30,000 to have a hybrid carnation named for his wife, Mamie resolved to become the first socialite to have a new dance named in her honor. Irene and Vernon Castle, the leading waltz team of the day, were commanded to appear at the 78th Street residence after a formal dinner (to which they were pointedly not invited). Only after the dessert course had been cleared did Mrs. Fish inform them of what she had in mind. The Castles protested that they could hardly evolve a whole new routine on such short notice.

"But you've got to, Mr. Castle," Mamie barked. "Releases have already gone out to the newspapers saying the new dance is a *fait accompli.*"

The dancers, spurred on by the promise of $10,000 for their footwork, executed a number of familiar paces in complete reverse, giving the appearance of total novelty. A great success, the "new" step was dubbed the Fish Glide.

"I'm so tired of being hypocritically polite," Mrs. Fish once lamented to a close friend. Thereafter, she did her best to break down civility at her parties and make bad manners fashionable. "Make yourself perfectly at home," she told one dinner guest. "And, believe me, there is no one who wishes you there more heartily than I do." To another gentleman she remarked: "Oh, how do you do! I had quite forgotten I

170

asked you." And when she suffered from boredom at one of her own affairs, she ordered the band to play "Home Sweet Home" continuously until everyone got the hint.

BILL FITCH "People are vain," Bill Fitch mused philosophically. "They're afraid of a little pain. Me? I don't give a damn."

Then to illustrate his point Fitch proceeded to jab dozens of hat pins into his arms, neck, mouth, ankles, and ears without a wince. Fitch, in case you've never caught his act, is the "Human Pin Cushion," the sole surviving practitioner of a masochistic art.

"You've gotta have guts to make money," Fitch declares, and for the past 27 years his sticky profession has brought in about $700 a week at fairs and circuses all around the country. His wife Alice also works the sideshow circuit, billing herself as "Zoma, the Jungle Girl."

Fitch willingly offers how-to advice to young, up-and-coming pin cushions: "I have to stick the pins in a different place each time so I don't get scar tissue. And I have to switch arms every week to avoid complications." Since the early 1950s, however, he has had the field entirely to himself.

Has he somehow become inured to the pain? "No," he says, "it hurts the same every time."

JIM HOGG Big Jim Hogg, who served as governor of Texas from 1891 to 1895, named his only daughter Ima; she grew up to be a much-admired philanthropist. There is absolutely no truth to the story that he had two other daughters called Ura, Wera, or a son named Hesa.

DAVID KENNISON In the Battle of Sackett's Harbor during the War of 1812, David Sackett's hand was blown off. He was 76 years old at the time. Some years later a tree fell on his head and fractured his skull, and a few years after that, while he was in the Massachusetts State Militia, both his legs were splintered by a blast from a misfiring cannon. The fractures healed but Kennison's legs were forevermore riddled with festering sores and soon thereafter he fell prey to rheumatism. Then a horse kicked him in the face, causing permanent disfigurement. When he died in bed in Illinois in 1851, Kennison was 115, the longest-surviving veteran of the Boston Tea Party.

LILLIAN KOPP When Lillian Kopp died at age 69 in 1978, she became the first human to be buried in Paw Print Gardens, a pet cemetary just outside Chicago. "She wanted to be near her pet German shepherd, Rinty," Mrs. Kopp's daughter, Barbara, explained to the Associated Press. "Rinty died in 1972. We have three other German shepherds left— Cindy, Dutch, and Jamie. All will be buried side by side, in the cemetery. So will I, my father, Henry, 72, and my brother, Ron, 45." When the late Rinty barked his last, Miss Kopp said, "the family sat down and discussed burial in Paw Print Gardens. Mother was in failing health the last two years and we all made definite plans to be buried in the cemetery near our pets." Funeral services and a wake were conducted by a Catholic priest in a chapel on the grounds of the cemetery.

STANLEY MARSH The one-of-a-kind spectacle on U.S. Route 40, five miles west of Amarillo, Texas, has been described as a "pop art whimsy" and "a monument to the decline of automobile culture." Stanley Marsh, the wealthy businessman who designed and owns the display, prefers to call it his "Cadillac Ranch." It is, quite simply, ten Cadillacs

Stanley Marsh's Cadillac ranch *(Stanley Marsh/McSpadden Photography)*

ranging from a 1949 fastback coupe to a 1960 Sedan de Ville, planted hood-end-down in a fertile wheat field with the tail fins sticking high into the air. Lined up in a straight row, the automobiles look like a surrealistic crop sprouting from the dark soil. Marsh doesn't pretend to be making any kind of statement. He just likes to hear what people say when they see his extravagant roadside joke.

MIKE MARYN   The most versatile of all crime victims is no doubt Mike Maryn of Passaic, New Jersey. Over the course of five years he endured 83 muggings and was hospitalized 20 times. In achieving that record he was knifed, shot at twice and bludgeoned with a metal pipe, lost several teeth, and was robbed of $2,000 in cash, several bags of groceries, and four automobiles. According to newspaper reports, Passaic police offered Maryn a walkie-talkie as a quick way of summoning help, but he turned them down. "It would only be taken from me," he explained.

HOMER MOOREHOUSE   In 1923 Homer Moorehouse became the first fatality of the marathon craze when he dropped dead after 87 hours of dancing in North Tonawanda, New York.

PAUL MORPHY   When Paul Morphy (1837–84) was ten years old, his father taught him the game of chess. Three years later, still so short that "he was obliged to have a couple of books put on his chair to bring him up to the right height for the table," Morphy catapulted into international prominence by winning two games and drawing one in a three-game match against the famed Hungarian master J. J. Lowenthal. He was the archetypical adolescent prodigy, defeating all comers with an aggressive, reckless, open style that left the experts gasping in amazement. "When one plays with Morphy," an opponent said, "the sensation is as queer as the first electric shock, or first love, or chloroform, or any entirely novel experience." His photographic memory enabled him to play and win as many as eight games simultaneously—while blindfolded. And in 1858 a triumphant tour of Europe, during which he routed Harrwitz, Mongredien, and finally Anderssen (the Continent's foremost player), established him as the undisputed world's champion and "the greatest genius in the history of the game."

Intellectuals everywhere hailed his magnificent achievement. He was invited to dine with Longfellow, Holmes, Lowell, and Agassiz. Then, almost without warning, he announced his retirement from the game. Rumor had it that he had fallen in love with an exquisite, haughty Creole girl, who had refused the proposal of a "mere chess player." With more certainty we know that his mother regarded chess as no fit occupation for a grown man and made him promise "never again to play for money or other stake, never to play a public game or a game in a public place, and never again to encourage or countenance any publication of any sort in connection with your name."

Morphy yearned for another kind of success. He wanted to make his name as a jurist, like his father. But people would not take him seriously as a lawyer; they persisted in regarding him as a kind of gambler who played with rooks and knights instead of hearts and spades. A failure at his profession, Morphy occupied himself by going every evening "in a cloak and monocle" to the opera. Slowly, irreversibly, he lapsed into melancholia and developed a textbook persecution complex. He was afraid that people were trying to poison him or burn his clothes. He imagined that his brother-in-law had cheated him out of his rightful inheritance from his father's estate. At night he paced back and forth on the veranda shouting: *"Il plantera la banniere de Castille sur les murs de Madrid, et le petit roi s'en ira tout penaud!"* ("He will plant the banner of Castille on the walls of Madrid, and the little king will take himself off abashed," a reference perhaps to the king piece in chess.)

On July 10, 1884, the demented genius went for a long walk in the blazing New Orleans sun and returned for a bath. Hours later his mother found him dead in the tub, surrounded by dozens of women's shoes. Doctors established the cause of death as "congestion of the brain" or apoplexy brought on by the shock of cold water on an overheated body.

ONE ZERO SIX NINE   Michael Herbert Dengler seems a nice enough name, but the man it identified, a 32-year-old unemployed college professor, insisted on changing it in 1977 to "1069." The Social Security Administration figured it a harmless act and duly issued Dengler a new card with his new four-digit name. Two banks imprinted his checkbooks with "1069" and various utility companies recognized the name change, but the Minnesota Motor Vehicles Department, the telephone company, and the state government itself all balked.

With that, 1069-née-Dengler, whose friends call him "One-Zero," went to court to sue for an official change. Before a Hennepin County (Minnesota) district judge, Dengler asserted that his choice of a new name was not capricious. The first digit, he said, represented life's basics: nature, political sophistication, food, clothing and shelter. The "zero" stood for time, color, motion, emotion, magnetism, and gravity. Growing more mystical by the digit, he explained that "6" symbolized the universe, harmony and disharmony, accord and discord. And "9" stood for "relationship to essence in the difference in the meaning when actualizing the spatially everpresent nature of life." Although state laws are lenient regarding name changes, approval was withheld pending clarification of the word "name." Resolute to the end, Dengler paid his court fees with a check he signed "1069."

JOHN LANGDON SIBLEY   An overabundance of school spirit motivated John Langdon Sibley to undertake a project awesome for its monumental impracticality. As head librarian at Harvard, he set out to write a biographical sketch of every man who attended the university from its founding in 1636 right on through to the present. Sibley worked doggedly on the research effort for 25 years despite failing eyesight that forced him to wear three pairs of spectacles at once. By 1885, the year of his death, he had gotten as far as the Class of 1689. In his will, he left $161,169 to the Massachusetts Historical Society—a bequest that has now compounded to $400,000—to carry on the Sisyphean task. The problem is, Harvard keeps turning out new graduates at a rate of 3,000 each year, and the biographers keep falling further and further behind. In all, there are now approximately 160,000 Harvard degree holders, of whom about 158,000 still lack biographies.

JOE SIMPSON Today Skidoo 23 is a ghost town. But until the gold mines were exhausted, it was a thriving little village of some 700 souls, situated high in the Panamint Mountains of California. With a modicum of wit, the settlement derived its unusual name from the turn-of-the-century fad expression "23 Skidoo" and the fact that the nearest water supply was exactly 23 miles away.

Skidoo's finest hour came in 1908, when the town's most dissolute citizen, Joe "Hoach" Simpson, shot and killed Jim Arnold, a wealthy and respected banker. As soon as the news of the sensational murder reached the editor's desk at the *Los Angeles Herald,* a reporter was dispatched to cover the story. But justice was swift and sure in Skidoo, even if all the legal niceties were not always observed. By sundown Simpson was hanging from a telephone pole and twisting slowly in the wind; and by the time the *Herald* reporter arrived, Simpson was resting peacefully under six feet of soil at the local cemetery.

The newsman was desolate. His editor had instructed him not to come back without photographs and a first-hand account of the trial and execution. In the face of such disappointment, the townspeople regretted their unseemly haste, and for the benefit of the press they exhumed the body and lynched Joe Simpson a second time.

ROSS STERLING Fifty years ago, former governor of Texas Ross Sterling decided to build a new house—just a modest little bungalow with 21,000 square feet of floor space, fifteen tile bathrooms, and three kitchens. He asked a Houston architect to draw up several alternative plans, but somehow none of them quite suited his fancy. Reaching for his wallet, Sterling pulled out a crisp new $20 bill and pointed to the back side. "Make it look like that," he ordered.

That's how the pleasant town of La Porte on Galveston Bay came to have an exact model, in three-fifths scale, of the well-known structure at 1600 Pennsylvania Avenue in Washington. Sterling's White House has the same simple and stately lines that distinguish the original, but the resemblance only goes so far. The much-admired north facade of the executive mansion was copied to the last detail, whereas the other three sides of Sterling's pretentious home are done in a rambling, eclectic style modeled after no particular building. Nonetheless, for an aging politician with more ambition than brains it was the fulfillment of a lifelong dream.

Incidentally, as of this writing, the White House is for sale by its current owner, Paul Barkley. There may never be an opportunity like this again.

FRANCIS JOHNSON and FRANK STOEBER Just as music lovers are forever arguing whether Beethoven or Bach was the greater composer, so are twine fanciers divided into two warring camps—those who say that Francis Johnson has accumulated the world's largest ball of string and those who champion the claim of Frank Stoeber.

Johnson, a retired carpenter living in Darwin, Minnesota, has enjoyed most of the publicity. As far back as 1958, he appeared on the television show *I've Got a Secret* with an ample orb weighing 2,490 pounds. Since then, thanks to years of diligent scrounging, it has swollen into a gargantuan five-ton spheroid that can only be rotated with a railroad jack. Johnson has also collected 5,000 pens and pencils, 1,700 carpenter's aprons, 84 Steam Engine Show buttons, 140 Seven-Up bottles, 1,000 wrenches, and a good deal more. If you're ever passing through Darwin, you can see it all in Johnson's private museum. Admission is 50¢.

In 1953, the late, great Frank Stoeber, Johnson's only serious rival, tripped over a length of twine lying near his cow barn in Cawker City, Kansas. It was a momentous misstep. Beginning with those few seemingly insignificant inches, Stoeber went on to amass an estimated one and a half million feet of string, enough to stretch from Chicago to Cincinnati. The Cawker City Community Club, which now has custody of the ball, claims the total weight is 8,953 pounds, which is roughly commensurate with Johnson's collection. In circumference their measurements are nearly the same. Today, the Stoeber ball is housed in a special shelter and illuminated with floodlights at night.

Stoeber or Johnson: whose ball comprises more string? The one way to tell for sure is to place the two balls side by side and start unwinding. No one is very keen on that.

BARONESS ELSA von FREITAG von LORINGHOVEN

Even by the outlandish standards of Greenwich Village, the Baroness Elsa von Freitag von Loringhoven was as eccentric as a comet. Abandoned by her husband, a wealthy German industrialist, at the outbreak of World War I, she squandered a small fortune, then moved into a tiny downtown apartment. For a while she worked as an artist's model and later she took a job in a cigarette factory. Her haughty, patronizing, aristocratic manner once prompted a fellow employee to bash out her two front teeth. She never bothered to have them fixed, but according to one observer of the Bohemian scene, "This in no way detracted from her distinction."

The baroness occupied her spare moments with writing Dadaist poetry and painting cubist canvases. Ultimately, though, she was her own greatest work of art. During one memorable phase, she shaved off all her hair and applied brilliant vermillion lacquer to her bare skull. She wore a peach basket for a hat and pasted pink postage stamps to her cheeks in place of rouge. (She was inordinately fond of postage stamps in all denominations and completely papered the walls of her studio with them.) An artist described her as "a walking assemblage."

178

Her distinctively outrageous attire never prevented her from being invited to all the most fashionable parties. To a reception for a leading soprano of the day she wore an irridescent blue-green gown, a coal bucket for a chapeau, two mustard spoons bent to look like feathers, and an elegant peacock fan. Her lips were painted black, her face powdered bright yellow, and 27¢ worth of cancelled stamps adorned her right cheek. The guest of honor was taken aback by the baroness's singular appearance, but she made a brave attempt at polite conversation. "My art is only for humanity, I sing only for humanity," the prima donna declared. "I wouldn't lift a leg for humanity," the baroness replied, a remark that was widely admired and repeated.

ROBERT MANNAH   Heartbeak is one of Robert Mannah's middle names; the other is *meshuganah.* Gunning for a berth in *The Guinness Book of World Records,* Mannah had himself buried alive in Dover, Delaware, on April 1, 1977, intending to stay buried for at least the 102 days he'd need to break the world's record. But Mannah had barely made himself comfortable when he learned that he had erred about the record, that it wasn't 101 days but 217. Still reeling from that blow, he was then informed that the editors of *Guinness* had decided to exclude burials from all forthcoming editions because they are too dangerous. "After that I didn't see any sense in staying down," Mannah said, cutting short his effort after 12 days.

EVANDER BERRY WALL   Every morning Evander Berry Wall was confronted with a decision of awesome proportions, i.e., what to wear. As the trend-setter in men's tailoring at the turn of the century, and quite probably the best-dressed American male of all time, he possessed a wardrobe of 500 suits and changed his attire at least six times a day. Each change could easily occupy him for half an hour or more. There was much to be negotiated—detachable collars and cuffs, spats, stickpins, vests, watch chains and fobs, studs, cufflinks, and a great many other intricate accessories that would have driven a lesser man to distraction. Accordingly, fashion-conscious people will never forget the summer's day at Saratoga when, to win a bet, Wall changed into 40 entirely different outfits between breakfast and dinner, each impeccably matched and selected. The deed earned him the honorific title King of the Dudes. Later he abandoned his native New York for the more splendidly accoutered society of Paris, where he became known as the Prince of the Boulevardiers, a stunning achievement for an expatriate.

JOHN WATSON   Like the English poet Alexander Pope, John Watson (appointed Surveyor General of Pennsylvania in 1760) could write and *speak* in spontaneous rhymed couplets, carrying on the most ordinary conversations about hog prices or the weather in perfectly metrical verses. He was a well-known figure in colonial Philadelphia, not least of all for his habit of going barefoot all summer long, even to formal dinners and dances. Watson supplemented his surveyor's income by practicing law. On one memorable occasion he defended a thief who had been caught red-handed. The jury was so delighted with Watson's final summation, delivered in impromptu iambic pentameter, that they disregarded the evidence and acquitted his client.

ROBERT C. WEISZMAN   Prime candidates for the over-reachers of the decade award: the Robert C. Weiszman family of Spokane, Washington. Desiring a "less alien sounding" name, husband, wife, and five children legally changed their names to the Robert C. America family.

One year earlier, a Boston College student, seeking a name that would make people "take plenty of notice," asked a court to change his name to Sir Adolf Hitler.

JAMES MARION WEST, JR.   Almost single-handedly James Marion West, Jr., established the public image of what a Texas oil millionaire should be. He owned 30 cars (11 of them Cadillacs), lived in a castle, wore cowboy boots, a gold belt buckle, and a stetson hat, and spent money like it was going out of style. He earned the monicker "Silver Dollar" Jim because of his fondness for scattering rolls of silver dollars in the streets and watching people scramble for them. When dining out at a fancy restaurant, he generally brought a tub of butter, churned from the cream of his own cows, to spread on his biscuits. If the service was good, he tipped the waitress with a pile of 80 silver dollars.

West suffered from chronic insomnia and spent his nights cruising the streets of Houston, responding to police radio calls. On these nocturnal outings, West wore a diamond encrusted Texas Ranger badge on his chest and a .45-caliber pistol on his hip. His car was equipped for any eventuality with a 28-gauge shotgun, a 30–30 rifle, a Tommy gun, and a cannister of tear gas. The Houston police indulged his adolescent fantasies to the extent of assigning him a uniformed partner, Lieutenant A. C. Martindale. It was rumored that during one late-night shootout West fired at a fleeing robber, not too accurately, wounding Martindale in the foot. Another incident involving West erupted into a minor civic scandal. On Halloween night a playful group of trick-or-treaters in costume "ambushed" the self-appointed lawman in his traveling fortress. West, carrying the joke one step further, broke out the tear gas and fired into the crowd of youngsters. Their parents were not amused.

When "Silver Dollar" Jim cashed in his chips in 1957 the mourning was tinged with a definite note of relief.

SANDRA ILENE WEST　And then there was another eccentric Texan, Sandra Ilene West, the only person ever to be buried in a sportscar. Shortly before her death in 1977 at age 37, Mrs. West directed that she be interred "next to my husband . . . in my Ferrari, with the seat slanted comfortably." Uncertain of the legality of it all, the executors of her estate, which was estimated at between three and six million dollars, turned to the Los Angeles Superior Court, which ruled that the request was "unusual but not illegal."

While the matter was still being bandied about, Mrs. West's body was shipped to San Antonio, where it lay entombed in a local funeral parlor; the car, awaiting shipment, was held in a Los Angeles parking garage.

(Mrs. West's subterranean preferences turned out to be the first signs of an epidemic of Ferrari-burying in Los Angeles. In February, 1978, children digging in a backyard in that city unearthed an improbably large and mysterious object which they immediately called to the attention of the police, who brought it to the surface using heavy excavation machinery. It was Rosando Cruz's 1974 green Ferrari, stolen three years earlier.)

BILL WILLIAMS   To win a $500 bet in 1929, Bill Williams of Hondo, Texas, spent 30 days pushing a peanut 22 miles up to the summit of Pikes Peak with his nose.

H. P. WILLIAMS   The marathon craze reached its peak in 1929. There were marathon dances, marathon cross-country races, marathon stints atop flagpoles. H. P. "Hoppie" Williams of Texas City, Texas, is credited with one of the most extraordinary and unheralded achievements of this mad era. On July 31, he left Galveston, propelling before him a 12-inch diameter iron hoop by means of a bamboo cane. Six months later the marathon hoop roller arrived in Manhattan, having traveled a round-about route of nearly 2,300 miles—a feat the *Guinness Book of World Records* has yet to acknowledge.

ZACHARY ZZZZRA   The ultimate name belongs to Zachary Zzzzra of San Francisco, California. If you were to call every person listed in every United States telephone directory in alphabetical order, Mr. Zzzzra would be the last person you would dial. To spare you the trouble of looking it up, his number is (415) 928-1717.

182

Performing and Creative Artists

HADJI ALI Turn-of-the-century sensation-seekers queued up for hours at a time to view the peristaltic prowess of Hadji Ali, "The Amazing Regurgitator." His act never varied: having swallowed, in full view of the audience, a succession of small objects—peach pits, pennies, rhinestone rings, watermelon seeds—Ali would then bring up specific items on request from the audience.

But that was merely a warm-up for his pièce de résistance: While his assistant set up a miniature castle, Ali drank a gallon of water and then a pint of kerosene. To the accompaniment of a protracted drum roll, he would spit out the kerosene in a six-foot arc across the stage, setting the castle afire. Then, with the flames shooting high into the air, he would vomit up the water and extinguish the blaze.

DELIA BACON Delia Bacon took nothing for granted. As a student at Connecticut's finest private schools in the 1840s she'd been taught that the author of Shakespeare's plays was, well, Shakespeare. Drivel, she said. By her mid-20s, she was convinced that this Shakespeare fraud was an ambulatory illiterate and a slavering fool who could not possibly have penned a laundry list much less the 37 plays commonly attributed to him. Who, then? A committee of six, consisting of Sir Francis Bacon (no relation), Sir Philip Sidney, Lord Buckhurst, Lord Paget, the earl of Oxford, and Sir Walter Raleigh.

When her obsession ripened like a burgeoning boil, the

183

sickly Miss Bacon took to lecturing and raging splenetically against the bard at every opportunity, prompted, some said, by a hatred of *all* men generated by her disastrous romance with an elderly Protestant clergyman. As she explained it, the evil Sir Francis & co. had slipped a deadly dose of radical politics into the plays by means of a secret code, then hired Ben Jonson to act as public relations man and introduce the plays to a gullible public.

Furthermore—and of this she was *certain*—the key to the mysterious code lay buried with Shakespeare in Stratford, England. She traveled there in 1853 to pursue her theories in earnest, and once managed to wheedle the vicar of the Stratford church into letting her pry open Shakespeare's tomb for a quick peek inside, only to lose her nerve in a fit of nausea.

Finally, in 1857, she brought out *The Philosophy of the Plays of Shakespeare Unfolded,* 700 pages of sludge-like prose, ideas strewn wildly about and toppling on each other like an idiot child's playthings. The book was an overnight commercial failure and its author was hailed widely as a lunatic. "Hawthorne [a sympathizer] in later years averred that he had met one man who had read it through," notes *The Dictionary of American Biography.* "There is no record of another."

Miss Bacon, who, by her brother's admission, "had been verging on insanity for six years," finally went over the edge soon after her book was published. She died in an insane asylum the following year.

JOHN BANVARD Quantitatively, John Banvard was the world's greatest artist. At the age of 22, he was fired from his job as a drugstore clerk in Lousiville, Kentucky, for chalking caricatures on the wall. Pharmacy's loss was beaux arts' gain. Soon afterward, he embarked on an open raft to explore the channels and sandbars of the Mississippi, making thousands of preliminary sketches for a proposed work "of major scale." He traveled the river for over 400 days before he slapped the first dab of paint on his chef d'oeuvre in 1841. By the time he called it quits three years later, he had covered a

John Banvard painted a three-mile-long landscape *(Minnesota Historical Society)*

strip of canvas twelve feet high and three miles long with a vast "Panorama" depicting some 1,200 miles of Mississippi shoreline—the largest picture in history.

From all accounts, Banvard's style was monumentally so-so; his talents, if any, were geographical. But, in terms of sheer size, Banvard's "Panorama" merited comparison with the Colossus of Rhodes and the brontosaurus. Two uniformed attendants wound the enormous landscape from one huge spindle to another, like a 3,657 mm roll of film. And every day hundreds of people paid 25¢ apiece to watch the countryside slide by, waiting patiently for the good parts. It took two hours to view the entire show, from the Minnesota headwaters to the levees of New Orleans.

Banvard toured all 29 states and England with his "Panorama," netting over $200,000 in admissions. President Polk and Queen Victoria both endured it from start to finish and politely expressed their admiration.

In middle age, having overwhelmed the art world, Banvard turned his prodigious energies to literature and composed over 1,700 melancholy poems. When he died in 1891, the "Panorama" was hacked into pieces, and, for many years, parts of it were used as backdrops in South Dakota theaters.

THE GREAT BLATZ   Billed as The Human Fish, Blatz was a popular fixture of the New York vaudeville stage in the 1890s. He would appear on stage submerged in a tank of water alternately munching on a banana and playing a trombone. For his finale, he would fall asleep reading a newspaper.

CHARLES BROCKDEN BROWN   Pretend for just a moment that the year is 1959 and you're representing your alma mater on the old College Bowl television program. For 20 bonus points Allen Ludden asks you, "Who was the father of the American novel?" Confidently you reply "———." Wrong!

Well, the next time you'll remember Charles Brockden Brown (1771–1810), a man whom Keats and Shelley hailed as a "powerful genius" comparable to Schiller, the first American to earn his living exclusively from writing fiction. Today his half dozen major novels are disparaged for their hasty style, stilted language, and ghoulishness, but back in 1789 he kept his readers in a perpetual cold sweat. *Wieland,* his masterpiece, is the lighthearted story of a religious fanatic deluded into butchering his family by a villain who practices ventriloquism. In one remarkable scene Wieland's father dies of spontaneous combustion.

SOLYMAN BROWN   In the 1830s Dr. Solyman Brown of New York was a veritable walking Crest commercial who spent as much time as he could spare from his busy practice to preach the new gospel of Oral Hygiene to the unwashed millions. He became in 1839 one of the founding editors of the world's first dental magazine, *The American Journal of Dental Science* In 1841 he authored the first text on orthodontia: *An Essay on the Importance of Regulating the Teeth*

*of Children Before the Fourteenth Year, or the Period of Life
When the Second Set of Teeth Become Perfectly Developed.*
But history remembers him best for his epic *Dentologia: A
Poem on the Diseases of the Teeth,* published in 1840 and
thoughtfully annotated with a list of 300 qualified dentists
throughout the United States. Herewith the tale of Urilla's
Sorry Plight, excerpted from Canto the Third:

> [Urilla] is fair in form and face;
> Her glance is modesty, her motion grace.
> Her smile, a moonbeam on the garden bower,
> Her blush, a rainbow on the summer shower. . . .

> When first I saw her eyes' celestial blue,
> Her cheeks' vermillion, and the carmine hue
> That melted on her lips:—her auburn hair
> That floated playful on the yielding air. . . .
> I whispered to my heart:—we'll fondly seek
> The means, the hour, to hear this angel speak. . . .

> Twas said—'twas done—the fit occasion came,
> As if to quench betimes the kindling flame
> Of love and admiration:—for she spoke,
> And lo the heavenly spell forever broke!
> For when her parted lips disclosed to view
> Those ruined arches, veiled in blackest hue,
> Where love had thought to feast the ravish'd sight
> On orient gems reflecting snowy light,
> Hope disappointed, silently retired,
> Disgust triumphant came, and love expired!. . . .

> Let every fair one shun Urilla's fate,
> And wake to action, ere it be too late:
> Let each successive day unfailing bring
> The brush, the dentifrice, and the spring,
> The cleansing flood:—the labor will be small,
> And blooming health will soon reward it all. . . .

CONARD CANTZEN   At the time of his death in 1945 Conrad Cantzen, a bit part actor on Broadway, had all of $11.85 in his pockets. There was an additional 11¢ scattered around his apartment. Friends who attended the reading of his will in September 1945 were shocked to learn that he had established a fund of nearly a quarter of a million dollars to provide shoes for needy actors.

"I leave the Conrad Cantzen Shoe Fund for the people who can't buy shoes," he wrote, "even if they are not paid up members [of Actors Equity Association]. Many times I have been on my uppers, and the thinner the soles of my shoes were the less courage I had to face the manager looking for a job."

The president of Actors Equity recalled that Cantzen had lived as a pauper, begged for food, and slept on newspapers in a barely furnished room in Jersey City. Once he had asked a Broadway producer to allow him to sleep in a dressing room. The most anyone could remember him earning was $55 a week when he appeared in "The Good Earth" on Broadway. No one could figure out how he managed to stash away huge sums of money in 18 different bank accounts.

ELIZABETH, EFFIE, JESSIE, and ADDIE CHERRY "I've been putting on the best talent and it hasn't gone over," impresario Oscar Hammerstein announced in 1896. "I'm going to try the worst." Ferreting out the most abominable entertainment on the American stage took several months of wide-ranging searching, but on November 16 Hammerstein presented Elizabeth, Effie, Jessie, and Addie Cherry to audiences at his Olympia Theater in New York. Fresh from the vaudeville houses of the Midwest, the Cherry Sisters strutted out onto the Olympia's stage garbed in flaming red dresses, hats, and woolen mittens. Jessie beat time on a bass drum while her three partners did their opening number: "Cherries Ripe Boom-de-ay!" It was ghastly.

At first New York audiences seemed more tolerant than those in the Great Plains. They restrained themselves from showering the girls with beer bottles and rotten tomatoes,

188

gawking slack-jawed in disbelief. "It is sincerely hoped that nothing like them will ever be seen again," *The New York Times* said. Another commentator offered that "A locksmith with a strong rasping file could earn ready wages taking the kinks out of Lizzie's voice." The inevitable hail of garbage and slops ultimately materialized, forcing the sisters to perform behind a wire screen. The screen became their trademark, but in later years the girls would insist that they'd never been fired upon.

THOMAS HOLLEY CHIVERS Cydonian suckets indeed! Thomas Chivers was a nineteenth-century Georgia physician who proclaimed himself a poet of the highest order. But the verses he penned between patients were, we suspect, merely a ploy to create sickness where none existed and thereby drum up new business. Consider these lines:

> Many mellow Cydonian suckets,
>   Sweet apples, anthosmial, divine,
> From the ruby-rimmed beryline buckets,
>   Star-gemmed, lily-shaped, hyaline:
> Like the sweet golden goblet found growing
>   On the wild emerald cucumber-tree,
> Rich, brilliant, like chrysoprase glowing,
>   Was my beautiful Rosalie Lee.

TED DeGRAZIA Ted DeGrazia's a painter, and a successful one at that, who had made a small fortune with depictions of Indian children and chubby-faced angels. But we salute him here for playing a plucky David to the Internal Revenue Service's Goliath. At age 68, DeGrazia was incensed at a new IRS ruling socking his heirs for half the worth of his paintings on his death. As a first step, DeGrazia stopped painting, period, cutting the Feds off from any additional revenues they might hope to gain. Then he carted 100 of his pictures on horseback high into the Superstition Mountains in California, where he set them afire, more as a grand display of nose-thumbing at the IRS than anything else. But that wasn't the end of his ploy. DeGrazia made several subsequent visits to the Superstitions, each time bearing a cartload of his pictures, which he hid in caves. To keep the pictures safe from thieves, government-employed or otherwise, he dynamited the entrances to the caves.

ANNE SHAW FAULKNER   While serving as music chairperson of the General Federation of Women's Clubs, Anne Shaw Faulkner defined the important ethical distinction between ragtime, which merely "quickens the pulse" but "does not destroy," and that hideous new music called jazz, which was "originally the accompaniment of the voodoo dancer stimulating the half-crazed barbarian to the vilest deeds . . . its demoralizing effect upon the brain has been demonstrated by many scientists." At the urging of Mrs. Faulkner and others with discriminating taste, the federation voted during its 1923 convention to wage a national crusade to "annihilate" jazz, adopting the motto "Make Good Popular Music and Popular Music Good."

In the long run, of course, the antijazz forces lost the war, but they did win a few moral victories along the way. In Cincinnati a judge enjoined construction of a movie theater next to the Salvation Army's maternity hospital on the grounds that it might cause "the implantation of jazz emotions" in newborns. The superintendent of public schools in Kansas City, Missouri, called on Congress to act by Constitutional amendment if necessary, to outlaw the menacing new rhythms, as it had recently outlawed booze. And in Los Angeles a woman chiropractor announced that jazz produced cancer in laboratory animals. Fortunately, the malignancies could be cured with doses of light classical music.

SARAH FERGUSON   Miss Ferguson is the author of *A Guard Within,* unfortunately billed in the spring, 1974, catalogue of Pantheon Books as "an account of Miss Ferguson's painful adjustment to the sudden death of her psychiatrist."

WOLLCOTT GIBBS   Wollcott Gibbs, a longtime theater and movie critic for the *New Yorker,* established an unexcelled standard for brevity with his review of the Broadway farce *Wham*. The full text of his notice ran as follows: "Ouch!"

ELIZABETH GOOSE

There was an old woman who lived in a shoe.
She had so many children she didn't know what to do.

Change the word "shoe"in that couplet to "Boston" and you spoil the rhyme, but you have an apt description of the life of the real Mother Goose. Kids usually picture Mother Goose as a benevolent, somewhat simple-minded bird in a bonnet. In point of fact, there is ample reason to believe that a flesh-and-blood Massachusetts woman named Elizabeth Goose may have compiled or, at least, contributed to a book called *Songs for the Nursery, or Mother Goose's Melodies for Children,* published in 1719.

Born Elizabeth Foster, she married a widower named Isaac Goose in 1682 and suddenly found herself the step-mother of ten children. Soon she added six natural children of her own to the ever-growing gaggle, two of whom died in infancy. To keep all the little goslings entertained and quiet, she relied on her tenacious memory for old stories, fables, and rhymes, occasionally making up a few of her own.

One of Mrs. Goose's daughters married Thomas Fleet, a printer, who, it is said, could hardly endure his mother-in-law's nonstop singing and storytelling. Resolving to make the best of a bad situation, Fleet drew on Elizabeth Goose's repertoire of tales, and other sources, to assemble an edition of children's nonsense—*Songs for the Nursery*. (No copy is known to have survived.)

The American Mother Goose's collection of tales is believed by some scholars to predate by ten years the translation of Frenchman Charles Perrault's *Tales of My Mother Goose* into English; the Perrault work is the source of "Old King Cole," "Sing a Song of Sixpence," and other perennial nursery favorites.

The Mother Goose rhymes that have come down to us are

traditional; like old folk songs they have no known author. But Elizabeth Goose—the real American Mother Goose—may have played a role in helping to preserve them. She died in 1757 and you can still visit her grave in the Old Granary Burial Grounds near the Park Street Church in Boston.

ZIGGY GRABOWSKI You won't see any Mail Pouch chewing tobacco advertisements on the barns in Fenton, Michigan. What you will see are exact copies of John Singleton Copley's "Paul Revere" and Raphael's portrait of Baldassare Castiglione; two stories tall. It's the prodigious handiwork of a barn-painting artist who goes by the pseudonym Ziggy Grabowski.

GREELER, THE COMPOSER Periodically a bill is introduced in Congress to replace "The Star Spangled Banner" with a more singable melody, such as "America the Beautiful." But perhaps the chef d'oeuvre of an obscure Boston composer named Greeler would be the most suitable national anthem of all.

According to the journal *Music World,* Maestro Greeler set the entire United States Constitution, including the Bill of Rights, to music in 1874. "The performance did not last less than six hours. The preamble of the Constitution forms a broad and majestic recitative, well sustained by altos and double basses ... the Constitutional Amendments are treated as fugues." The passages on states' rights were in a minor key for bass and tenor.

The Constitution was performed numerous times before enthusiastic audiences. Then sometime in the 1880s the score disappeared, never to be heard again.

HORATIO GREENOUGH Commissioned to produce a marble statue of George Washington in 1823, sculptor Greenough let his artistic vision run wild, fashioning a statue too heavy for the Capitol floor to support. The piece was instead displayed outdoors, where it was ravaged nastily by the elements. In its third niche, in the Smithsonian Institution, it sparked the anger of bluestockings who felt that the classically half-nude representation of Washington was unpardonably lewd. For years tucked away in a corner of the original Smithsonian "castle" building, the draped, seated figure is now on prominent display in the Museum of History and Technology.

JOHN GUEDEL   John Guedel, who produced such long-running television series as "You Bet Your Life" and "Art Linkletter's House Party," originated the radio and TV summer rerun as well as the singing commercial, and still had the courage to show his face in public.

SADAKICHI HARTMANN   Hartmann was the flower of the New York vaudeville stage around the turn of the century: touting himself as a Japanese-German inventor, he would appear on stage manning a battery of electric fans, with which he would waft clouds of scented smoke over the audience. In barely discernible English Hartman would explain that each aroma represented a different country. Despite his evident sincerity, Hartmann was a tempting target for hecklers and seldom got beyond Germany (violets) and England (roses) before being hooted from the stage.

HENRY HETZEL   Henry Hetzel costarred with Germaine Chomette in the first talking motion picture in Esperanto. The film premiered in 1929.

ADRIAN HILL   The summit of Hill's creativity was a 381-page biography of Ulysses S. Grant in verse. Entitled *The Grant Poem, Containing Grant's Public Career and Private Life from the Cradle to the Grave,* it was published in 1886.

FLORENCE FOSTER JENKINS   Florence Foster Jenkins emerged from a taxi collision in 1943 with no lasting traumas save one: the ability to sing and sustain a higher if scratchier F than ever before. Joyfully, the Pennsylvania socialite banished all thoughts of lawsuits and instead sent the driver a box of expensive cigars. It was an appropriately grand gesture for the woman hailed universally as the world's worst opera singer.

Mrs. Jenkins's unique career for many years prompted knowing giggles and smirks among cognoscenti and music critics who wrote wonderfully ambiguous reviews of the performances she gave regularly in salons from Philadelphia to Newport: Edward Tatnall Canby spoke of "a subtle ghastliness that defies description," and *Newsweek* noted that "In high notes, Mrs. Jenkins sounds as if she was afflicted with low, nagging backache." On October 25, 1944, the well-padded matron, well into her 70s, made her Carnegie Hall debut before a packed house. As always, Mme. Jenkins went through numerous costume changes, appearing first as the bewinged "Angel of Inspiration," then as the Queen of the Night from Mozart's *The Magic Flute,* and later as a Spanish coquette, showering the front rows with rose petals plucked from a wicker basket. This last was a favorite of her admirers, and newspaper accounts the following day were quick to point out that for once Mme. Jenkins remembered not to toss the basket as well.

JAMES JOHNS It's a little known fact that Johann Gutenberg was born Johann Gensfleisch—which means "gooseflesh" in German. For obvious reasons, the inventor of movable type preferred to go by his mother's surname; after all, who could take a Gooseflesh Bible seriously? As it was, Gutenberg had plenty of opponents. Monks feared, with justification, that printing would destroy their means of livelihood. Even as late as 1883 there was one last holdout: James Johns of Huntington, Vermont.

Make no mistake. Johns gave Gutenberg his chance. In 1828 Huntington's greatest poet and journalist published a little volume called *Green Mountain Muse.* It was about as popular as anthrax. Rightly or wrongly Johns blamed the book's failure on the typesetting. Never again would a confounded machine interfere with his literary career. Johns would do his own printing—with pen and ink.

Years before, at the age of 13, he had begun to write and edit his own newspaper, the *Vermont Autograph and Remarker*. Like every journal it was filled with public and private happenings: births, deaths, weather reports, and outcries against political corruption. The printing was clear and regular; on first glance one could hardly recognize that every word was laboriously hand-lettered. It took Johns five hours to pen-print each copy, which was then posted for the public to read. He published five times weekly for 63 years, ceasing only in August, 1883, eight months before his death.

In addition to his amazing gift for penmanship, Johns also excelled as a musician and inventor. He sang his own poems in a high, quivering voice, played the violin at local square dances, and devised a new instrument combining the features of windchimes and the pianoforte. Thin glass plates of various lengths were suspended from wires; when a key was depressed, a hammer struck the glass, sending forth tinkling sounds.

At the age of 60 Johns did compromise somewhat with modern technology. He purchased a miniature press and published a three-by-four inch book burdened by the lengthy title: *A Brief Record of the Various Fatal Accidents Which Have Happened from the First Settlement of the Town of Huntington to the Present Time.* It remains the classic work on the subject.

GEORGE JONES English-born George Jones settled in the United States in 1828 and soon became hailed widely as the worst dramatic actor in the history of the American theater. He was also a man of singular unversatility, immersing himself in the role of Hamlet and refusing to play anything else. Over the next few years Jones deteriorated into gibbering insanity, and his performances drew raucous laughter. Finally he became too mad to act any longer—too mad, as one contemporary observer put it, to play the role of the Mad Prince.

Known familiarly as Count Johannes, Jones was also a writer of sorts. His *Original History of Ancient America*

195

(1843) claimed that Phoenicians and Israelites were among the first people to inhabit the Americas.

DR. JACK LEEDY "There are no reported deaths from an overdose of poetry," Dr. Jack Leedy mused recently. In fact, an occasional dose of iambic pentameter can do a world of good for persons suffering from neurotic anxiety, chronic depression, and psychosomatic ailments such as peptic ulcers, according to the head psychiatrist at New York's Poetry Therapy Center. Like Aeschylus, Leedy believes that "Words are the physicians of a mind diseased," and he encourages his patients to write poems about their symptoms, fears, fantasies, conflicts, and dreams as a means of overcoming their problems. He also has observed that the reading and recitation of certain poems can have a soothing effect on the psyche. For insomnia he suggests Longfellow's "Hymn to the Night," Wordsworth's "To Sleep," and Swinburne's "A Ballad of Dreamland." For depression: Milton's "On His Blindness," Shelley's "Ode to the West Wind," and Stevenson's "The Celestial Surgeon." And for alcoholism and drug addiction: the works of Kahlil Gibran, William Blake, Lewis Carroll, Langston Hughes, and John Keats.

AL MARTIN When Al Martin and his traveling theatrical show came to town it was no secret. They kicked things off, in the spirit of P. T. Barnum, with an uproarious parade featuring:

A Lady Zouave Drum and Bugle Corps, 18 Real Georgia Plantation Shouters, Mlle. Minerva's New Orleans Creole Girls Fife and Drum Corps, The Original Whangdoodle Pickaninny Band, Eva's $1,500 Gold Chariot, A Log Cabin, Floats, Phaetons, Carts, Ornate Banners, Dazzling Harnesses and Uniforms, 3 Full Concert Bands, the Drum Major, an 8-Foot Colored Boy, 10 Cuban and Russian Ferocious Man-Eating Hounds, 25 Ponies, Donkeys, Mules, Horses, Burros, All Trained as Entertaining Tricksters.

196

Incredibly enough, the occasion for all this hoopla was a production of *Uncle Tom's Cabin.*

"Tom Shows" were an enormously popular form of entertainment in the 1890s, when no fewer than 400 troupes toured the country performing Harriet Beecher Stowe's abolitionist tear-jerker. Al Martin's production—billed as "Too Big for Imitators, Too Strong for Rivalry"—was easily the most lavish and most successful. And to enhance the box office appeal of the show, Martin was not averse to taking a few liberties with the tragic storyline, transforming it into a "laff riot." As Heywood Hale Broun described Martin's *Uncle Tom* in *American Heritage:* "Sometimes two Topsies alternated the lines, or one sang while the other played the banjo, and sometimes two Simon Legrees simultaneously whipped a pair of Uncle Toms."

Another group took this wretched excess one step further and put three Little Evas on stage at once.

JOHN McCORMICK John McCormick—*Professor* John McCormick to his followers—was the first person ever to walk upside-down on the New York stage.

Billed as "The Great Philosophical Antipodean Pedestrian from Ohio," he first demonstrated his sticky-footed prowess by shuffling across the highly polished underside of a hanging platform at the Bowery Amphitheatre on February 16, 1852. The New York *Herald* the next day called the Professor's feat—and his feet—"astonishing."

MARK McKINLEY Mark McKinley's first record doesn't lend itself to disco dancing and it doesn't get much play on AM radio. To be completely honest, his *Crybaby* LP, featuring protracted high-fidelity whining, squealing, mewling, bawling, puling, and screeching, may be the most strident 30 minutes ever preserved in vinyl. And yet McKinley insists that expectant mothers and fathers would do well to suffer through it. As a professor of psychology at Lorain Community College in Ohio, he became interested in the ability of mothers to interpret their babies' cries. There is, he says, a kind of "cry language." A hungry cry (short and loud) is easily distinguished from a (shrill) cry of pain. A trained ear can also identify a "burp me" cry, an "I'm sleepy" cry, and many more. Distributed by Folkways Records, *Crybaby* includes explanatory narration and a challenging test-yourself section.

TED MIKELS Ted Mikels is a low-budget filmmaker whose finest efforts—*The Corpse Grinders, Children Shouldn't Play with Dead Things, The Undertaker and his Pals,* and *Up Your Teddy Bear*—would hardly rate mentioning much less enshrinement in these pages. But he and his colleague Herb Robins won our hearts and minds (albeit at the price of our appetites) by staging the first public diet of worms since the Protestant Reformation. Before a thicket of television cameras, reporters, and several hundred admirers in Kansas City in 1977, Robins downed four eight-inch Canadian night crawlers and Mikels two. Assistant Howard Hall gorged himself on six and was promptly elected president of the Worm Eaters Society of America by its other two members, Mikels and Robins.

All this public gourmandism was by way of plugging their latest film, *The Worm Eaters,* billed by Mikels as a comedy. In the first five weeks of production, he said, the cast ate some $200 worth of worms, all provided gratis by the Minnesota Worm & Fly Corporation. According to *Variety,* Mikels planned also to offer free admission to anyone willing to swallow a worm prior to entering the theatre. "They're not bad," he said. "I've eaten raw oysters and I prefer the worms."

JULIA A. MOORE "Literary is a work very difficult to do," poet Julia A. Moore once told her critics, who ranged from Mark Twain to President Grover Cleveland. Still, Mrs. Moore, a farmer's wife whose admirers dubbed her the "Sweet Singer of Michigan," soared like a wombat high above the banal conceits and tired rhythms of her contemporaries, penning deathless odes on war, child-rearing, sickness,

198

Julia A. Moore, the "Sweet Singer of Michigan" *(Michigan Department of State)*

congenital idiocy, and patriotism. Sample these lines from "The Brave Page Boys:"

> Enos Page the youngest brother—
> His age was fourteen years—
> Made five sons in one family
> Went from Grand Rapids here.
> In Eight Michigan Cavalry
> This boy he did enlist.
> His life was almost despaired of
> On account of numerous fits.

In an 1878 collection of her verse entitled *A Few Choice Words to the Public and New and Original Poems,* she waxes lugubrious over the fate of Little Libbie:

> While eating dinner, this dear little child
> Was choked on a piece of beef.
> Doctors came, tried their skill awhile,
> But none could give relief.

It was in the preface to that collection that Mrs. Moore issued the first of many rebukes to her detractors: "Although some of the newspapers speak against it," she wrote, referring to an earlier volume of her works, "its sale has steadily progressed. Thanks to the Editors that has spoken in favor of my writings. May they ever be successful. The Editors that

199

has spoken in a scandalous manner have went beyond reason."

Still, Mrs. Moore knew that to be scorned by critics in one's lifetime only to be exonerated by future generations was often the poet's lot:

> "Lord Byron" was an Englishman,
>   A poet, I believe,
> His first works in old England
>   was poorly received.
> Perhaps it was "Lord Byron's" fault
>   and perhaps it was not.
> His life was full of misfortunes.
>   Ah, strange was his lot.

But Mrs. Moore was at her finest in drawing truth and beauty from hideous calamities both man-made and natural, as she did in "Ashtabula Disaster." On December 29, 1876, the bridge spanning the Ashtabula River, in Ashtabula, Ohio, collapsed under the weight of a speeding passenger train, plunging 85 passengers to an icy death. Herewith an excerpt from Mrs. Moore's rendering:

> Have you heard of the dreadful fate
>   Of Mr. P.P. Bliss and wife?
> Of their death I will relate,
>   And also others lost their life. . . .
> Among the ruins are many friends,
>   Crushed to death amidst the roar,
> On one thread all may depend,
>   And hope they've reached the other shore. . . .

Mrs. Moore died in 1920 at age 73. Perhaps her aptest epitaph is the instructive quatrain with which she concluded her autobiography:

> And now, kind friends, what I have wrote,
>   I hope you will pass o'er

> And not criticize as some have done,
>> Hitherto herebefore.

CHARLOTTE MOORMAN For the past decade, Charlotte Moorman has been attracting a kind of admiration, if not critical acclaim, for her classical cello recitals, performed in various stages of undress. Early in her career she performed Saint-Saën's *Le Cygne,* garbed only in *cello*phane, taking time out in the middle of a movement to execute a *swan* dive from a six-foot ladder into an oil drum filled with water. Then in 1967 she was arrested for indecent exposure during a concert in which she played topless. As recently as February 1977 she was at it again, sawing away at her cello at the Carnegie Recital Hall in New York with twin propellers on her naked breasts, which spun on cue. Quoth Miss Moorman: "The propellers remind one of Vietnam, the bombings and the airplanes. It is all more symbolic than anything else."

JOSEPH NAGYVARY A professor of biochemistry at Texas A&M University, Dr. Nagyvary had long sought to know the last secret of violin making, the unknown element with which masters such as Amati and Stradivarius had given their violins the rich, golden burnishes that have lasted till this day. Now, says Dr. Nagyvary, he thinks he knows what the mystery ingredient was: chicken feces.

"The science of materials through that time remained fixed on the old alchemistic framework," he explains. "Their goals were pursued with ingredients of midnight moon, witchcraft, lead oxide and chicken manure." Beer and blood also figured in the recipe, says Dr. Nagyvary, and although he cautions that there is no existing formula for violin finishing, he's pretty certain that Stradivarius kept his recipe in the family Bible, destroyed long after his death by his great-grandson.

HARRY PARTCH Most composers are content to limit themselves to a 12-tone scale. Not so the late Harry Partch.

201

Decrying "the tyranny of the piano scale, a wholly irrational, oppressive lid on musical expression," he invented his own 43-note octave and an assortment of musical instruments to do it justice. They included the Whang Gun, a 72-stringed surrogate cithara, a strange, marimba-like instrument called a "boo," glass bells which he dubbed "cloud chamber bowls," and his most prized innovation, the bloboys.

Born in California in 1901, Partch earned little money from his music, although he was able to attract enough support from foundations to continue his work. Some of his compositions were recorded on Columbia Records and they included, "Visions Fill the Eyes of a Defeated Basketball Team in the Shower Room," "And on the Seventh Day Petals Fell on Petaluma," "Daphne of the Dunes," "Water, Water," and "U.S. Highway," which includes the chatter of rail-riding hoboes.

JOHN LOUIS ROVENTINI   Roventini was the smiling bellhop who spent 41 years shouting "Call for Philip Morris" in radio and TV commercials. Barely four feet tall, he was forbidden by his employers from riding subways during rush hours, and his voice was insured for $50,000. He retired in 1973.

DEBORAH SCHNEIDER   On a per word basis, who is the highest paid writer in the United States? a) Jacqueline Susann. b) Erle Stanley Gardner. c) Wayne Dyer. d) Norman Mailer.

If you answered "none of the above," you cheated and should be ashamed of yourself. Nevertheless, you're right. When it comes to earning megabucks at the typewriter, Mrs. Deborah Schneider of Minneapolis, Minnesota, surpasses all the better-known wordsmiths. In 1958 she wrote 25 words to complete a sentence extolling the merits of Plymouth automobiles. Her prose fragment was selected over those of 1 million other entrants in the contest, and she was awarded the grand prize—$500 a month for life. If she lives out her normal life expectancy, that works out to about $12,000 per word.

TOM SHANNON   Taking a leaf from Cleve Backster (q.v), Tom Shannon, a television celebrity from Denver, pressed a long-playing record for indoor gardeners wishing to serenade their Swedish ivy. "We know our music will stimulate a favorable response in plants," he declared. "Serious plant lovers think the idea is beautiful." Some representative cuts: "Ode to a Philodendron," "Moses on a Raft," "March of the Chocolate Soldiers," and "Silver Queen."

JOHN STETSON   John Stetson, a prominent Boston theatrical director during the 1890s, specialized in elaborate productions with lots of extras. Once while staging a Last Supper tableau in a religious play, he complained there weren't enough actors to "fill the stage." His stage manager meekly pointed out that the Bible only mentions 12 disciples, but Stetson overruled him. "I know what I want!" he shouted. "Gimme twenty-four."

RICHARD LLEWELLYN WATSON   The bargain was too good to pass up: an evening on the podium of the Houston Symphony, conducting the orchestra in a program of your choosing in front of a packed house, all for a mere $14,500. It was, of course, no more than an ingenious fund-raising stratagem to beef up the orchestra's sagging profits, but Richard Llewellyn Watson, an aspiring conductor from New York, was biting. He got 60 backers to supply the necessary cash, flew to Houston, and led the musicians through a program of Paganini, Rossini, and Shostakovich.

And was another star born? Hardly. *Houston Post* critic Carl Cunningham wrote that Watson's style was "tedious" and riddled with "energy-lacking tempos." Watson returned to New York to sharpen his baton stroke.

Physical Specimens

DOROTHY MAE STEVENS ANDERSON Chicago temperatures fell to 11 below on the night of February 1, 1951, and by the time police discovered Dorothy Mae Stevens Anderson, who had passed out from drinking and lay all night unprotected in an alley, the woman's body temperature had plunged to 64.4 degrees, her blood and legs had long since frozen solid, and her eyeballs had all but turned to ice. Her pulse rate was barely 12 beats a minute, breaths came at three to the minute, and there was no measurable blood pressure. Doctors at Michael Reese Hospital saw little chance that she would survive; still they did what they could. They administered cortisone and swaddled her arms and legs in gauze to keep the flesh from chipping off. Within 24 hours Mrs. Anderson was conscious and taking liquid nourishment; a week later she was eating solid food, her body temperature having risen to 100.2 degrees. No one had ever before survived such a catastrophic loss of body heat.

Ultimately both of Mrs. Anderson's legs and all but one finger had to be amputated. But she was able to leave the hospital after six months and lived till 1974.

E. G. ATLOY It was a *New York Times* story, but the headline was pure *Police Gazette:* "Electrically Charged Boy Furnishes Power for Fan and Lights." On an afternoon in 1908, seven-year-old E. G. Atloy of Houston returned home from a visit to the dentist to find that the fresh metal fillings in his teeth had transformed him into a human storage battery. We won't speculate, nor does the *Times* story enlighten us, on what prompted the boy to place the plug from an electric fan into his mouth, but when he did, his head snapped back and the fan began to turn, first arthritically, then faster and faster till it was going at top speed. Scientists studying young E. G. found that he could magnetize so powerfully an iron-handled hammer merely by grasping it a few seconds that it could suck up carpet tacks from a distance of four feet.

"The mother was frightened and feared witchcraft," the *Times* reported, "but the boy seemed pleased at the reaction ... [and] says that he feels only an agreeable sensation. He has red hair of the reddest possible hue, large freckles and blue eyes."

BILL CARSKADON   While taking part in a psychology experiment at the Chicago campus of the University of Illinois on February 15, 1967, Bill Carskadon experienced the longest dream in the annals of sleep research. Rapid eye movements were observed continuously for two hours and 23 minutes.

CELESTA GEYER   Celesta Geyer, known as Dolly Dimples to her public, decided to chuck her career as circus fat lady in 1950 and trim some of the flab off her 553-pound frame. Trim she did: within 14 months, under close medical supervision, Mrs. Geyer lost 401 pounds and exchanged 79-84-84 measurements for a 34-28-36. By 1967 she had dieted down to 110 pounds and written a book, *How I Lost 400 Pounds.*

MARGARET GORMAN   The first Miss America, crowned on September 7, 1921, at Atlantic City, was Margaret Gorman, a 15-year-old high school student from Washington, D.C. The five-foot one-inch, blue-eyed blonde remains to this day the youngest, shortest, and flattest (30–25–32) contestant ever to win the title.

DAVID JONES   An Anderson, Indiana, farmer named David Jones first startled the medical world in 1893 by going

Margaret Gorman, the first Miss America *(The Miss America Pageant / Mrs. Margaret Gorman Cahill)*

93 days without a wink of sleep; a year later he went 131. To date he remains the most famous of compulsive nonsleepers.

In 1895, while serving on jury duty, Jones embarked on a lengthy bout of insomnia that he predicted would be "more serious than the preceding ones." Surprisingly, Jones could eat, talk, work, and walk with the zest of an acrobat during his waking jags and often spent his middle-of-the-night hours on farm chores. According to a local newspaper account of the day, "Mr. Jones thinks his abnormality was probably induced by the use of tobacco while very young."

HANS LANGSETH The longest beard on record, now preserved in the Smithsonian Institution, belonged to Hans Langseth (1846–1927) a native of Norway who emigrated to the United States in 1912. It has been officially measured at 17 feet 6 inches in length. *(See also:* Joseph Palmer.)

FRANCISCO LENTINI Born in Siracusa, Sicily, in 1889, Francisco Lentini was a double-bodied freak from the waist

Hans Langseth owned the world's longest beard *(The Smithsonian Institution)*

Francisco Lentini, the "Three-Legged Wonder" *(Circus World Museum, Baraboo, Wisconsin)*

down, possessed of three legs, four feet, 16 toes and two sets of genitalia. For years American circus-goers knew him variously as "The Three-Legged Wonder," and "The King of Freaks."

"I am often asked the question, What is the cause of my strange condition?" Lentini said in 1954. Physicians on both sides of the Atlantic asked it too, ultimately deducing that Lentini would have been *twins* but for an embryonic foul-up that produced one child with the equipment of two. At the moment of his delivery the attending midwife hid him under the bed and ran screaming from the room.

Lentini came to the United States with his parents in 1898 and went into show business as a child. He appeared with the Ringling Brothers, Barnum and Bailey Circus for 19 straight seasons, and also with Buffalo Bill's Wild West Show. Later he ran a touring carnival side-show of his own, often bringing down the house by using his powerful third leg to kick a football the length of the side-show tent. And while that extra leg was no good for walking—it was a full six or seven inches shorter than the other two—it served him well as a stool. Said fellow circus star Harry Lewiston, "He was the only man I ever knew who could sit down anytime, any place, without bothering to drag up a chair."

Essentially a private man, Lentini often confessed he would gladly have swapped his fame and riches for a less conspicuous life. But his personal physicians feared that amputation would surely result in death or total paralysis, so he retained the extra member instead, eating 15 percent more than the average man to nourish the extra muscles and blood vessels. His favorite dishes, incidentally, were chicken, spaghetti, and salads. He hated liver.

Lentini was married—quite happily, too—and raised four perfectly well-developed children. His excess anatomical baggage notwithstanding, he was a handsome man, congenial, well-read, and fluent in four languages. David Hilton, another of his circus compeers, said, "He was one of the best-natured men I ever knew. When he needed shoes, he'd buy two pairs at a time—he'd have to—and give the extra left shoe to a one-legged friend of his. He was truly a prince among freaks."

SHARON MITCHELL   A teller in a New York City bank politely informed Ms. Sharon Mitchell, star of the x-rated movie *Captain Lust,* that he could not cash her check unless she could present a driver's license or some other form of positive identification. As it happened, Ms. Mitchell was carrying a copy of a current magazine in which she appeared in the nude. Handing the magazine to the teller, she hiked her sweater up to her chin and struck a pose from the photospread. After careful examination (according to the *London Sunday Telegraph Magazine)* they honored her check, with interest.

JOSEPH PALMER   Joseph Palmer was a farmer and gentle abolitionist who dared to wear a flowing Old-Testament beard in a militantly clean-shaven age. On a spring afternoon in 1830, as Palmer was leaving a hotel lobby in Fitchburg, Massachusetts, he was set upon by four men armed with scissors, brush, soap, and razor—and so began one of the strangest civil liberties cases on record.

Palmer defended his magnificent growth with the ferocity of a mountain lion protecting its young. Though outnumbered and injured in the furious scuffle, he managed to pull out his pocketknife and stab two of his assailants in their legs, driving them off before they could shear so much as a single whisker. The wounds were superficial, but the attackers avenged themselves by swearing out an official complaint. The next day Palmer was charged with committing an "unprovoked assault," found guilty by a pogonophobic judge, and fined ten dollars.

It was a barbarous miscarriage of justice, and Palmer vowed to spend the rest of his life in jail rather than pay the court. For over a year he languished in a dreary underground cell, where he wrote a series of eloquent letters proclaiming his constitutional rights to life, liberty, and hirsute happiness. The letters, smuggled out by his son, were pub-

Joseph Palmer's tombstone
*(Fruitlands Museums,
Harvard, Massachusetts)*

lished in newspapers all over New England and attracted the attention of Bronson Alcott, Henry Thoreau, and other notables. Palmer's chinpiece became a national issue.

Finally, the public outcry prompted the Fitchburg sheriff to suggest that Palmer run along home and forget the whole affair; the fine, he said, would be forgiven. But Palmer declared, "I won't walk a single step toward freedom." The judge, his wife, and his aged mother all implored him "not to be so stubborn." Still he wouldn't budge. In desperation, the sheriff and jailer entered his cell, hoisted him up in his chair, carried him out of doors like a sultan, and gently deposited him on the sidewalk a free man.

MARY HARDY REESER Nobody knows why, even to this day, but sometime during the night of July 1, 1951, 67-year-old Mary Hardy Reeser burst into flames while sitting in an easy chair in her St. Petersburg, Florida apartment. The flames raged unnoticed through the night and the following morning wisps of smoke caught the attention of Mrs. Reeser's landlady, who tried the doorknob and found it too hot to handle. According to Michael Harrison in his book *Fire from Heaven, or, How Safe Are You from Burning?*, the landlady was struck full in the face by a blast of hot air when she finally pried open the door. In the apartment, "within a blackened circle about four feet in diameter were a number of coiled seat springs and the remains of a human body . . . and a small pile of blackened ashes."

Despite numerous investigations, the mystery remains un-

210

solved. "As far as logical explanations go," St. Petersburg Police Chief J. R. Reichart said, "this is one of those things that just couldn't have happened but it did."

CHARLIE SMITH As of this writing, former slave Charlie Smith is the oldest person in the United States, and perhaps the oldest person in the world, according to the Social Security Administration. On July 4, 1978, he celebrated his 136th birthday at a convalescent home in Bartow, Florida. Smith was kidnapped from Liberia when he was a teenager and sold at auction in New Orleans on July 4, 1854. He was a full-grown man when President Lincoln issued the Emancipation Proclamation giving him his freedom.

A. W. UNDERWOOD What can we write here that will comfort the troubled wraith of the late A. W. Underwood, who was marked by that most repellent of social blemishes, worse even than halitosis or chronic flatulence: an innate compulsion to set afire anything he breathed on? A 24-year-old native of Paw Paw, Michigan, Underwood was examined by Dr. L. C. Woodman, who later published his findings in the *Michigan Medical News:* "Underwood will take anybody's cotton handkerchief, hold it tightly against his mouth while breathing through it," the doctor wrote. "After a few seconds it bursts into flames. . . . He will undress completely, rinse out his mouth thoroughly and submit to the most rigorous examination to preclude the possibility of any humbug. He can collect dry leaves and start a fire by breathing on them."

Prophets and Moralists

EVANGELINE ADAMS On her first visit to New York City, Mrs. George E. Jordan (1865–1932), better known professionally as Miss Evangeline Adams, checked into the ultra-fashionable Windsor Hotel on Fifth Avenue. The proprietor, delighted to have America's foremost astrologer under his roof, asked for and received a 30-minute private consultation. Pulling no punches, Miss Adams advised her hotelier that he was "under the worst possible combination of planets, bringing conditions terrifying in their unfriendliness." A bit shaken, he returned to the lobby whereupon the desk clerk informed him that the east wing of the hotel was in flames. The Windsor burned to the ground in short order, incinerating the proprietor's wife and in-laws, numerous guests, and all of Miss Adams's possessions. Despite the loss of life and wardrobe, the astrologer later told the press she had to count her prognostication as a "grim success."

The stars were kind to Miss Adams. Over the next 30 years she personally cast over a quarter of a million horoscopes, earning $20 for a half-hour face-to-face reading or $5 for a mail-order ministration. Eight hours a day, six days a week she approved and vetoed marriages, divorces, investments, steamship trips, and assorted surgical procedures. Among her regular clients were J. P. Morgan, Enrico Caruso, and two presidents of the New York Stock Exchange. She netted millions.

There were disappointments, of course. "I'm only right about 95 percent of the time," she confessed, and once she lost a chief executive. Asked in June of 1923 about the astrological well-being of Warren G. Harding, Miss Adams stated, "He is safe and under favorable auspices." Within a matter of days the President was as dead as a smoked salmon. But no one could say she lacked the courage of her convictions. She selected George Jordan as her mate, sight-unseen, solely on the basis of his astrological chart; even the wedding day was set according to the exigencies of the zodiac. It was literally a marriage made in heaven. She used the same occult means to choose her pet griffin terrier.

At times she was harassed by skeptics, but she always triumphed in the end. In 1914, for instance, the astrological counselor to royalty and millionaires was arrested in a general round-up of tea-leaf readers, magnetic healers, gypsies, and phony spiritualists. Brought to trial in Manhattan's West Side Court, she was given an anonymous horoscope to interpret. Afterward, the judge announced that the horoscope was his own son's, that Miss Adams's comments had been absolutely correct, and that in his opinion she had "raised astrology to the dignity of an exact science." The case was dismissed.

As an "esoteric scientist" she closely followed developments in related fields. When the planet Pluto was detected in 1930, she was asked how her previous horoscopes could possibly be accurate, based as they were on an eight- rather than nine-planet solar system. "Every new discovery by astronomy makes us very happy," she patiently replied. "They're finding us more tools to work with."

JAMES RENSHAW COX Father Cox of Pittsburgh was the first American priest to conduct a Roman Catholic mass in a dirigible over the Atlantic. He achieved the distinction aboard the ill-fated *Hindenburg* on August 6, 1936.

THEOPHILUS GATES "The orgasm," Malcolm Muggeridge recently declared, "has replaced the Cross as the focus of longing and the image of fulfillment." Maybe so. But the orgasm is hardly a twentieth-century discovery; and, in point of fact, throughout American history there have been a number of missionary spirits who have striven lustily

213

to combine worship with pleasure. Theophilus Gates was one of these hot-blooded apostles; John Humphrey Noyes, *(q.v.)* was another.

Gates was the father, in more than one sense, of an unconventional religious sect known as the Battle Axes ("Thou art my battle axe and weapon of war," *Jeremiah* 51:6). The center of this theological movement was the Shenkel Reformed Church, a handsome stuccoed-stone structure erected near Pottstown, Pennsylvania, in 1838, where Gates and his followers customarily worshipped in the nude.

Gates must have been a difficult child. Born in Connecticut in 1787, he experienced visions and hallucinations with alarming frequency. As a young man, he was variously employed as an itinerant school teacher, law student, and freelance writer of religious prophecy. It was in this last capacity that Gates authored the *Battle Axe,* a tract in which he predicted that "among the present fashions and usages of this world that will fade away is that of man and wife so-called, living in strife and disagreement." While hawking copies of the *Battle Axe* on the streets of Philadelphia for "five cents a copy or a dozen for a quarter," he first met Hannah Williamson, a woman of religious disposition and ill-repute.

Together Gates and Williamson established a church in Shenkel to propagate their erotic faith. They gathered around them a congregation of about 45 men and women who would gather in each other's homes, shed their secular garments, and exercise religious freedoms such as the Founding Fathers had not imagined when they drafted the First Amendment. Any Battle Axe felt free to call at another member's house and, after explaining about a Heavenly Voice, walk out the door with the householder's wife; women enjoyed the same privileges. In *Around the Boundaries of Chester County,* W. W. MacElree mentions one Magdalena Snyder, who entered the home of William Stubblebine, informing him that he was her divinely selected mate. "Immediately William complied ... shifting his wife to the end of the table and installing Magdalena in her seat."

The Battle Axes were given to experimentation of all sorts. One day it occurred to Gates that the quickest way to heaven might be to fly there; he was nearly right. Strapping a pair of wings made of light shingles to his arms, he jumped off a roof and started flapping. It took him over a month to recover from the fall.

Despite harassment from the authorities and neighboring townspeople, the sect grew and flourished; after all, what did the Methodists and Baptists have to offer in comparison? Gradually the Battle Axes did away with all restraints and allegedly communed in the aisles of Shenkel's church with either sex at either end.

GEORGE W. HENRY Shouting in church seems to be making a tumultuous comeback these days as the "born-again" movement wins more and more adherents. Perhaps, then, the time has come to take another look at a long-forgotten theological classic of 1859 entitled *Shouting: Genuine and Spurious in All Ages of the Church: Giving a History of the Outward Demonstrations of the Spirit, such as Laughing, Screaming, Shouting, Leaping, Jerking, and Falling under the Power,* by George W. Henry of Oneida, New York.

Henry was a stalwart believer in the spiritual value of robust, heartfelt, outspoken Hallelujahs and Amens. But he despised the hypocritical shouter: "Men may pass counterfeit money on ignorant men," he writes, "but it is not so easy to deceive a sanctified ear in regard to a genuine shout.... There is as much difference between the true and counterfeit shout and song as between the sounds of a maniac dancing to the music of his own chains and the sweet music that enraptures the saints in heaven."

His own religious conversion took place at an ecstatic camp meeting. The next morning he awoke, his mouth "filled with great laughter," even though nothing was particularly funny. Thereafter, when Henry became a famous circuit preacher, he welcomed the outbursts of snickering and guffaws that greeted his Sunday sermons, and often joined in the general hilarity.

Jerks, too, were openly encouraged: "I have seen more than five hundred persons jerking at one time in my large congregations," he said. And a bout of jerking was always good for a few more holy laughs. "To see those proud young gentlemen and young ladies, dressed in their silks, jewelry, and prunella, from top to toe, take the jerks, would often excite my risibilities. The first jerk or so you would see their fine bonnets, caps, and combs fly; and so sudden would be the jerking of the head, that their long loose hair would crack almost as loud as a wagoner's whip."

Henry's sermons combined the attractions of vaudeville, primal scream therapy, and St. Vitus's dance; there's never been another quite like him.

MOTHER ANN LEE First there was Bethlehem. Then there was Toad Lane in Manchester, England. At the latter, less-celebrated location, on the magical date of February 29, 1736, Ann Lee was born, the woman whom thousands would acknowledge as the second (this time female) incarnation of Christ.

A key event in her quirky religious development occurred in 1762 when she married a blacksmith named Abraham Standerin, by whom she had four children; all four died in infancy. Subsequently, she developed a violent repugnance to sexual intercourse, which, in the end, drove her husband to leave her for another woman. Coitus, she proclaimed, was "filthy gratification" ... "a covenant with death and an agreement with hell" ... "the root of all depravity." In the afterlife she warned, all copulators would be tied up and tortured in the genitals. An enthusiastic member of a sect known as the Shaking Quakers, she was imprisoned in 1770 for "profanation of the Sabbath," in essence, refusing to conform to the dictums of the Church of England. Two years later, she emerged from jail convinced of her own divinity. "I am Ann the Word," she said, and a number of people believed her.

A vision, in 1774, convinced her to emigrate to America in 1774 along with eight disciples. They established a colony at

216

Watervliet in upstate New York where they practiced absolute celibacy and communal ownership of property. Soon after their arrival, Mother Ann, as she now called herself, spoke out against the War of Independence and stated that the Shakers would never bear arms or take oaths. She and her followers were arrested in 1780 on charges of high treason and jailed for six months without trial, probably the first prosecution of conscientious objectors in the New World.

Ann Lee continued to make a noise in the world and win new converts until 1783, when she disappointed many of the faithful (who thought her immortal) and died. Suffering under Mother Ann's stern commandment not to be fruitful or multiply, the Shakers nevertheless survived and prospered, adding to their numbers by adopting homeless orphans. By 1826 there were 18 Shaker communities in eight states, as far west as Indiana. To the end, the sect maintained its firm belief in the dual nature of the Deity, the male principle embodied in Jesus; the female principle, in Mother Ann.

PAUL LITKEY Litkey voiced his outrage at the legalization of abortion in 1977 by walking from his Green Bay, Wisconsin, home to the steps of the United States Supreme Court building in Washington, carrying a large wooden crucifix. It took him three months.

WILLIAM MILLER By close reading of the Bible and a series of painstaking mathematical calculations, the seventeenth-century Irish bishop James Ussher was able to demonstrate that God created the earth in the year 4004 B.C. A formidable accomplishment, to be sure; but it took the apocalyptic genius of William Miller, a Baptist farmer from upstate New York, to figure out the exact day and hour when the trumpet would sound announcing the end of the world and the Second Coming of Christ. From the Book of Daniel, chapters 8 and 9, he deduced that the big event would occur at 3 A.M. on March 21, 1843. (To arrive at this number he assumed every biblical "day" was actually equivalent to an

217

earthly year. Napoleon, he reasoned, was the Anti-Christ heralding the impending Last Judgment.)

Miller's fire and brimstone preachings, aided by his widely distributed newspaper called *The Midnight Cry,* won him an estimated half million converts. His following grew as the fateful day approached and numerous signs and omens were reported: strange rings around the sun, crosses in the sky, birds falling dead in mid-flight. Miller personally delivered over 300 sermons during the last six months, which produced "much excitement, a great breaking down, and much weeping." Then in March, 1843, the brightest comet of the century appeared in the sky, visible even at high noon, and seemed to hang ominously over the sinful earth "like a threatening sword."

Terrified believers asked "How shall I be saved?" Speaking in tongues and religious conniptions reached epidemic proportions. Miller was accused of raking in thousands of dollars from the sale of white "ascension robes," the recommended attire for the great "Going Up." Others preferred to meet their Maker in the nude. On the appointed evening, thousands assembled on hilltops and in graveyards for convenient transportation to heaven. Gerrit Smith, a famed abolitionist and devout Millerite, wrote a poignant farewell letter to his wife, who had been called away from home: "My dearly Beloved: We have just had family worship—perhaps for the last time.... I know not, my dear Nancy, that we shall meet in the air."

Nothing much happened on March 21. The embarrassed evangelist went back over his figures and discovered a simple mistake in addition; a new, revised date for the end of the world was set: October 22, 1844. Incredibly, the whole scene was played out a second time. Crops went unharvested, stores closed, positions were resigned, debts forgiven, entire herds of animals were slaughtered for lavish last suppers. The demand for ascension robes exceeded the supply.

As the reader is probably aware, the millenium was not *usshered* in that day. But despite the "Great Disappointment," as it is known in the history of the Adventist church, many souls retained their faith. The Jehovah's Witnesses and other sects that look forward to an imminent Second Coming trace their origins back to William Miller's fanatical movement.

C. W. RALSTON   East of San Francisco, near the northern end of the San Joaquin valley, there is a town of 62,000 souls named for C. W. Ralston, a generous and well-liked nineteenth-century financier. You won't find "Ralston" mentioned on any map or street sign, though. A simple, unassuming man, he found that kind of publicity embarrassing; so, after thanking the townspeople for their tribute, he asked them not to use his name. Accordingly, the village was incorporated in 1884 as "Modesto," from the Spanish word meaning "modest man."

DR. ROBERT H. SCHULLER   Fresh from divinity school, Dr. Robert H. Schuller adopted the unorthodox tactic of going from house to house, ringing doorbells and trying to round up a congregation for a new Dutch-heritage Reformed Church in Garden Grove, California. "Good intelligent people told me they felt closer to God out of doors," he recollects. And so Dr. Schuller decided to bring the Ford to the Lord.

In 1955 he established Christendom's first drive-in sanctuary, where commuters-turned-communicants might worship in the comfort and privacy of their own automobiles. Initially he delivered his sermons from the rooftop of a drive-in movie theater; before long, however, the offering plates were filled to overflowing by prayerful motorists, and Dr. Schuller was able to finance his current 14-story skyscraper-church, topped with a neon cross, and surrounded by a carefully manicured 22-acre campus. No other house of God even remotely compares with it. Within the sanctuary there are 1,700 indoor seats, which are jammed whenever Dr. Schuller preaches; and the east wall is fabricated entirely of glass so that hundreds of drive-in congregants can watch from a terraced parking lot while listening to the service on their radios. And that's just the beginning. . . .

Every Sunday over 1.2 million television viewers now tune in Dr. Schuller's "Hour of Power" program, carried on 160 local stations nationwide. The broadcast pulls $8.9 million in donations annually. He has also authored 14 books on what he calls "possibility thinking," a philosophy of personal optimism that echoes Norman Vincent Peale. But his most ambitious project is still on the drawing boards. As of this writing, Dr. Schuller hopes to break ground shortly on his planned $12.5 million Crystal Cathedral that will be wider and taller than Notre Dame in Paris. "If this building were not a work of art, it wouldn't be worth it," Dr. Schuller confided to a *New York Times* reporter. "But this building will stand for 500, 600, 700 years, and it will be a super-bargain."

CHARLES SMITH   The American Association for the Advancement of Atheism was founded in October 1925 by Charles Smith "to educate the people as to the falsity and superstition of all religion." The New York State Supreme Court at first refused to issue the organization a charter, but later relented. (Parenthetically, in a rare display of wit, Dwight Eisenhower once defined an atheist as "a guy who watches a Notre Dame–SMU football game and doesn't care who wins.")

FRANCES WILLARD   In her family Bible the indomitable Frances Willard inscribed and signed the pledge that was to influence the drinking habits of the nation:

> A pledge to make
> No wine to take
> No brandy red
> To turn the head
> No whiskey hot
> That makes the sot
> Nor fiery rum
> That ruins home
> Nor will we sin

By drinking gin
Hard cider too
Will never do
No brewer's beer
Our hearts to cheer

To quench our thirst
We always bring cold water
From the well or spring
So here we pledge
Perpetual hate
To all that can intoxicate.

Admittedly no great shakes as a poet, the teetotaling Miss Willard was a holy terror when it came to organization. The one-time dean of women at Northwestern University was the moving force behind the creation of the Women's Christian Temperance Union, and under her presidency it became a formidable institution to battle vice wherever it reared its ugly head. She was the architect of the WCTU's "Do Everything" policy, expanding its concerns far beyond mere abstinence from alcohol. There was a separate agency to combat "Social Evil" (a euphemism for prostitution); an agency for promoting purity of thought and action in young boys; a "flower mission" assigned to visit jails on Sundays presenting each prisoner with a pretty posy and a biblical tract.

Miss Willard pulled off her most brilliant coup in organizing the WCTU Department of Scientific Temperance Instruction; by 1902 she had succeeded in making "alcoholism education" a compulsory subject in most American public schools. Using WCTU-provided materials, temperance instructors taught young school children "facts" about demon rum—"a drunkard's blood is so rich in alcohol that it will catch fire from a match"—all at the taxpayers' expense.

Scientific Figures

ALBERT ABRAMS   A physician of imposing credentials, Dr. Albert Abrams raised eyebrows in the early 1900s by asserting that a sample of Henry Wadsworth Longfellow's handwriting proved the poet had syphilis and that that disease and others could be cured over the telephone.

In 1909–10, Abrams published his first findings on the efficacy of tapping on the spine—later he found the abdomen would do just as nicely—as a way of charting the body's infirmities. The tapping, he said, would induce a characteristic spinal vibration associated with a specific illness. But tapping by itself wasn't enough: Abrams invented a mechanical "dynamizer" that ran on house current and was, he proclaimed, the ultimate in sure-fire medical diagnosis. It was a metal box crammed with wires and bejewelled with switches and dials. A long wire leading from the device was fastened to the head of a healthy person who had stripped to the waist for the occasion and was facing west. Dr. Abrams would place a sample of the patient's blood within the box, throw the switch, beat his diagnostic tattoo on the abdomen of his healthy confederate, whose spinal vibrations would reveal not only the disease in question but exactly where it was located and its severity, as well as the patient's age, sex, and religion.

As he sharpened his technique, Dr. Abrams found he could replace the blood with a handwriting sample, a breakthrough enabling him to examine dead patients as well as the living. Autograph letters of Samuel Johnson, Edgar Allan Poe, and Oscar Wilde all revealed anatomies wracked with syphilis, and this, to a literate public, was no surprise. The Longfellow diagnosis, however, was something of a shocker.

Dr. Abrams devised an "oscilloclast" in 1920, which treated and cured diseases vibratorily, just as the dynamizer diagnosed them. Next came the Abrams "reflexophone," which made telephone therapy possible. Other electric marvels poured forth from the doctor's busy workshop, and they made him a rich man. What with machine rentals to other doctors, instruction courses, lecture tours, and a wide-selling magazine, he amassed an estate of $2 million by the time of his death in 1923.

Of course, none of this cut much ice with the A.M.A. Once they tried to topple Abrams's mechanical empire by sending one of his physician-subscribers a blood sample taken from a "Miss Bell," concealing that it had really been extracted from a healthy guinea pig (male). By return mail the A.M.A. was told that Miss Bell was suffering from cancer, a sinus infection, and a streptococcic infection of the fallopian tube. Another time, a doctor in Michigan sent Abrams himself a vial of rooster's blood and was informed by the master that it showed malaria, cancer, diabetes, and venereal disease.

A postscript: one of Abrams's most outspoken supporters was the novelist Upton Sinclair, who attributed his hero's occasional failure not to incompetence and chicanery, but rather to interference from the "complex vibrations of I know not how many radio stations."

GEORGE ADAMSKI UFOs were already old hat by the early 1950s, but only a handful of self-claimed eyewitnesses reported to have had personal dealings with extraterrestrial beings. One of the earliest "close encounterers" was handyman George Adamski, who offered that he had first shaken hands with a visitor from Venus in the California desert in November, 1952. According to Adamski, his Venusian friend was five-foot-six, wore his hair long, had gray eyes, and was given to oxblood shoes and brown jump suits. Later, he would ride with the Venusians aboard their magnetically-powered aircraft, chatting telepathically—as if there were any other way—with an especially ravishing, full-breasted member of the species (presumably a woman).

What Adamski reported, in accounts to the press and later in his books *(Behind the Flying Saucer Mystery* was his first), was that Martians, Venusians, and the denizens of the other planets—and they are *all* crawling with life, make no mistake about *that*—resemble earthlings as closely as, say, Californians resemble Midwesterners. In fact, Adamski learned from his Venusian hosts, there are doubtless legions of extraterrestrials on earth right now, posing as humans, assigned to study man-made nuclear explosions, a source of deep anxiety beyond this planet. What Venusians want most, he said, is to live in peace and harmony with Earth's millions.

CLEVE BACKSTER Does the philodendron in your kitchen window cry out inwardly with pain when you prune it? Does the oak tree on your front lawn feel deep-rooted revulsion every time a full-bladdered dog comes near? Can a turnip find true love? Those are just a few of the momentous questions raised by Cleve Backster's investigations into the emotions of potted plants.

Backster, a former interrogation specialist with the Central Intelligence Agency, obtained the first scientific evidence of intense feelings among flora when on a lark he attached a lie detector to the *Dracaena massangeana* in his office:

> I decided to try to apply some equivalent to the threat-to-well-being principle, a well-established method of triggering emotionality in humans. I first tried to arouse the plant by immersing a leaf in a cup of hot coffee. But there was no measurable reaction. After a nine-minute interim, I decided to obtain a match and burn the plant leaf being tested. At the instant of this decision.... [there was] a dramatic change in the PGR tracing pattern in the form of an abrupt and prolonged upward sweep of the recording pen. I had not moved or touched the plant, so the timing of the PGR [i.e., polygraph] pen activity suggested to me

that the tracing might have been triggered by the mere thought of the harm I intended to inflict upon the plant.

Apparently the *Dracaena* was gifted with mental telepathy as well as simpler emotions.

When these results were first reported in 1969, *National Wildlife* magazine dispatched a team of skeptical staff members to evaluate the man and his methodology. They concluded: "Cleve Backster is not some kind of nut. He really knows his business and is pursuing his investigations with great care to avoid any chance of criticism from the doubting scientific community." Since that time Backster's findings have been replicated by some scientists and scoffed at by others. We still don't know for sure whether a lettuce has a heart.

Epilogue: In 1975 Backster reported to the annual meeting of the American Association for the Advancement of Science that he had detected evidence of sympathetic communication between two containers of yogurt culture placed at opposite ends of his laboratory.

EDWARD GARRISON BALLENGER You-Oughta-be-in-Pictures Department: Dr. Ballenger, working in concert with Drs. Harold Paul McDonald and Reese Clinton Coleman, took the world's first full-color cystoscopic photographs. The historic blow-ups, suitable for framing, were publicly exhibited in March, 1940, at the Postgraduate Surgical Assembly of the Southeastern Surgical Congress, in Birmingham, Alabama.

DR. ADAM BARBER

Make Thee an Ark of Gopher Wood, Genesis 6:14

They laughed at Noah. And there are those who scoff at Dr. Adam Barber of Washington, D.C., when he warns that the earth may soon experience an inundation that will make the Noahian deluge seem as but a drop in the bucket.

As Dr. Barber explains in his book *The Coming Disaster*

225

Worse than the H-Bomb, there is danger that the earth may at any moment tilt crazily to one side. Specifically, what worries Dr. Barber is the wobbling of the earth's axis known as the precession. Each wobble takes 26,000 years to complete, but Barber believes this chronic instability portends the earth will soon fall over like an exhausted toy top. When the axis shifts there will be some kind of trouble! The oceans will come spilling over the continents in a colossal tidal wave, and within an hour and a half the geography of the earth will be completely rearranged. Like Atlantis, entire cities and nations will sink beneath the waters.

Now before dismissing this curious Apocalyptic vision, consider the fact that Dr. Barber is a gyroscope engineer by profession. Who could be better qualified to assess when the planetary carousel is showing signs of winding down? Note also that he doesn't expect that the earth will stop rotating altogether; these things take time. He merely claims we're due for a major axial readjustment, the first since Noah's time.

Dr. Barber has made every effort to alert the world to the impending catastrophe. In 1954 when *The Coming Disaster Worse than the H-Bomb* first appeared, he sent copies to Winston Churchill, Charles DeGaulle, Dwight Eisenhower, and the emperor of Japan, as well as to the Mount Palomar, Mount Wilson, and Royal Greenwich Observatories. The response he received from geophysicists and astronomers ranged from skeptical to scathing.

Undaunted, Dr. Barber went ahead with plans to install an Early Warning System in every American home. It works like the "tilt" mechanism on a pinball machine. The home-owner hangs a large metallic ball from the ceiling of his living room; then if the earth should suddenly totter, the ball will swing, thus closing an electrical circuit and causing an alarm bell to ring. Except in low-lying coastal areas this alarm would give everyone in the house ample time to scramble on board a boat, which should always be anchored in the back yard for just such emergencies. Taking no chances, Dr. Barber has constructed a seaworthy ark of his own. Alternatively, he says, helium balloons might serve as airborne life rafts.

But must we stand idly by while the world lists and founders? No, by god! Dr. Barber proposes that rockets be installed on mountaintops (for maximum leverage) at the North and South Poles. Then when the Great Tilt occurs, the rockets would be fired and the earth nudged back into its accustomed position.

The days of maximum hazard, according to Dr. Barber's calculations, are December 21 and June 21; the year is less certain. But if once again "the waters prevail and increase greatly upon the earth," remember you were forewarned.

JOSEPH BATTELL A wealthy Vermont farmer and breeder of horses, Joseph Battell is best known as the author of *Ellen, or the Whisperings of an Old Pine,* a three-volume discourse on the mysteries of mathematics and the physical universe between a teenage girl and a Vermont pine tree (who, incidentally, is the narrator). A sampling:

> June again was blossoming above our hills. . . . At this moment the golden rim of the sun was lifted above the eastern horizon. . . . For many minutes Ellen watched the wondrous scene, then turning again, came towards me. A little laugh shook the newborn leaves. . . . She threw aside the light shawl that she carried on her arm, and again seated herself upon the rocks near me.
>
> "And now, Mr. Pine," she said, "Ellen will criticize the theory of sound which has been accepted substantially by all the scientists. . . ."

ALBERT K. BENDER Albert K. Bender, who ran a space-saucer watchers' club in the early 1960s and wrote books on UFOs, wanted nothing more than to have a meaningful dialogue with extraterrestrial creatures. Figuring telepathy to be the most likely interplanetary *lingua franca,* he had his followers concentrate in unison on this message, while he himself lay down with his eyes shut tight and intoned it three times: "Calling all occupants of interplanetary craft.... Please come in peace and help us with our earthly problems. Give us some sign that you have received our message. Be responsible for creating a miracle here on our planet to wake up the ignorant ones to reality. Let us hear from you. We are your friends."

Bender's extraterrestrials, to hear him tell it, picked up before the second ring. A voice as even as a railway terminal announcer's sounded in his head with this reply: "We have been watching you and your activities. Please be advised to discontinue delving into the mysteries of the universe. We will make an appearance if you disobey." Writes John Sladek in *The New Apocrypha,* "I believe that poor Mr. Bender was so advised."

RUTH DROWN What made being a patient of Ruth Drown's so appealing was never having to shlep your complaints to her office. She healed by beaming radio signals to your home. A licensed osteopath, Mrs. Drown did her wondrous work from a one-of-its-kind broadcast studio in downtown Los Angeles whence she treated each of her patients via his or her own radio channel, first slotting into her transmitter the patient's identifying blood sample, then tuning in one of the dozens of dials that festooned the walls.

All this started in the late 1920s when Mrs. Drown, fresh from a few years' on-the-job training in the electrical assembly division of the Southern California Edison Company, scored her first successes with wireless healing and set up shop as an over-the-air osteopath. Her inventions found a ready market among chiropractors, osteopaths, and other quasi-medical men, despite the more-than-occasional accusation that she was less than straightforward in her diagnoses.

"Her technique is to find so much trouble in so many organs," a team of University of Chicago doctors reported after one investigative session with Mrs. Drown in 1950, "that usually she can say, 'I told you so' when she registers an occasional lucky positive guess." The team had submitted for Mrs. Drown's analysis a sample of blood taken from a woman who, unbeknownst to Mrs. Drown, was tubercular. Her findings: "a type IV cancer of the left breast with spread to ovaries, uterus, pancreas, gall bladder, spleen and kidney." Additionally, she found, the woman was plagued by an impaired pancreas, pituitary gland, uterus, right ovary, parathyroid, spleen, heart, liver, gall bladder, kidneys, lungs, stomach, spinal nerves, ears, and intestines—and was blind in her right eye. During that same examination, Mrs. Drown trained her magic radio waves on the bleeding wound of an anesthetized laboratory animal. The more she transmitted, the more the animal bled until, the team reported, "her friends found the sight beyond their capacities."

DR. LYDIA EMERY When Lydia Emery established a medical practice in Yoncalla, Oregon, in 1946, she decided a dollar per office visit and two dollars per house call were reasonable rates. They were and still are. As of 1977 Dr. Emery had not increased her rates, prompting write-ups in such national publications as *Modern Maturity* and *Saturday Review*. *Fortune* has yet to run a story.

DR. BETTY LANE FABER "They eat anything," said Dr. Betty Lane Faber, describing her favorite animal. "They are cheap, easy to raise—and I don't have to worry about disposing of the body. I just throw it out in the garbage." Does it sound like the ideal pet for your house or apartment? Well, maybe you have swarms already.

Dr. Faber, an entomologist with the American Museum of Natural History, is the world's foremost authority on *Periplaneta americana*—cockroaches, that is. She has spent over 600 nighttime hours during the past two and a half years observing the private habits of this shy night-active species in the museum's infested greenhouses. To watch them without disturbing their lifestyle, she employs an invisible infrared scanning device similar to those used by the military. She has affixed tiny numbers to their backs, like the numbers on a football player's jersey, to document their migrations and help her distinguish one little bugger from another.

Her uncommon fondness for roaches was born within the clean walls of a dissecting laboratory. "It was exciting to see that it wasn't just mush inside," she told a reporter from *People* magazine. "There is an organism, and it's even pretty."

It remains a mystery, even to Dr. Faber, how roaches can reproduce in such profusion when they seem to have a rather lackluster sex life. Only twice during her studies has she witnessed a sexual coupling, which among roaches is consummated end-to-end with male and female facing opposite directions. "The pair remain together for thirty to forty minutes," she explains. "During courtship, males flap their wings and run around erratically."

Cockroaches are very old. Fossil evidence indicates that they were the dominant species during the Carboniferous period, about 350 million years ago. And unlike the familiar household variety, these ancient cockroaches were able to fly and were probably the first flying animals. As for their reputation for filthy living and carrying diseases, Dr. Faber says, "Cockroaches have had a bad press."

ORSON SQUIRE FOWLER "No quackery," said H. L. Mencken, "is ever rejected by the American public until a more scientific sounding but inherently less plausible quackery is ready to take its place." In the mid-nineteenth century the reigning nonsense in the United States was phrenology, a pseudoscience that purported to discern human character from the bumps and depressions of the skull. It seems ludicrous today that Clara Barton took up nursing and Bernard Baruch went into finance on the counsel of their phrenologists, and yet they did. General George McClellan recruited spies for the Union Army on the basis of their phrenological profiles, insisting on a prominent secretiveness faculty. Horace Greeley, the editor of the *New York Tribune,* seriously suggested that accidents might be reduced if railroad engineers were selected by the shape of their crania. Presidents Tyler, Grant, and Garfield all had their heads examined.

The self-proclaimed "great gun of Phrenology in America" was Orson Squire Fowler (1809–87). With no training whatsoever in science, medicine, or physiology, he and his younger brother Lorenzo established an office at 135 Nassau Street in New York City and began reading heads. For a comprehensive private examination they charged three dollars, quite a sum in those days, but then it brought several pages of personality analysis and some Ann Landers-style advice on conduct. If a patient lived too far away to come in to the office for a palpation, the brothers Fowler would assess his character by mail "from a good daguerrotype, the three quarter pose preferred." Mark Twain was one of the thousands of men and women who came to Nassau Street for a reading; he was told he had an "underdeveloped mirthfulness faculty."

Fowler supplemented his considerable income by opening a school for would-be bump-readers, the American Institute of Phrenology, and by selling his students the macabre paraphernalia of the profession. For $25 one could buy a set of 40 choice plaster casts, including the notable noggins of John Quincy Adams, Voltaire, Sir Walter Scott, Napoleon, Sylvester Graham (q.v.), and Aaron Burr ("secretiveness and destructiveness faculties much enlarged"). Of course, advanced students required hands-on experience with real skulls and Fowler obliged by importing crania from European battlefields, retailing them for five dollars a head. Skulls of "rare races" went for premium prices of $30 and up.

Business boomed and Fowler was able to open the Phrenological Cabinet, one of the showplaces of Old New York. On display were the skulls and skeletal remains of famous men contrasted with those of "savages," animals, and assorted murderers and pirates. It combined the charms of Madame Tussaud's with those of a dissecting laboratory.

It was only fitting that such an unconventional man should live in an unconventional house. In fact, Fowler was the world's first and foremost octagonal architect; the mansion he built in Fishkill, New York, was widely acclaimed as one of the most original and daring structures of the century. "The octagon," he said, "is a spiritually beautiful shape.... The quality of living is much improved in rooms without right angles." He went so far as to design an entire city laid out in an octagonal pattern. Over 60 colonists joined the Octagon settlement scheme and migrated to the banks of the Neosha River in Kansas Territory. The leader of the expedition was the Reverend Henry Stephen Clubb, a Fowler disciple, who frequently posed in his sermons the rhetorical question, "Is Edenic life practical?" The answer turned out to be: not in Kansas! The settlement was a dismal failure.

RICHARD LYNCH GARNER Garner (1848–1920) was a nineteenth-century zoologist whose consuming passion was learning to speak the language of the apes. He spent a lifetime at it, ultimately claiming fluency. Transcripts of meaningful conversations with apes, along with Garner's overall findings, appear in his three major books: *The Speech of Monkeys* (1892), *Gorillas and Chimpanzees* (1896), and *Apes and Monkeys* (1900).

DINSHAH PESTANJI FRAMJI GHADIALI On trial for medical fraud in the 1940s, Colonel Ghadiali paraded through the witness stand some 112 satisfied users of his "Spectro-Chrome Therapy," including former syphilitics, asthmatics, cancer victims, and epileptics, one of whom exclaimed, "I tell you I had fits all my life till Doctor Ghadiali cured me," and then promptly had a seizure. It did not speak well of the colonel's practice. In the end he was fined $20,000 and received a suspended three-year jail sentence. The presence in the courtroom of the Colonel's seven young sons, all wearing identical purple beanies, as did their father, elicited no sympathy from the court.

It was in 1920 that the Bombay-born Ghadiali, who lived most of his life in Malaga, New Jersey, and established the Spectro-Chrome Institute there, first dabbled in Spectro-

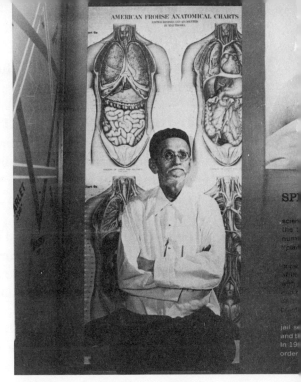

Dinshah Pestanji Ghadiali, the father of "Spectro-Chrome Therapy" *(St. Louis Museum of Medical Quackery)*

Chrome therapy. (His military title derived from a brief volunteer stint with the New York Reserve Air Service during World War I.) While its proper application required one of the colonel's patented Spectro-Chrome Machines, its principles were much the same as those of other cure-by-colored-light practitioners. Diabetes, for instance, could be cured by alternating rays of yellow and magenta light and a diet heavy in starches and brown sugar. Green rays were best for gonorrhea. Whatever the ailment, the colonel counseled, avoid meat, tea, coffee, strong drink, eggs, honey, and tobacco, and keep your head pointing north when you sleep.

The Colonel first ran afoul of the law while on the lecture circuit in Seattle in 1925; he was convicted under the Mann Act and drew five years in Atlanta penitentiary. (His case was no doubt weakened by his teenage secretary's testimony that he had required her to join him in unnatural sexual practices.) Later he protested his treatment in *Railroading a Citizen,* two volumes of rage against an anti-Ghadiali conspiracy of Catholics, blacks, the medical establishment, the

United States Department of Justice, the government of England, and Henry Ford.

GEORGE FRANCIS GILLETTE   George Francis Gillette made insulting Albert Einstein—the man, his theories, and everything he stood for—his life's work. Born in 1875 and educated at the University of Michigan, Gillette was an engineer with various American corporations and a sometime author whose four books, all published at his own expense, rang with these sentiments and others of their ilk: "Einstein a scientist? It were difficult to imagine anyone more contrary and opposite to what a scientist should be. . . ." And, "As a rational physicist, Einstein is a fair violinist." Relativity, of course, was the main target of Gillette's rage. He called it "the moronic brainchild of mental colic," "voodoo nonsense," and "the nadir of pure drivel," and in 1929 predicted that the theory would "be considered a joke" ten years hence, its author's reputation "dead and buried alongside Andersen, Grimm, and the Mad Hatter."

What prompted Gillette's ragings against the gentle Einstein was the fact that relativity was so laughably, impossibly inconsistent with Gillette's theory of the universe. He called it his "spiral universe" theory, based it on the teachings of Newton, or so he claimed, and it goes something like this: "Each ultimote is *simultaneously* an integral part of zillions of otherplane units and only thus is its *infinite* allplane velocity and energy subdivided into zillions of *finite* planar quotas of velocity and energy." Pretty nifty, no? There's also some talk about "bumping," to which, in Gillette's universe, all movement and energy can ultimately be reduced. "All motions ever strive to go straight—until they bump," he writes. Well, fine, that sounds admirably like Newton's Third Law of Motion. But there's more. "In all the cosmos, there is naught but straight-flying bumping, caroming, and again straight flying. Phenomena are but lumps, jumps and bumps. A mass unit's career is but lumping, bumping, rejumping, rebumping and finally unlumping."

Gillette is best known for his "backscrewing theory of

gravity," the linchpin of his vision of a "spiral universe." As he explained it in *Rational, Non-Mystical Cosmos* (1933), "Gravitation is the kicked back nut of the screwing bolt of radiation." If that seems a bit muddy, this may help: "Gravitation and backscrewing are synonymous. All mass units are solar systems . . . of interscrewed subunits. . . . Gravitation is naught but that reaction in the form of subplanar solar systems screwing through higher plane masses."

Understandably, it made Gillette angry to see his theories scorned and ignored by what he labeled the scientific establishment's "orthodox oxen." "There is no ox so dumb as the orthodox," he wrote in *Orthodox Oxen* in 1929. And why are most scientists so narrow of vision? It's because they are "cramped within Homoplania, ignorant of ultimotically related sub and supraplanes." *Orthodox Oxen* incidentally, is a good introduction to Gillette's thinking. Briefer than his other works, it is blissfully free of "hi-de-hi mathematics" according to the title page, and is illustrated with drawings of such Gillettian constructs as "the all cosmos doughnut" and the "laminated solid, solid, solid, solid." Many of the diagrams are hand-colored by the author himself.

JOHN GREENWOOD John Greenwood is the man behind George Washington's stoic grimace: he was the dentist who fashioned Washington's notoriously ill-fitting false teeth (made, no doubt of green wood). The dentures were soaked by Washington in port wine each night in a futile attempt to deodorize them. As for Greenwood, whatever his failures as a craftsman, Washington did offer this sincere if tepid endorsement for use in the doctor's advertisements: "Sir, I fhall alwayf prefer your fervicef to that of any other in the line of your prefent profeffion."

GERALD HEARD Gerald Heard is no hoaxer. The celebrated writer of a dozen or more books of theological, psychological, anthropological and mystical interest, he has often concerned himself with the origins of UFOs, in which he believes wholeheartedly. In his 1951 work, *Is Another*

World Watching? he says that flying saucers are piloted by bees.

Of course, these are bees such as no earthbound picnic has ever been disrupted by. They are actually a race of "super-bees," endowed with lightning speed, superhuman intelligence, and the toughness to endure endless interplanetary journeys. What might one look like? "A creature with eyes like brilliant cut diamonds," says Heard, "with a head of sapphire, a thorax of emerald, an abdomen of ruby, wings like opal, legs like topaz. . . . In its presence we would feel shabby and ashamed and maybe, with our clammy, putty-colored bodies, repulsive."

The magnificent bees and their flying machines are of Martian extraction, Heard believes, and were brought close to earth by a mother ship which hovers in space while smaller saucers go on reconnaissance missions to study atomic explosions on this planet. To prove he's not kidding around, Heard includes photographs of real-life flying saucers in his book, although most are too muddy to show anything discernible. One of the clearer ones, says science writer Martin Gardner, "bears a striking resemblance to the top of a garbage can tossed into the air."

GEORGE and MOLLY HUNT   Their shocking but scientifically verifiable disclosure of rampant homosexuality among California seagulls won notoriety for the Hunts, both researchers at the University of California. "We were absolutely astounded," confessed George who, with wife Molly, had spent three years observing 2,400 seagulls on Santa Barbara Island, an otherwise scarcely tenanted rock near Los Angeles. Fourteen percent of the females, it developed had paired off in lesbian unions, simulating the mating and reproduction patterns of their more orthodox sisters. Invariably, one of the gulls would play the male role, the other act the female, ultimately laying a nest of chickless eggs which she would guard as jealously as if they bore live offspring.

"This sort of thing has not been found before and was clearly not what we anticipated," George said. Oh, well, gulls will be gulls.

ALFRED WILLIAM LAWSON   Although Alfred William Lawson played many roles in his lifetime—physicist, professional baseball player, economist, novelist, nutritionist—ultimately only two things mattered to him: Suction and Pressure. Every movement, he insisted, every force in the universe, from a grasshopper's belch to the earth's progress around the sun, was a form of one or the other. It's all spelled out in Lawson's 1939 book, *Penetrability.*

Light, for example, is merely "a substance drawn into the eye by Suction," just as the sounds of Christmas carols or radio programs are sucked into the ear, oxygen into the lungs, food into the mouth. Excretion, of course, is Pressure at its most efficient, and the "attraction of one sex for the other is merely the attraction of Suction for Pressure." The planet earth, in fact, is the ultimate pressing and sucking machine. As Lawson pictured it, the earth sucks in life-supporting gases and proteins from the sun through a mouth-like orifice at the North Pole. From there they pass through a pole-to-pole digestive tract, with wastes excreted at the South Polar anus.

Lawson's vision of an endlessly sucking and pressing cosmos is but one component of his great "Zig-Zag-and-Swirl" theory, which in turn is the cornerstone of "lawsonomy," his all-encompassing vision of the universe or, as he once somewhat grandly stated it, "The Knowledge of Life and everything pertaining thereto." Grand statements, to be sure, were as vital to Lawson as the side dish of fresh-mown grass he ate at every meal. "When I look into the vastness of space and see the marvelous workings of its contents," he once wrote in a rare reference to himself in the first person, "I sometimes think that I was born ten or twenty thousand years ahead of time." But his biographer, the mysterious Cy Q. Faunce, who wrote the prefaces to many of Lawson's 50 books, thought more positively: "The birth of Lawson," he wrote, "was the most momentous occurrence since the birth of mankind."

Born in England in 1869, young Lawson grew up in Detroit and signed on with a minor league baseball club in Goshen, Indiana, when he was 19, leaving in 1907 for a career in aviation. In the years before the Great War he founded *Fly,* America's first popular magazine devoted exclusively to airplanes. The cover of the first issue showed a young lady soaring through the heavens on the back of an eagle.

Later Lawson invented first the word "aircraft," then the double-decker passenger plane. In 1919 he formed his own airline, the Lawson Aircraft Corporation, piloting many of the longer flights himself, and did very well until a crash forced him out of business.

During the Depression Lawson was the guiding light of a quick-cure economic scheme called "Direct Credits" that demanded an end to the gold standard and its replacement by "valueless money with no purchase power." Its twin bibles were Lawson's *Direct Credits for Everybody* (1931) and *Know Business* (1937). His faithful turned out by the tens of thousands at Direct Credits rallies and parades throughout America. Some 16,000 jammed Detroit's Olympia Auditorium in 1933, waving banners bearing such sentiments as "All nations need direct credits for little children and feeble old folks." When Lawson stepped to the podium, the crowd went berserk and the orchestra struck up *Hail to the Chief.* At that meeting and others, the faithful sang such anthems as *Hark to Lawson* and *God's Gift to Man.* (The final line of every stanza is "Alfred William Lawson is God's great eternal gift to Man.")

It was also during the 1930s that Lawson spelled out his life's thinking in a three-volume work called *Lawsonomy.* Along with its Suction/Pressure chapters, it set forth Lawson's theory of how the human brain works. The brain, he said, is run by menorgs (short for "mental organizers"), tiny thinking organisms that power all constructive voluntary actions. "To move your arm requires the concentrated efforts of billions of Menorgs working together under order from one little Menorg," Lawson explained. Unfortunately, every brain is riddled with an opposing army of Disorgs, or "mental disorganizers," who are "microscopic vermin that infect the cells of the mental system and destroy the mental instruments constructed and operated by the Menorgs."

238

With money earned from his writings and elsewhere, Lawson purchased the long-defunct University of Des Moines in 1943 and reopened it as the Des Moines University of Lawsonomy. The course of studies was ten years and limited exclusively to Lawson's works. Even a non-Lawsonian basketball rulebook was once declared taboo. Instructors were known as "Knowlegians," senior professors as Generals, and the founder himself was revered as "Supreme Head and First Knowlegian." It cost nothing to attend the school, this in keeping with Lawson's frequently proclaimed aversion to acquiring wealth. In fact, he would often turn his pockets inside out at public meetings, a gesture which was to become his trademark.

Campus proscriptions against tobacco and strong drink grew out of Lawson's concern for the Body as Temple of the Soul. His recipe for good health: sleep in the nude (changing bed linens daily), avoid meat, and feast instead on raw fruits and vegetables, making sure to swallow seeds, pits, and skin. "Under no circumstances," he counseled, "should anyone breathe through the mouth." The best beverage is warm water, although he advised dunking the head in a basin of *cold* water every morning and night. ("The eyes should be opened under water and rolled around ... and the ears should be allowed to suck in the water until pressing against the eardrums.")

Kissing, Lawson believed, bred disease, and should be avoided at all costs.

CHARLES WENTWORTH LITTLEFIELD Charles Wentworth Littlefield, born in 1859 and raised on a farm in Muncie, Indiana, first made his mark as a gifted homeopathic physician who could stanch the most profuse bleeding by reciting a mysterious Biblical incantation he'd learned as a child.

Now Littlefield's medical training was solid—he was an 1896 graduate of Kansas City Homeopathic Medical College—and however wondrous the effects of his magic charm, he knew its secret could ultimately be explained scientifically. In a 1905 experiment the doctor, now moved to Seattle, trained his microscope on a specimen of the organic salt that figures crucially in the clotting of blood. Gazing steadily at the drying solution, Littlefield intoned his ancient charm while forming the picture of a chicken in his mind. Before his squinting eyes, the crystals took the shape of the very fowl he imagined. In subsequent experiments Littlefield would induce his obedient crystals to transform themselves into other species of poultry, seashells, fish, lizards, octopi, gorillas, various saints, Uncle Sam, the devil, printed words, the state of Rhode Island, and a woman walking against the wind with a poodle tucked under her arm.

Black magic? Not at all, Littlefield insisted. As he explained it, the drying of the salt solution left it easy prey to the power of mind control. He wrote up his findings in a 656-page volume called *The Beginning and Way of Life* (1919), illustrated with over a hundred photographs of his quasi-living microscopic beasties. The preface includes a verbal tip of the hat to Sts. Paul and John and to the eighteenth-century English physicist Michael Faraday for contributing to Littlefield's research from beyond the grave.

Littlefield did not put all his stock on Biblical surgery. Just after the close of World War I he patented his "Rainbow Lamp," with which he cured an unlikely range of diseases from gout to gonorrhea. Indeed, much of *The Beginning* is given to a lengthy discourse on his wonderful lamp, and the reader's special attention is directed to a series of unre-touched photographs of a waitress's nastily burned backside. Littlefield had played his rainbow lights on the burn and within ten weeks his patient was totally recovered. He made known his wish that profits from the sale of *The Beginning*, unwisely limited to 1,000 copies, might finance the creation of a Rainbow Temple, equipped for both individual rainbow light treatment and group therapy in a central rotunda.

DR. CRAWFORD LONG   The teenage residents of Jefferson, Georgia, were feeling no pain—thanks to Dr. Crawford Williamson Long. Early in 1842, the fun-loving general prac-

240

titioner had purchased a bottle of sulphuric ether from a traveling science lecturer, and thrill-seeking youngsters soon discovered that Long was willing to give them a whiff, inducing a mild state of drunkenness. From these dizzy, clandestine experiments, the doctor concluded that a stronger dose could render someone as unconscious as a statue.

On March 30, Dr. Long poured a small amount of ether onto a towel and held it over the nose of James Venable, then proceeded to carve off a half-inch cyst from the back of Venable's neck. At the time, neither doctor nor patient realized that this was the earliest use of an anaesthetic during a surgical procedure. Long charged two dollars for the excision and fifty cents for the ether, and he went on to perform at least nine more operations with ether as an anaesthetic, including the amputation of a black child's finger.

Meanwhile, the respectable, church-going folks of Jefferson were up in arms because Doc Long was using charms and potions to put people out of their senses. A "delegation" went to his house late one night and told him that the practice of sorcery must stop or there would be a lynching. Long, unwilling to stick his neck out, suspended his research.

CARL MOORE   Next time you trim your toenails, why not give Dr. Carl Moore a call before you chuck the clippings in the dustbin? He may need them.

Dr. Moore, who chairs the Chemistry Department of Chicago's Loyola University, placed an ad in the college paper asking for donations of clippings—in full sets of ten only—from the student body (and the students' bodies.) He was neither prey to some arcane addiction nor joking. In fact, toenail envelopes were placed conveniently throughout the campus along with questionnaires on the donor's medical history, race, and other vital statistics. He asked that clippings be scoured of dirt and nail polish, noting that "They're easier to wash while still attached."

Of course, Dr. Moore had good reason to covet his neighbors' toenails: with them he would investigate the presence of such trace elements as zinc, iron, and mercury in human tissue. Students not only at Loyola but as far afield as California came through with daily sackfuls of fresh clippings. Actually, he had wanted only 1,000 sets; he got far more. Then, a newspaper reporter erroneously identified Dr. Moore as a teacher at neighboring Northwestern University, and that school too was swamped with unsolicited toenails, all of which were turned over to Dr. Moore for filing.

ROBERT T. NELSON   There were actually two Robert T. Nelsons, father and son. Nelson senior was a Chicago businessman who in the 1920s contrived and marketed a brass cylinder about the size of a man's thumb and packed with a mysterious radioactive element called vrilium. Wear the vrilium tube around your neck, said Nelson, or pin it to your blouse or shirtfront like an American Legion button, and its potent emanations would banish viruses, bacteria, and other vermin forever.

Nelson senior died in 1935, before the vrilium tube really got off the ground, but Nelson *fils* renamed it "The Magic Spike," formed the Vrilium Products Co. in 1944, and made a small fortune, sometimes charging as much as $300 for the strange device. Chicago Mayor Kelly showed up at the 1948 Democratic National Convention with the thing dangling from his neck, and said, "I don't pretend to know how it works, but it relieves pain like all get-out."

In 1950 the federal government moved in on Nelson and his Vrilium Products Company, first subjecting the Magic Spike to the ruthless gaze of the geiger counter. When the needle failed to budge, Nelson futilely offered that "an unrecognized form of radioactivity" was at work. Charged in Chicago Federal District Court with "false and misleading" advertising, Nelson produced legions of happy customers to testify on his behalf, including one man who claimed that prior to purchasing a Magic Spike 11 years earlier, he had been chronically short of breath and unable to walk against the wind. "After he got the spike," *Time* magazine reported, "he said he walked against the wind fine." Later the same spike brought relief to his pet dachshund, Hector, suffering from a paralyzed backside. Another user told the court how the spike had cured his arthritis as well as breathed new life into his wife's drooping violets; still another offered that his wife was easier to live with thanks to the spike's mysterious charm.

But the Feds weren't buying. When one of the tubes was broken open for analysis, the vrilium turned out to be rat poison.

CHARLES OSBORNE While slaughtering a hog in 1922, Charles Osborne of Anthon, Iowa, contracted the hiccups. He has been hiccupping ever since, the longest continuous case on record.

Experiments conducted by Dr. Edward Engleman, a researcher at the California Medical Center in San Francisco, have demonstrated that a teaspoonful of sugar swallowed dry can be effective treatment for spasmodic glottal closures. Sugar worked immediately in 15 out of 17 hiccuppers who had been afflicted for only a few hours. For patients suffering chronic attacks, lasting anywhere from 18 hours to six weeks, the treatment brought relief in 16 out of 22 instances. Dr. Engleman theorizes that the sugar irritates the nerves at the back of the throat, counteracting the hiccup reflex. Sand or salt, it is said, would provide the same results.

So far, neither sugar, nor breathing into a paper bag, nor a sudden fright, nor drinking ten swallows of water has done Mr. Osborne a bit of good.

RAYMOND PALMER In the mid-1940s Raymond Palmer edited a sci-fi pulp magazine called *Amazing Stories* that was not above fobbing off the occasional fabrication as unvarnished truth. But Palmer carried off the greatest ruse of his career in 1945 with a series of stories, "articles" he called them, about life among the *abandoneros,* a subterranean race of malevolent and misshapen dwarves whose only fun is in making life hell for us surface-dwelling folk.

Based on a series of mysterious visions by Richard Shaver, a welder from Pennsylvania, the stories explained that the *deros,* as they were known, had once been the slaves of Lemuria, a now-defunct land-mass in the South Pacific *(or the Indian Ocean, depending on which theorist you've signed on with).* What drove the deros underground in the first place was a spate of unbearably strong solar radiation. What keeps them occupied now that they're there is a variety of technologically sophisticated, mechanical mischief makers, such as tractor raybeams good for derailing trains, surgical ray cannons capable of performing long-distance surgery on unwitting humans, a mechanical nightmare inducer, death ray devices, and a "stim machine" that drives men and women to the height of unbearable passion. This apparatus, coupled with innate telekinetic powers, has enabled the deros over the years to cause—ready?—shipwrecks, fires, air disasters, nervous breakdowns, floods, mass thievery, epidemic impotence, fractured toes, and gas attacks. Judge Crater was stolen away by the deros, Shaver reported, and Palmer claimed they'd even had the gall to swipe copy from his typewriter.

Palmer snowed thousands of readers with the "Great Shaver Mystery," and was ultimately ordered by his publisher to end the nonsense. In later years he owned and ran the Venture Bookshop in Evanston, Illinois, stacked with such nonliterary wares as "Aura Goggles," which makes visible to the wearer auras of "the human body, animals, and inanimate things."

SETH PANCOAST Born in 1823, Dr. Pancoast wrote *The Kabbala: or the True Science of Light* (1883). A sequel to the work of Augustus J. Pleasanton, it was printed in blue with a red border girding each page, and explained how the ancient Jewish mystics had used blue and red light as a cure for diseases. A special chapter on "Light in the Vegetable Kingdom" is included. Pancoast died in 1889.

LYDIA ESTES PINKHAM The most famous female face of the nineteenth century belonged to Lydia Estes Pinkham, the self-proclaimed "mother to the women of the world," whose matronly countenance appeared on every bottle of her patented, wonder-working Vegetable Compound. From 1875 right on through the 1920s, druggists and grocers sold millions of gallons of this high-potency syrup, guaranteed to cure such mysterious female complaints as "falling of the womb" and "weakness of the generative organs."

Despite rigorous testing, doctors were never able to discover any genuine therapeutic benefits attributable to unicorn root, pleurisy root, and the other exotic ingredients contained in the mixture. In fact, the only active "active ingredient" was alcohol—a staggering 18 percent by volume. Mrs. Pinkham, a stern W.C.T.U. member, always insisted that alcohol was added "solely as a solvent and preservative," and many prominent Temperance leaders used and endorsed the Compound. The company always maintained that Prohibition had nothing to do with the sudden boom in sales, to men as well as women, after 1919.

An important sideline of the business was the "Department of Advice" that Mrs. Pinkham personally directed. Thousands of women, reluctant to discuss their gynecological problems with male doctors, wrote in requesting medical counsel. She was not at all reluctant to diagnose and prescribe by mail, usually recommending a change in diet, frequent exercise, cleanliness, and a tablespoon of Vegetable Compound every four hours. Judging from the testimonials that poured in, this regimen was effective in a surprising number of cases.

So popular was kindly Mrs. Pinkham that her company was reluctant to part with her. In 1905 the advertisements for Vegetable Compound clearly implied that she was still in the pink of health and dispensing her wonderful advice to women all over the world. Edward Bok, the editor of *The Ladies Home Journal,* grew suspicious. When Bok uncovered the truth, he ran the Pinkham advertisement side-by-side with a photograph of the good woman's grave; the legend cut into her tombstone indicated she had gone to glory 22 years previously.

245

AUGUSTUS J. PLEASANTON   Many thousands of health-conscious Americans during the 1870s looked at the world through blue-colored glass, a craze incited by a Civil War general turned medical authority, Augustus J. Pleasanton. In his popular volume entitled *The Influence of the Blue Ray of Sunlight and the Blue Color of the Sky* he demonstrated with a kind of scientific sleight of hand how sunlight passing through a pane of blue window glass could cure everything from warts to blindness to gangrene.

E. H. PRATT   In the 1920s a Chicago physician named E. H. Pratt spread the gospel of "orificial therapy," which promised relief from a catalogue of illnesses by relaxing the body's orifices.

MR. and MRS. FREDERICK H. PRINCE   The Roman Emperor Vespasian won few friends when in 70 A.D. he imposed a tax on the use of public urinals. His own son Titus was one of those who protested that taxing basic bodily functions was a heartless and undignified way to raise revenue. In reply the aged emperor is supposed to have held some coins to the youth's nose and said, "See, my child, money doesn't smell." It should be noted, however, that the absence of an odor is no proof that money is sanitary; and the nasty possibility that germs were lurking in the millings of a quarter or in the fabric of a $100 bill obsessed Mr. and Mrs. Frederick H. Prince.

Frederick Prince had good reason to worry. He was probably the wealthiest man in New England in 1929 even after the Wall Street debacle; he owned the Chicago stockyards outright and was on the boards of some 20 different railroads. That meant exposure to a lot of money and a lot of germs. To protect his wife's delicate health, he never allowed her to handle coins or currency for fear she would come down with chronic septicemia, venereal disease, or worse. Everywhere she went, a French-born Irishman named Thomas accompanied her, disbursing filthy lucre when necessary.

There were other risks, of course. Due to the possibility of infection, Mrs. Prince would not sleep on the same bedroom two nights in a row. She slumbered in a specially-constructed oversized cradle which could be wheeled from room to room, outfoxing the predatory microbes. As an additional precaution the walls of the bedroom she selected were draped with fresh sheets and drenched with antiseptics before she retired.

FRANCIS I. REGARDIE   Freud had his couch, Reich his orgone box, and Francis Regardie his tongue depressor, bedpan, and mop. A psychotherapist on the West Coast—Studio City, to be exact—Regardie has proven that the most effective way to treat an uncommunicative patient is to make him vomit. Or, to use his more clinical language, "to induce a gag reflex."

"My procedure," Dr. Regardie wrote in an article in the Winter, 1952, issue of *Complex,* "is to let him gag anywhere up to a dozen times. . . . In itself, the *style* of gagging is an admirable index to the magnitude of the inhibitory apparatus. Some gag with finesse, with delicacy, without noise. These are, categorically, the most difficult patients to handle. Their character armor is almost impenetrable. . . . They require to be encouraged to regurgitate with noise, without concealment of their discomfort and disgust. Others will cough and spit, yet still remain unproductive. Still others sneer and find the whole procedure a source of cynical amusement. . . ."

DR. BENJAMIN RUSH   In his position as Surgeon General of the Continental Army, Dr. Benjamin Rush was quite possibly the most influential physician practicing in eighteenth-century America. A greatly gifted and benevolent man, he did much to improve the conditions in mental hospitals, promoting cleanliness and occupational therapy for his patients. Regrettably, however, he also championed the use of terror as a treatment for insanity. With an eye toward frightening schizophrenics into the pink of mental health, Rush advised pouring water down their sleeves "so that it may descend into the arm pits and down the trunk of the body" for 15 or 20 minutes. If that didn't work, Rush tried death threats, or starving the patient for weeks at a time, or the "bath of surprise" in which the unsuspecting patient was dropped through a trap door into a tub of cold water, or the "well cure" which entailed confining the patient in the bottom of an empty well and pouring water down on top of him. Barbaric as this regimen may seem today, it was considered a progressive amelioration in the treatment of the insane, who had previously been locked in chains and subjected to dungeon-like conditions.

Rush also deserves to be remembered for a paper he presented at a 1797 meeting of the American Philosophical Society, wherein he argued that black skin color was a disease akin to leprosy. To support his novel contention, he cited the case of one Henry Moss, a Virginia slave, whose skin supposedly turned white when he moved to Pennsylvania.

FREDERICK SMITH If you secretly chew your toenails, there's no reason to be ashamed. Professor Frederick Smith, a psychologist at Brigham Young University, was doing a study of fingernail biting in 1978 when he inadvertently discovered that up to 15 percent of all Americans may also take an occasional nibble at their toes. Professor Smith is concerned that many toenail biters think of their habit as "an abnormal practice that would invite the scorn of others." He hopes that his findings will help the nearly 30 million closet chewers to recover their self-esteem and think of themselves as healthy, normal individuals once again.

JAMES E. SMITH In the expert opinion of James E. Smith, Buffalo, New York, doesn't need a weatherman to know which way the wind blows. On February 8, 1977, Smith, a 56-year-old meteorologist with the National Weather Service, put in for immediate retirement, calling Buffalo's severe winter "the final straw." At the time of his announcement the city had already received 160 inches of snow, its worst winter on record, and residents were bracing for at least six more weeks of hard weather.

Smith said he first started to think about early retirement when he was trapped in a November blizzard while driving his car to work. He was trapped again a block from his house when another blinding snowstorm struck on January 28. "After all this, I just asked myself, What am I doing here?" he said.

CYRUS TEED Most hollow-earth theorists are conservative folk, content with their notion that the planet's interior is home to a civilization vastly more interesting than our own. But Cyrus Teed was a hollow-earther who marched to a different drummer. He was certain that *we're* the ones on the inside, and he spent a lifetime spreading that truth.

A Union Army private during the Civil War, Teed had been quietly practicing herb medicine and alchemy in Utica, New York, in 1869 when his pursuits were interrupted by a beautiful, if hallucinatory seeress who told him that (a) we inhabit the earth's interior and (b) it was up to him to assume the role of messiah and bring this truth home to mankind. It made sense to Teed, perhaps because it was comforting to think the earth surrounds and protects us like a womb or a sealskin coat. Within a year he had published two works on the subject: the immodestly titled, *Illumination of Koresh: Marvelous Experience of the Great Alchemist at Utica, New York,* and *The Cellular Cosmogony,* wherein he explained that the hollow shell we call earth has 17 concentric layers of rock, minerals, and metal; that the continents and oceans are distributed about the surface of the innermost layer, and that the sun hangs in the center of the void, showing us first its fiery side, then its black one to create the illusion of sunrise and sunset. Whatever else we might see shining in the heavens—a full moon, for example, or the Big Dipper—is an optical joke played by a mirthful sun. And if you're wondering why you can't look skyward on a clear day and see China, it's because the distance is too great and the atmosphere is too thick. What keeps us on the ground is centrifugal force, not gravity, and *outside* the earth there's just nothing at all. As Teed himself writes, "Life Develops and Matures in a Shell, Egg, or Womb; Hence We Are Inside of It."

Teed left Utica in 1886 for Chicago, which became the headquarters of his astonishingly broad-based quasi-Christian Koreshan movement. Besides establishing a magazine called *The Guiding Star* and a "College of Life," he attracted scores of followers to his commune, Koreshan Unity. Although his wife had left him years before when his neighbors in Utica accounted him mad, Teed was sufficiently of this world to dress nattily—he was given to Prince Albert coats and white silk bow-ties—and the *Chicago Tribune* credited him with "a strange mesmerizing influence over his converts, particularly the other sex," who, not unimportantly, comprised 75 percent of his following.

In 1897, Teed, accompanied by the Koreshan Geodetic Staff, ambled down to the Old Illinois Drainage Canal and measured the shoreline with T-squares, thus proving to the world that the earth's surface was indeed curved upward like a raccoon's smile. It was an experiment he was to reproduce a few years later near Fort Myers, Florida, where he established the town of Estero, billed as The New Jerusalem, the future capital of this inside-out world. By the time of his death in 1908, 200 people had settled in Estero. Teed had expected 8 million.

But what a faithful 200 they were. Heeding his vow to rise Lazarus-like from his coffin and lead the way to Paradise, they kept watch over his unburied corpse for two days until it began to rot. When the county health officer ordered him buried, they sealed their prophet in a concrete sarcophagus. Thirteen years later it was washed out to sea by a tropical storm.

(In the 1930s the Nazi Admiralty dug up Teed's old theories, gave them a German name, *Hohlweltlehre,* and tried to deploy them militarily against the British. In an experiment described in the June, 1946, issue of *Popular Astronomy,* a party of ten men, under the leadership of Dr. Heinz Fischer, an infrared expert, "was sent out from Berlin to the isle of Rügen [in the Baltic Sea] to photograph the British fleet with infrared equipment at an upward angle of some forty-five degrees." The experiment failed.)

CHARLES H. T. TOWNSEND Even before 1926, the name Charles Henry Tyler Townsend was one you mentioned only with the utmost caution if at all in the highest entomological circles. Despite impeccable credentials—graduate and doctoral degrees from George Washington University, articles in the field's most prestigious scholarly journals, a lifetime's work as a professional bug-watcher in the jungles of Brazil—Townsend's colleagues accounted him an incorrigible gadfly, a nitpicker, a bee in the bonnet of science, and an altogether ornery little bugger who had once publicly railed at the work of colleague Daniel Coquillet with such waspish invective that a third entomologist, W. R. Walton, was moved to sputter, "He would better not have been born insofar as the interests of science are concerned."

A year after that set-to, in April, 1926, Townsend embarked on the grandest folly of his career when he insisted that a certain species of deer botfly—namely, that of the genus *cephenemyia*—was the fastest creature found in nature, bar none. Now a Thomson's Gazelle has been clocked at 50 m.p.h. on a fast track and a cheetah at 70, but the insignificant *cephenemyia*, not a whole lot bigger than the period at the end of this sentence, could do 818 miles per hour, Dr. Townsend averred, without even panting.

In those pre-sonic boom days, when airplanes lumbered along at barely 250 m.p.h., it was astonishing to hear the good doctor posit that a magic aircraft endowed with the swiftness of the *cephenemyia* could circle the globe at 40 degrees above the equator in just 17 hours, thereby outracing the sun and remaining in daylight throughout the trip. The dreamers among his readership were duly enchanted, but others were skeptical. Howard Rappelye of the Coast and Geodetic Survey pointed out that Dr. Townsend had erred in putting the earth's circumference at 40°N latitude at 13,855 miles. It was actually *over 19,000* miles, he said, and a plane flying at 818 miles per hour would make it back to the starting point in 23.4 hours, not 17, outracing the sun by a far less dramatic 36 minutes. Too, Dr. Townsend had apparently gotten his east mixed with his west when he'd made his claims for the *cephenemyia:* another reader observed that an aircraft flying west faster than the sun would remain in *darkness,* not daylight, throughout the journey.

No matter, Dr. Townsend said. Such cavilling hardly undermined the wondrousness of the supersonic botfly, and in the September, 1927, issue of the *Journal of the New York Entomological Society,* he envisioned the future skies filled with mechanical "myiopeters" built, like insects, to flap their wings and attain speeds comparable to the *cephenemyia's.* It was in that article that he specified that only the male of the species flew at 818 miles per hour. "The males are faster than the females," he explained, "since they must overtake the latter for coition."

Although the entomological establishment ignored his absurd claims for the *cephenemyia,* the nonentomological world seemed only too thrilled to take them at face value. On August 18, 1929, for example, when a new world's airspeed record of 318 m.p.h. was established, *The New York Times* proclaimed idiotically, "Speed of Deer Fly Sets New Goal for Airplanes." Nine years later, so highly acclaimed a naturalist as Roy Chapman Andrews was writing in *Natural History* magazine, that "neither fins, feet, wheels, nor propeller-driven airplanes can compete with Nature's tiny speed champion." That article was reprinted the following New Year's Day in the *Illustrated London News,* where Irving Langmuir, a 1932 Nobel Prize winner in chemistry saw it, did some quick pencil-and-paper figuring, and concluded that Townsend's brain was full of bubbles. In a letter to *Science* magazine, he pointed out that at 818 miles per hour, a botfly would be moving against an air pressure of eight pounds per square inch, easily enough to crush it. Too, the fly would need to consume 1.5 times its own weight in food *every second* to keep up the speed. No doubt the botfly is a fast little devil, Langmuir conceded. On a good day, with the wind at its back, he allowed, it might get up to 25 miles per hour. The notion of 800 m.p.h. was insane.

Science writer William L. Laurence of *The New York Times* picked up on the Langmuir correspondence and on March 13 debunked Townsend's claims in print. Townsend tried twice to get a response printed in *Science,* and then, in March '39, a refutation of sorts appeared in the *Journal of the New York Entomological Society.* By now Townsend's prose had deteriorated as sadly as his reason ("When a man can jump as twice as high as the Washington Monument and live a year and a half without a bite or a drink, it will be time to judge insect metabolism and mechanics by man metabolism and mechanics"). Unable to refute Langmuir's argument, he bravely lopped 68 miles per hour off the insect's speed. Three years later he reduced it by another 50 m.p.h., still insisting that at 700 miles per hour the fly was uncatchable. In his *Manual of Myiology,* he wrote, "The writer and his father before him had exceptional eyesight . . . which may be compared to the superlative eyesight possessed by Percival Lowell, who saw and mapped many markings and objects on Mars that were wholly invisible to other astronomers."

It was an unfortunately chosen analogy at best; for the markings with which Lowell had earned his honor points with Townsend—which Lowell claimed were sure signs of life—ultimately turned out to be optical illusions. No matter, by now no one was listening to Townsend. Two years later he was dead.

WILBUR GLENN VOLIVA Columbus be damned! Any fool can see that the world is as flat as a filet of sole. But it took a man of gumption like Wilbur Glenn Voliva to say what many of us have secretly believed all along.

Assuming the world isn't spherical (how comforting to lay that old superstition to rest), one minor question remains: What shape is it? "Circular," Voliva stated flatly, quoting from memory long biblical passages to prove his point. What some people call the North Pole is actually the center of the circle, and the outer edge is bordered by a towering wall of ice, mistakenly referred to as the South Pole. God, in His infinite wisdom, put an insurmountable barrier there to keep the oceans from spilling into space and to prevent crazy Antarctic explorers from sailing right over the brink and killing themselves. As for Magellan and all the others who claim to have circumnavigated the globe, they merely cruised around the outer circumference of the disk, a commendable achievement, but hardly proof that the world is round.

Once we've corrected our misconceptions about terrestrial geography, the organization of the rest of the universe falls neatly into place. The sun, Voliva said, is 3,000 miles away, not 93 million; like the moon, it hovers in a continuous circle above the pancake-shaped earth. And the ancients were right about the sky: it's an arching blue-black vault to which the stars are fastened like so many Christmas tree ornaments.

Never guilty of false modesty, Voliva once said: "I can whip to smithereens any man in the world in a mental battle. ... I have never met any professor or student who knew as much on any subject as I do." To turn the cliché around, he was so smart that he was rich; and for many years the millionaire fundamentalist exercised complete ecclesiastical and secular authority over the small theocratic community of Zion City, Illinois. He ran an annual advertisement in the Chicago and Milwaukee papers offering $5,000 to anyone who could prove to him that the world was not flat. The award went uncollected.

ROBERT J. WHITE A Cleveland neurosurgeon, Dr. Robert J. White jolted an international gathering of organ transplant specialists in Fiuggi, Italy, with this rallying cry: "We must, we *want* to think of transplanting the head."

That was in 1974 and Dr. White has since shown himself to be as much a doer as a talker. To date he has successfully performed ten successful head transplants on monkeys, some of which continued functioning for as long as 36 hours. In his latest efforts, Dr. White managed to keep the relocated head seeing, smelling, hearing, and responding to stimuli.

254

ROBERT A. WOOD   Find yourself short of breath lately? Or just dog-tired, headachy, and out of sorts? Maybe you're having no luck fighting off a nasty bout of syphilis, TB, cancer, appendicitis, gout, or incipient madness. If so, said Dr. Robert A. Wood, the great Chicago naturopath, chuck your prescription medicines in the dustbin and banish the surgeon's scalpel. All you really need is an enema.

Dr. Wood, who rose to become president of the American Naturopathic Association, was a lifelong champion of chlorophyll, vegetable and fruit juices, raw cow's milk, and distilled water as the ultimate balm for nature's woes. But above all he believed in "colonic irrigation, the greatest fever reducer of them all." A brief fast, followed by a daily enema— and make it a *cold* one—for four days will clear up all but the stubbornest cases of appendicitis, he offered, and he once used the magic bag to cure an elderly man of syphilis, although he'd been infected 49 years before.

(In England, Dr. Wood's counterpart is Barbara Cartland, who urges her countrymen to scour their bowels clean as a hound's tooth every 12 hours. "We all know that the setting sun of the British nation is constipation," she says.)

DR. DORAN D. ZIMMER   After five years of exhaustive laboratory study sponsored by the United States Public Health Service, Dr. Doran D. Zimmer of Daytona, Florida, has concluded that kissing can cause tooth decay.

Sexy People

DR. RONALD BARFIELD   Might there be an element of truth in the Pied Piper legend? Two Rutgers University biologists, Dr. Ronald Barfield and Lynette Geyer, think so.

While making "a standard observation of sexual behavior," they found that male rats, after a bout of sexual intercourse, emit a contented high-frequency snore. Apparently this is the male's way of saying "I've had it, baby, leave me alone," or to put it more scientifically, "The call functions as a signal of social withdrawal while the post-ejaculatory male is recuperating." So long as the male sings this drowsy song, the females refrain from the hopping, darting, and ear wiggling that are considered sexually provocative among rats.

The signals, at a frequency of 22 kilohertz, accompany the rat's contented sigh-like breathing. And this call continues throughout the male's refractory period when he is incapable of renewed sexual response. The signal is also characteristic of males that have been defeated in a fight or females who are trying to discourage the unwanted advances of rodent romeos, which leads Barfield and Geyer to speculate that 22 kilohertz may be a general carrier frequency for rats who want to avoid social contacts. A loudspeaker broadcasting a continuous 22 kilohertz signal (a pitch too high for humans to hear) could serve as a kind of ultrasonic contraceptive for rats, the researchers say.

But ultrasound may also have a positive roll in the sex life of rats. Dr. Barfield is now investigating the possibility that another song may be used to woo the female and ensure a fruitful coupling. One imagines a modern Pied Piper playing an ultrasonic love song to charm the rats out of infested tenements and dock areas.

256

Dr. John R. Brinkley, scourge of Toggenburg goats *(The Kansas State Historical Society, Topeka)*

DR. JOHN ROMULUS BRINKLEY   How fitting that Dr. John Brinkley, M.D., Ph.D., M.C., LL.D., D.P.H., Sc.D., Lieut. U.S.N.R., should wear a goatee! In the 1930s, at the height of his outrageous career, Brinkley and his scalpel-happy staff were engrafting some 500 pairs of "goat glands" (i.e., testicles) a day into the groins of grateful male patients. His operation, which promised sexual rejuvenation, sorely disappointed many transplant recipients when tissue rejection set in. But financially his "private" hospitals in Kansas and Texas were a howling success; at $750 per gland, $1,500 for a matched set, Brinkley was grossing over $1 million a year. Entire herds of Toggenburg goats were decimated. The doctor always used Toggenburgs because "other breeds, while effective, may give the patient a permanently goaty smell."

With the enormous profits from his potency factories, Brinkley bought twelve Cadillacs, three yachts, a goat farm in Oklahoma, a flock of penguins (for medical research), a trove of diamonds, and XERA, the most powerful radio station on the North American continent. Every night thousands of rural families from the Mississippi to the Rocky Mountains tuned-in to "The Question Box Hour" to hear Dr. John read letters from ailing listeners. Sight unseen, he diagnosed everything from cancers to "elliptical epizootia," and prescribed—by number—one of his 50 patent medicines. Number 36 was typical of the lot; especially concocted for "miseries of the back," it consisted of blue dye mixed with hydrochloric acid.

By 1932 his popularity was so great that he decided to run for governor of Kansas on the slogan "Let's pasture the goats on the Statehouse lawn." Although he narrowly lost to Alf Landon, Brinkley could take some consolation from the fact that he carried four counties in neighboring Oklahoma, where he wasn't even a candidate. True to form, his politics were as bad as his medicine. While claiming to be a populist Republican, he secretly bankrolled a number of fascist causes including the Silver Shirts, a native anti-Semitic organization modeled after Hitler's Brown Shirts.

ELLEN COOPERPERSON   At first Judge Scileppi denied the petition on the grounds of "inanity," but 31-year-old Ellen Cooperman of Babylon, New York, finally won the right in 1978 to change her name legally to Ellen Cooperperson. The business cost her $350 but it was worth every penny.

"I wanted to show my strong feelings about the sexist nature of our language," Ms. Cooperperson explained. "I think when you change the language, you change people's attitudes."

THOMAS EWELL   A United States Navy surgeon, Thomas Ewell, proposed an original and, no doubt, effective "remedy or corrective for fruitful nature" in 1806. Black slaves, he erroneously believed, were as fertile as the delta of the Nile; moreover, they were wont to copulate out-of-doors; this led to the "inescapable" conclusion that "coition will always be unfruitful unless it be done in pure air." Carrying this fascinating logic one step further, he advised couples who did not wish to conceive to embrace "in vessels filled with carbonic acid or azotic gas." (Had more young men and women heeded his counsel there would indeed have been a drastic decline in population.)

JOHANN HOCH "Women are all right in their place," Johann Hoch told reporters, "but marry only one." The dapper, nearsighted little German-American knew whereof he spoke. Over a span of 18 years he had married between 43 and 50 women of sundry ages, sizes, and descriptions, swindled them out of their savings, and, in at least a dozen instances, murdered them for their insurance money with toe-curling doses of arsenic. The newspapers styled him "the modern Bluebeard" and "America's greatest lady killer."

Hoch's homicidal love life was too long and complicated to describe in full detail; law enforcement officials could never be exactly sure how many spouses he had polished off. Rich widows were his favorite target. He would woo them with breathtaking haste, wed them, and promptly withdraw all the money from their bank accounts. If there was no further property to inherit, he would simply disappear. Otherwise there would be a highly profitable "undertaking." The clue that ultimately enabled the police to capture Hoch (variously known as Schmidt, Calford, Cudney, Dotz, etc.) was his sentimental habit of adopting as an alias the name of the deceased husband of the widow he had most recently abandoned or poisoned.

Arrested by New York City police, he confessed his multiple crimes and, as a legacy to would-be Don Juans, revealed six tried and true ways to win a woman:
1. Nine out of ten women can be won by flattery.
2. Never let a woman know her shortcomings.
3. Always appear to a woman to be the anxious one.
4. Women like to be told pleasant things about themselves.
5. When you make love, be ardent and earnest.
6. The average man can fool the average woman if he will only let her have her own way at the start.

Hoch was extradited to Chicago and hanged in 1905.

SOLOMON FEGION Solomon Fegion, 103, a resident of Stockton, California, was sued for divorce by his 100-year-old wife on grounds of adultery. The divorce was granted despite Mr. Fegion's protest that "a woman looks like a man to me now."

DR. SEYMOUR FISCHER In his diligently researched book *The Female Orgasm,* Dr. Seymour Fischer makes a plucky attempt to resolve the age-old mysteries of coitus. We pass along two findings which may or may not prove helpful in the bedroom: "The more sexually responsive a woman rates herself, the higher her rectal temperature." "The greater a woman's intercourse frequency, the greater is the temperature of her hand compared to her leg."

FREDERICK HOLLICK Frederick Hollick, a roving medical expert who lectured New Englanders in the 1840s on human anatomy, sexual dysfunction, and the importance of roughage in the diet, once got hold of the Annual Report of the Massachusetts State Lunatic Asylum and drew from it some remarkable lessons on the link between masturbation and the choice of profession.

Simply put, Dr. Hollick explained, young men placed in sedentary jobs are more likely to masturbate till they go mad than those who work out of doors. The statistics: "Among merchants, printers, students and shoemakers, fifty percent of the insanity arises from masturbation, and only twelve percent from intemperance; while among carpenters, blacksmiths, and others who are actively employed, thirty-five percent of the insanity arises from intemperance and only thirteen percent from masturbation." The lesson for parents is clear, Dr. Hollick concluded: guide your sons into strenuous work in the great outdoors, lest "the monotonous inactivity of a counting house desk, the distasteful plodding of an office or some merely intellectual profession" render him "listless, dogged, and self-debased," and likely to surrender to the siren call of self-abuse.

As for his own profession, Dr. Hollick is nothing if not

honest: "I can find physicians made insane by other causes," he said, "but [cannot] find a single case of one becoming insane from masturbation."

Of course, self-abuse was but one of Dr. Hollick's concerns; another was diet, and its relationship to the libido. To ward off impotence, he counseled, fill up on potatoes, celery, parsnips, onions, mushrooms, truffles if you can get them, olives, tomatoes, lima beans, and above all, *asparagus*. Canvasback duck also makes a potent pepper-upper, Dr. Hollick wrote; so does marijuana.

On the other hand, those who need restraining should avoid these foods and eschew coffee, particularly if they are "disposed to involuntary emissions." In all cases, avoid constipation, the hand maiden of impotence and derangement.

Timing is also important. "Sexual indulgence just after eating is nearly certain to be followed by indigestion, even if does not cause immediate vomiting," he stated. "Just *before* eating also the same evils may follow. . . ."

Dr. Hollick's lectures drew packed houses as well as rave notices in such responsible journals as the *Boston Post*, whose editorialists were greatly taken with Dr. Hollick's constant companion, an ingeniously crafted dummy containing "a facsimile of all the important machinery of the human body." The good doctor's best-known work is *The Male Generative Organs in Health and Disease, from Infancy to Old Age*. It went through 120 editions—or so Hollick claimed.

CAPTAIN KEMBLE Found guilty of "lewd and unseemly behavior," Captain Kemble of Boston was placed in the public stocks for two hours in 1656. His crime: kissing his wife in public on the Sabbath after a three-year sojourn at sea.

CHARLES KNOWLTON Dr. Charles Knowlton of Taunton, Massachusetts, was the "father of birth control" and a leading proponent of the vaginal douche. In 1832 he issued *The Fruits of Philosophy,* subtitled *The Private Companion of Young Married People,* which was the first clinical work on the taboo subject of contraception since a Greek tract from the second century A.D..

By today's standards many of Dr. Knowlton's prescriptions seem rather quaint. Vinegar, he said, is the most effective spermicide, although on cold nights it should be mixed with a little "spirits" to prevent freezing. But a few of his recommended preparations, such as "sugar of lead," sound distasteful at best, and possibly lethal.

Knowlton was no libertine; he warned young couples against the dangers of frequent "connexion" pointing out that the loss of an ounce of semen was as debilitating as the loss of 40 ounces of blood. Overindulgence might conceivably impair mental functioning, promote disease, bring on melancholia, or even destroy the partners' respect for one another. Bachelors, he advised, should eat a diet of vegetables and milk to suppress immoral urges, while the newly married should consume red meat, turtles, oysters, and red wine in moderation as an incitement to lovemaking.

Although *The Fruits of Philosophy* was couched in the most chaste of terms, it was far too daring for the fuddy-duddies of New England. One lawyer accused Knowlton of publishing a "complete recipe" for carrying on the trade of prostitution. The *Boston Medical and Surgical Journal* sternly denounced all contraception as "unnatural" and averred, "the less that is known about it by the public at large, the better it will be for the morals of the community." Knowlton was slapped with a number of indictments. A court in Cambridge, Massachusetts, sentenced him to three months hard labor in the House of Correction. Then, as now, nothing spurred book sales like a little notoriety. In Knowlton's home town of Taunton, where he was heavily fined, a gentleman of the jury approached him after the trial and said, "Well, we brought you in guilty—we didn't see how we could well get rid of it, still I like your book, and you must let me have one of them." Far and away the most popular sex manual in a bluenosed age, *The Fruits of Philosophy* went through nine printings and sold over 277,000 copies.

DR. COY LAY Coy Lay, M.D., is a recent past president of the American Fertility Society.

CARRICA LE FAVRE Miss Le Favre was the author of *Mother's Help and Child's Best Friend,* a boon to young parents determined to raise morally upright children amidst the lewd temptations of the age (1890). To keep the child's lower instincts in check, she counselled, forbid him to play marbles, eat between meals, or masturbate. Conversely, juggling Indian clubs in front of an open window and flying kites will do wonders for the child's loftier instincts.

ANN TROW LOHMAN The newspapers ungallantly referred to her as "the wickedest woman in the city" and "Madame Killer." It was a shabby way to treat a lady whose discretion and surgical skill had saved the reputations of many prominent families. By day she was an outcast. By night many glittering carriages came around to her large and dignified brownstone home on the corner of Fifth Avenue and Fifty-second Street in New York, and muffled female figures in fashionable dress would hurry into her basement office.

Mrs. Ann Trow Lohman (1812–78), or "Madame Restell" as she was known professionally, advertised herself in the *New York Herald* as a "professor of midwifery," but few of the pregnancies she attended ever went a full nine months. She was the country's most expensive and most sought-after abortionist. True, a good part of her income was derived from dispensing "infallible French female pills" through the mails. But if matters had gone beyond the point where pills could help, she guaranteed "a cure at one interview." There is no way of knowing how many young society women she "cured." It is recorded, however, that she gave her stepdaughter a $50,000 European honeymoon in 1854, and that she died leaving an estate officially valued at over $1 million.

So notorious was her "hospital" that the adjoining lots went undeveloped for decades, even though they were among the most attractively located parcels of Manhattan real estate. Ostracized from the polite society she served, Madame Restell made a public show of defiance every sunny afternoon by riding down Fifth Avenue in her opulent carriage, a liveried footman at the reins, past the site where her sworn enemy Archbishop John J. Hughes was erecting Saint Patrick's Cathedral. As the grim-faced woman passed through the streets, grubby urchins shouted at her, "Yah, your house is built on babies' skulls!" Once she was arrested in connection with the death of a young girl who had come to her for "treatment," and though there was plenty of evidence to convict her, she was acquitted. (The judge was politely reminded of skeletons lurking in certain high and mighty closets, and given a $100,000 present.)

God-fearing people concluded that she was too rich and politically powerful to be driven out of practice. George W. Matsell, the superintendent of police, was one of many public officials on her payroll. Then one day in 1878 a handsome, bewhiskered young man came to consult her about a personal problem. He was desperately poor, he confided; his wife was pregnant; and the birth of another child would bring them to financial ruin. Madame Restell listened sympathetically, gave him her professional advice, and provided him with medicine and instruments for his wife. At that moment, he ungratefully identified himself as none other than Anthony Comstock, the bluenosed secretary of the Society for the Suppression of Vice, a man who had personally incinerated 160 tons of obscene pictures and books. Comstock ordered a coach to convey the wealthy abortionist to the Tombs prison for arraignment. En route, she offered him $40,000 to drop his charges. He refused, but Madame Restell secured her release on bail. She returned to her Fifth Avenue home, where early one morning before her case came to trial she slit her throat with a carving knife and died in a pool of blood.

264

JOHN McDOWALL "O, the harlots!" Reverend John McDowall exclaimed to his diary just after his first soul-saving incursion into New York City's seamiest precincts in 1830. Intent on bringing "moral and religious improvement" to the area, the Reverend McDowall consorted with pimps, whores, thieves, and pickpockets, harangued them with endless sermons and pleas to reform, and occasionally induced a fallen woman to quit her work and enter one of the Magdalen Refuges, under the auspices of his Female Benevolent Society. Once he'd gotten them there, he would dose them with more religious persuasion. Most turned a deaf ear and ultimately returned to whoring.

The Reverend McDowall learned much about the New York underworld, and despite his protests that "modesty and purity forbid a minute detail," he published descriptions of the most lurid sort in his *McDowall's Journal.* For every New Yorker praising the reverend for his zeal there was one who damned him as a pornographer. In point of fact, *McDowall's Journal* was pretty spicy stuff. It boiled with accounts of the sexual excesses of Tahitian maidens brought to New York to work as prostitutes and contained such a complete list of bordellos that it was known informally as the Whorehouse Directory. Truth to tell, McDowall's insistence that the city's prostitutes numbered 20,000 seemed inflated. As one critic figured it, if there were as many as 20,000 and each entertained only three times a day, it would mean an astonishing 10 million illicit couplings annually—and that one out of every two adult males in the city was visiting a prostitute three times a week!

McDowall was as appalled by the easy availability of obscene materials as he was by the omnipresence of whores. In 1834 he organized an exhibit of pornography in its every form at a New York church—pamphlets, etchings, playing cards, music boxes and snuff boxes emblazoned with dirty pictures, even raunchy pastries. Three hundred clergymen came to ogle and gape.

Ultimately, McDowall was accused of embezzling funds

contributed to the ostensibly nonprofit publication and was indicted by a grand jury on charges of subverting the morals of the city. He quit his editorship, was soon defrocked, and died in obscurity in 1836.

DR. GREGORY PINCUS   Commissioned by Planned Parenthood to develop an ideal contraceptive "aesthetically satisfactory to both husband and wife," Dr. Gregory Pincus of Shrewsbury, Massachusetts, begat the oral contraceptive pill in 1954.

SUSAN GILBERT and ROXANNE RITCHIE   Consumerism reached a fever pitch at Massachusetts Institute of Technology when two coeds, Susan Gilbert and Roxanne Ritchie, published the results of some highly controversial research in *Thursday,* a campus newspaper. Their findings, headlined "Consumer Guide to M.I.T. Men," named names and provided x-rated ratings of the sexual methodology employed by 36 male undergraduates the two women said they had slept with. Around campus it quickly came to be known as the M.I.T. "coarse guide."

Each unwitting subject in the study was ranked on a scale from zero (" 'I did it! ' he said. 'Did what?' I asked.") to four stars ("Close your eyes and waves crash, mountains erupt, and flowers bloom"). The men, especially those who ranked near the bottom of the survey, were not amused. One whose prowess in bed was likened to "an energetic rock," retorted: "Roxanne Ritchie hardly deserved more than a half star." Meanwhile, M.I.T. president Jerome Wiesner (not ranked) called the report "a gross violation of our norms of taste and regard for privacy." Disciplinary proceedings were initiated against the two intrepid researchers, the editor of the paper, and another student who originally suggested the project.

Miss Ritchie aggressively defended the study on feminist grounds: "I was hoping to increase the sensitivity of men (all men, not just the ones mentioned) by turning the tables on them and showing them how it feels to be used, to be treated

266

as a sex object, and to be judged for their sexual performance."

DR. F. BRANTLEY SCOTT Bionics took a giant step forward with the invention in 1973 of the first man-made penis capable of erection. By merging the latest techiques of plastic surgery and micro-engineering, Dr. F. Brantley Scott, a urologist at the Baylor College of Medicine in Houston, was able to create from scratch a functional organ activated by a tiny hydraulic system. To make a short story long, fluid from a reservoir in the abdomen is pumped into the penis causing it to swell and rise on command.

The device was used successfully in April, 1977, in the first female-to-male transsexual operation. Dr. Joseph Montie, a urologist, and Dr. Charles Puckett, a plastic surgeon, the attending physicians in the case, described their patient as an "extremely intelligent" student of bacteriology at the University of Missouri.

"I've seen him around town several times," Dr. Montie told reporters, "and he always seems to be with reasonably attractive young ladies. What can I say? It looks like he's doing fine. The thing is working well. We're very pleased with how it's working." Neither doctor would reveal the dimensions of the implant.

ALLAN R. STAIB, D. R. LOGAN, and RICHARD D. WILLARD "A curved line," Mae West once said "is the loveliest distance between two points." And now, far-fetched as it seems, three scientists claim to have developed an effective method of adding lovely inches to even the flattest chest without silicone injections, without mail-order vacuum gadgets, and without repetitious "cheerleading exercises."

Allan R. Staib and D. R. Logan of the University of Houston believe that *hypnosis* may make falsies and A-cups as extinct as the pterodactyl in our time. According to a recent article in *The American Journal of Clinical Hypnosis,* the two mammary researchers were able to stimulate breast growth in mature adult women by putting them into a trance and suggesting that they were back in their teens. The average enlargement observed was a little over an inch and a half in circumference, and four out of five women retained the gain three months after the treatment ended.

An independent study by Dr. Richard D. Willard of the Institute of Behavioral and Mind Studies at Fort Wayne, Indiana, corroborated the Staib and Logan results. Simple suggestions of warmth or blood flow in the breasts are enough to promote growth, Willard found. The volunteers in the study used self-hypnosis and cassettes much of the time, and their average enhancement was also about an inch and a half.

The professional journal *Modern Medicine* cautiously concludes that hypnotism should be regarded as a promising "non-surgical, non-chemical, but still experimental therapy." If subsequent testing bears out these early findings, hypnotic breast development may bring recognition and prominence to Staib, Logan, and Willard, not to mention bevies of underendowed beauties.

ALICE BUNKER STOCKHAM Those who heeded the commandments of *Tokology,* the guide for living, written and made famous by Dr. Stockham in the 1880s, avoided meat, strong drink, and copulation as most adults know it. While sex for procreative purposes was an admirable enterprise, she said, husbands who forced themselves on unwilling wives were no better than white slavers. Moreover, such sex risked hideous birth defects and general ill health in the children. In 1896 Dr. Stockham sang the praises of "Karezza" a peculiarly motionless, nonorgasmic brand of lovemaking, in a book of the same name. After an hour's karezza, she wrote, "the physical tension subsides, the spiritual exaltation increases, and not uncommonly visions of a transcendent life are seen and consciousness of new powers experienced."

Karezza, Dr. Stockham felt, should not be overdone—

268

twice a month was more than sufficient. In fact, she said, "Many find that even three or four months afford a greater impetus to power and growth as well as more personal satisfaction during the interval, the thousand-and-one lover-like attentions give reciprocal delight and are an anticipating prophecy of the ultimate union."

DR. ERWIN O. STRASSMAN Like many men before him, Dr. Erwin O. Strassman has made a serious study of female anatomy. In his capacity as Professor of Clinical Obstetrics and Gynecology at the Baylor University medical school, he carefully surveyed the history of breasts and buttocks, correlating fashions in womanly beauty with the rise and fall of civilizations. His conclusion: The highest cultures tend to admire full-figured women, while skinny girls are preferred by societies in decline. Presumably, then, America enjoyed its Golden Age in the 1960s when Hugh Hefner's centerfolds were at their pneumatic maximum.

Another of Dr. Strassman's findings earned him national headlines. "The bigger the breasts," he stated, "the lower the IQ." Through the press, actress Mamie Van Doren replied that she had had the biggest bust and the lowest IQ of anyone in her high school class, but added, "Who cares about IQ?"

RUSSELL THACKER TRALL Trall was a 19th-century physician whose principal work, *Sexual Physiology,* became a runaway best-seller in 1867. In it he urged against early-evening sex (it inevitably leads to stomach distress, constipation, blindness and impotence, not to mention birth deformities of the vilest sort) and prescribed coughing and sneezing as useful if not always reliable methods of birth control. Having recently lived among the natives of both Iceland and the Friendly Islands and studied their mores, he wrote that "some women have that flexibility and vigor of the whole muscular system that they can, by effort of will, prevent conception. . . . Sometimes coughing and sneezing will have the same effect. Running, jumping, lifting and dancing are often resorted to successfully."

DR. MARY EDWARDS WALKER In 1865 Dr. Mary Edwards Walker (1832–1919), wearing a frock coat and striped trousers, was arrested in New York City for "masquerading as a man." It was not the first time her unconventional attire had caused her trouble. At the age of 16 she discarded her skirts and donned men's clothing, and ever after fashionable women snubbed her and little boys rotten-egged her in the streets. Her apparel was a national scandal. Humorist Billy Nye branded her "America's self-made man." And one editorial writer went so far as to say: "What must be demanded by all who have the interests of the Republic at heart is the refeminization of Dr. Walker. Her trousers must be taken from her—where and how is, of course, a matter of detail." But Dr. Walker's transvestism was a deeply held principle. In those days the bondage of women was very real, and Dr.

Dr. Mary Walker in top hat
(New York Public Library, Picture Collection)

Walker was a relentless opponent of "confining and un-hygienic fashions" such as the whalebone corset, which embraced the body like a boa constrictor.

At the trial Mary blasted the detested corset and excoriated the hoop skirt as an immoral and lascivious fashion conceived by "the prostitutes of Paris." In no uncertain terms she asserted her God-given and Constitutional right "to dress as I please in free America on whose tented fields I have served four years in the cause of human freedom." And as the finishing stroke she produced from her pocket the text of a special act of Congress, giving her permission to wear trousers in recognition of her heroic service in the Civil War. The judge had no choice but to acquit her, and he admonished the New York police force "never to arrest her again."

Everything about Mary Walker was unconventional. At a time when the professions were all but closed to women, she successfully completed her medical studies and in 1855 was awarded an M.D. degree from Syracuse University. It should also be remembered that she invented, among other things, the "Dress Reform Undersuit," a formidable female garment intended to thwart seduction and rape. It was, in essence, a baggy one-piece Union Suit made of linen, which covered the entire body from neck to ankles to wrists. A rabid feminist, she founded a Utopian colony, for spinsters only, called "Adamless Eden." But her particular enthusiasm was the crusade against "nicotine evil." She always carried a tightly rolled umbrella with which she would coldly knock offending cigarettes from the mouths of astonished male smokers.

Dr. Walker first achieved national prominence during the Civil War, serving as a nurse and later as a spy and surgeon (the first woman to hold a medical commission) in the 52d Ohio Infantry Division of the Union Army. In the field she dressed like her fellow officers, wearing gold striped trousers, a felt hat encircled with gold braid, and an officer's greatcoat. She did make some small concessions to femininity, though: Her jacket was cut like a blouse and fitted loosely at the neck, and she always wore her hair in curls so, she said, that "everybody would know that I was a woman." During the

Battle of Chattanooga, she was captured by a Confederate patrol and spent four months in the notorious Castle Thunder prison in Richmond. After the war she loved to tell how she was released from jail in a "man for man" swap for a Confederate officer.

For her service to the sick and wounded, President Andrew Johnson awarded her the Congressional Medal of Honor; she was the first and only woman in American history so recognized. Then in 1917, when Dr. Walker was 85, a government review board revoked her medal along with those of 911 other Civil War veterans on the grounds that there was "nothing in the records to show the specific act or acts for which the decoration was originally awarded." When the Army asked her to return her medal, she replied "Over my dead body!" True to her word, she wore her medal every day, and was wearing it when she took a fall on the Capitol steps (she was there to plead her case before Congress) which led indirectly to her death on February 19, 1919. And at her funeral it was still pinned securely to her Prince Albert coat.

Sports Heroes

FRANCES ANDERSON At the turn of the century Miss Frances Anderson, a handsome maiden from the Midwest, captured the imagination of sports fans with her standing offer of $5,000 to any woman who could defeat her at pocket billiards. For the next 25 years she systematically vanquished all comers, including many highly ranked male players, and received large sums for exhibitions in major European capitals. Then, at the pinnacle of her career, Frances Anderson made the startling announcement that her real name was Orie Anderson. She was a he.

T. L. BAYNE In an 1893 football game between Tulane and Louisiana State, T. L. Bayne served as umpire, ticket-manager, and coach for both teams. For service beyond the call of duty, the two schools presented him with a green umbrella.

JOSEPHINE BLATT Perhaps the greatest strongwoman in history, Mme. Blatt lifted 3,564 pounds in the Bijou Theater in Hoboken, New Jersey, in 1895. The record does not indicate how she accomplished this feat.

LYMAN J. BRIGGS As controversial as the authorship of the curve ball *(See:* Arthur Cummings and Jim Creighton) was the issue of whether there actually was such a thing. Outraged purists who felt there was no place in the game for anything but the Talmudically sanctioned underhand delivery insinuated that the curve was merely an optical illusion. They continued to carp even after George Wright demon-

Lyman Briggs (left) settled the great curveball controversy. *(National Bureau of Standards)*

strated that the curve was very much a reality, in Cincinnati in 1877. Even as late as the 1930s a popular magazine attempted to malign the curve, prompting New York Yankee moundsman Lefty Gomez to rue, "Here I am trying to make my comeback and they tell me my best pitch is an optical illusion."

It fell to Dr. Lyman J. Briggs, baseball fan, physicist, and former director of the National Bureau of Standards, to come out of retirement at 84 in 1959, to settle the great curve ball controversy. With an airgun, Dr. Briggs fired a series of spinning baseballs at a paper target 60.5 feet away through a wind tunnel filled with smoke; cameras caught the missile in midflight and recorded its effect on the surrounding smoke. The spin of the ball, Dr. Briggs saw, caused the air to rush past the ball faster on one side than on the other. Now, the faster the airstream, the weaker the pressure: anyone with a college freshman's familiarity with physics knows this. Hence the ball was deflected in the direction of the weaker pressure. Actually, said Dr. Briggs, this very principle had been worked out a century before by the German physicist Karl Magnus, who used it to explain why cannonballs curve in flight.

For the second part of the investigation, Dr. Briggs enlisted a pair of Washington Senators pitchers, Camilo Pasqual and Pedro Ramos. Briggs had the two moundsmen throw baseballs to which a long flat tape had been fastened. After each pitch, Briggs found that the number of twists in the tape ranged from seven to sixteen. A ball traveling at 100 feet per second and rotating 16 times thus spins at a rate of 1,600 revolutions per minute and produces a curve of 17.5 inches.

LARRY CANADAY Larry Canaday, who coaches varsity football at Eau Gallie High School in Florida, punctuates pregame pep talks by biting the heads off live frogs. "Our kids love it," he insists. "They say, 'Look how wild the coach is. Let's get wild too.' "

Lest you wince at this practice, rest assured that Coach Canaday's technique follows in the most hallowed traditions of the autumn game. It was the prestigious Ivy League that set the precedent. To stir up his 1908 Harvard eleven to victory over arch rival Yale, Coach Percy Haughton is reported to have throttled a healthy bulldog. Tossing aside the poor dead animal, the coach crowed, "There is what I want you to do to those Yale bastards out there this afternoon."

LINDY CHAPPOTEN You get what you pay for: Lindy Chappoten, a pitcher of middling talents who played for the old Shawnee Hawks in the Class D Sooner League, was once traded to the Texarkana Bears for 20 uniforms.

JIM CREIGHTON While Arthur Cummings is most frequently credited with inventing the curve ball, a commemorative plaque mounted on the portico of a Brooklyn brownstone scarcely three miles from Cummings's grave argues otherwise. "This was the home of James Creighton," it proclaims, "the baseball player who tossed the first curve-

Jim Creighton tossed the first curveball *(National Baseball Hall of Fame and Museum, Inc.)*

ball." Creighton died of a ruptured bladder at age 21 during a game against the Morrisania Unions in New York's Westchester County. That was in 1862, five years before Cummings threw his first breaking stuff, and many historians of the game say Creighton created the "wrist throw," the prototype of the curve ball. Others, however, argue that neither Cummings *nor* Creighton was the first man to impart a spin to the ball. Who was? Alphonse "Slow Ball Phonnie" Martin, of the erstwhile Brooklyn Eckfords, who had baffled batsmen with a floating, hesitating "drop pitch" while Creighton was still in knee pants.

However, in 1898, National League veteran Fred Goldsmith claimed publicly that all three stories were full of water and that *Charles Avery,* who had played at Yale and later taught classical literature there, invented the curve. Forty years later Goldsmith changed his story, forsook Avery, and told a sportswriter that he himself had contrived the pitch. He even produced a yellowed newsclipping from 1870 in

276

which Henry Chadwick, one of the game's earliest chroniclers, described seeing him throw the curve.

But in all fairness, Chadwick also said that he had seen *Cummings* throw the curve as early as 1867, but that neither he *nor* Avery nor any of the others was its inventor. (By now things were getting a bit silly.) Who, then, really did toss the first curve ball? An anonymous pitcher who played in Rochester, New York, in the 1850s, Chadwick insisted.

MONTY CROSS The Outlook-Wasn't-Brilliant Department: A first-string shortstop for Connie Mack's Philadelphia Athletics, Cross compiled a .182 batting average in 1904, the worst in the history of the major leagues for a player who played a full season's 154 games.

H. R. CULLEN Oilman H. R. Cullen customarily gave $20,000 to the Houston Symphony Orchestra every year. (To express its appreciation, the orchestra added Cullen's favorite tune, "Ol' Black Joe," to the program whenever he was in the audience.) Cullen's generosity was by no means limited to the arts. He once gave $100 million to the University of Houston, then in a moment of enthusiasm added an extra $2.25 million when the Houston football team scored an upset victory over Baylor.

ARTHUR CUMMINGS The man who tossed baseball's first bona fide curve ball was Arthur "Candy" Cummings, a tall, slim right-hander who hurled for the Brooklyn Stars in the late 1860s. The rulebook favored the batters in those years, forbidding overhead and sidearm pitching with a Calvinist fury normally reserved for buggery and incest. Thus, the principal problem with which Cummings busied himself during long hours on the bench during the summer of 1867 was this: How might a pitcher make the batter really earn his keep, yet still obey the rulebook's strictures to deliver the ball underhand, "swinging the arm as nearly as possible perpendicular to the ground and without jerk or throw"?

Well, he could make the ball *curve*. Why not? Outfielders did it all the time, even on the stillest of days, probably without realizing it. Too, he recalled that when a boy, he summered with his family on the Massachusetts shore and spent many an evening barefoot on the beach tormenting seagulls by tossing clamshells at them. When the novelty palled he tried imparting a backspin to the shells and, to his astonishment, they curved wickedly. Perhaps that same backspin would work now.

On a warm day in June, Cummings drafted a teammate catcher for some on-the-field labwork.

"A bit of straight pitching to start," he announced, and warmed up with a succession of garden variety underhand fast balls. "Now," he said, "for my dazzler." Gripping the ball across the seams, he whipped it sharply from right to left as it left his hand. No doubt about it: the missile tailed far off to the left, helped by a stiff headwind. Blessed with a rubber arm and a strong wrist, Cummings worked on his new technique all afternoon. The results were remarkable. And the catcher nearly wrecked his right hand trying to barehand some of the pitcher's wider-breaking throws.

Despite his own enthusiasm, Cummings's teammates wanted no part of his newfangled "curve pitching." By the time he convinced them to watch, the wind had died and his stuff wouldn't work. The doubting Stars walked off in disgust.

The Stars journeyed to Cambridge, Massachusetts that July to battle the Harvard nine. With Brooklyn's pitching mainstay bedridden with a virus, second-stringer Cummings started the game. No one expected much of a contest, for the Harvards were rated far above the misnamed Stars in all departments. Batting on their home turf against Cummings' tepid fare, they counted on a leisurely afternoon of home runs and easy money.

Instead they were fooled. Cummings had the headwind he needed to make his curves curve grandly and the collegians could do nothing but flail at the air. Brooklyn won, two to nothing.

"What were you pitching to us?" the Harvard shortstop asked Cummings after the game. "It came at us and then went away from us!"

In the years that followed, Cummings would milk much success from his brainchild. By 1877, his last year in baseball, he had posted a dandy record of 141–95, with such clubs as the New York Mutuals, the Baltimore Orioles, the Lynn (Massachusetts) Live Oaks, and ultimately with Hartford and Cincinnati in the fledgling National League. He died in Toledo, Ohio, in 1924, but was buried in Brooklyn's Greenwood Cemetery, barely a scratch single from the Stars' old playing grounds. *(See also:* Jim Creighton and Lyman J. Briggs)

C. B. DE WITT   A star pitcher for the Texarkana Texas Leaguers, De Witt was on the mound on June 15, 1902, as his team squared off against Corsicana. He was still on the mound nine innings later having yielded 51 runs, including 8 home runs to one batter, surely the most generous pitching performance on record. Final score: 51–3.

HESSIE DONAHUE   Mrs. Hessie Donahue, of Worcester, Massachusetts, was the only woman ever to knock out John L. Sullivan, fair and square. She floored the Boston Strong Boy with a single punch, a right to the jaw, in 1892.

Mrs. Donahue was the wife of Charles Converse, a boxing school owner who supplied training partners for the great John L. In 1892, Sullivan went on the vaudeville circuit, sparring on-stage with Converse's men and with Mrs. Donahue, who would go a couple of rounds with him clad in gloves, tights, blouse, skirt, and bloomers. One night the fakery turned real when Sullivan uncontrollably let fly a punch to Mrs. Donahue's face. Thus assaulted, she instinctively lashed out and knocked the champ on his ear. He was out for over a minute.

The freak knockout drew so much applause that Sullivan and Mrs. Donahue worked it into all ensuing performances. It wasn't until September of that year, when Sullivan was

Hessie Donahue knocked out
John L. Sullivan

bested by Gentleman Jim Corbett, that he was ever defeated
in the ring by a man.

HARVEY GARTLEY　In the 47th second of Round 1 of a
local Golden Gloves tournament, Harvey Gartley, of Saginaw, Michigan, was declared knocked out despite the fact
that he hadn't been so much as slapped by his opponent.
Eyewitnesses to the non-bout reported that Gartley had
"danced himself into exhaustion and fell to the canvas."

MIKE GRADY　While playing third base during a National
League contest in 1895, Mike Grady of the New York Giants
made four errors on a single batted ball.

GEORGE W. HANCOCK　For making company picnics
and senior class outings what they are today, thank George
W. Hancock, the inventor of softball. The game, originally
known as "indoor baseball," was first played on November
30, 1887, at the Farragut Boat Club in Chicago. But bear in

mind that in Hancock's version a boxing glove served as the ball, and a broomstick as the bat.

RICHARD HIGHAM In 1883 Richard Higham became the only major league baseball umpire ever to be thumbed out of the game permanently for dishonesty.

FRED LORZ Fred Lorz of the United States won the marathon at the 1904 Olympic Games in St. Louis and was crowned by the president's daughter, Alice Roosevelt. But Lorz's glory was short-lived, and deservedly so: a truck driver confessed that Lorz had hitched a ride with him over the last lap of the 26.2 mile course, and the champion was summarily de-crowned.

JACKIE MITCHELL Miss Jackie Mitchell enjoys the distinction of being the first woman to sign a professional baseball contract. Pitching for the Chattanooga club in April 1931, she struck out Babe Ruth and Lou Gehrig in succession during an exhibition game.

GARY MUHRCKE When a New York City running club announced a first-of-its-kind race up the stairs of the Empire State Building to the 86th floor observation deck, 37-year-old ex-fireman Gary Muhrcke was among the first to sign up. A fine specimen of a man with many swiftly-run marathon races under his belt, Muhrcke won the vertical sprint, clambering to the finish line in 12.32 minutes.

But Muhrcke's success was almost his undoing. He had retired from the New York City Fire Department just weeks before on a full disability pension, and now angry taxpayers were claiming that the city had been swindled, that any man who could scoot up so lofty a tower as the Empire State Building had no business collecting disability money. Muhrcke countered that a back injury he'd incurred on the job made it impossible for him to carry the heavy equipment basic to firefighting, but that running, rarely required of firemen, gave him no problem. Ultimately he was allowed to continue his pension.

Charles "Mile-a-Minute" Murphy preparing for his ride *(Long Island Railroad)*

CHARLES M. MURPHY What Roger Bannister is to track, Charles M. Murphy was to bicycle racing; each shattered a record which had become a psychological barrier. Murphy was 28 when he impetuously declared, "There is not a locomotive built which could get away from me." It was a mighty tall boast considering that the New York Central was averaging over 66 miles an hour on certain stretches of the Albany to Buffalo run. "I immediately became the laughing stock of the world," Murphy later said.

One man who didn't laugh was Hal Fullerton, an executive with the Long Island Railroad. He contacted Murphy and explained what a great publicity stunt it would be if Murphy could set a world record right behind an LIRR express.

"How fast would the train be going?" Murphy asked.

"About sixty miles an hour."

"I can do it," he said firmly.

A level three-mile straightaway between Farmingdale and Babylon was selected for the record attempt. Workmen laid down a smooth wooden runway between the tracks and painted a black line down the center. A special windscreen was built out from the rear of a railroad car. Experiments showed that confetti dropped inside the windscreen fell straight down. There was no aerodynamic suction to aid the cyclist; he would be riding in dead air.

At exactly 5:10 P.M. on June 30, 1899, with James E. Sullivan—the A.A.U. secretary—and a crowd of reporters on hand, the locomotive chugged forward and Murphy mounted his Tribune Racer. Over the first mile of the course man and train gradually accelerated so that when they crossed the official starting line both would be traveling at full throttle. The engineer, Sam Booth, was instructed to keep up a steady speed throughout the measured mile, then to apply his brakes gently so that Murphy (if he hadn't already been left in the dust) would not crash into the rear of the coach.

For the first quarter of a mile Murphy stayed right with the train, inside the protective shield. His head was down and his legs were pumping as regularly as pistons. Then inch-by-inch the cyclist began to fall behind. As Murphy told it, with no small measure of schmaltz:

Fred Burns (an official) asked me through the megaphone what was the matter. I raised my head from the bent position on the handlebars to reply. Quick as a flash I fell back fifty feet. With all the energy and power at my command I tried to regain the lost ground. It was no use. I was doomed to failure. . . . The suspense became maddening. I saw ridicule, contempt, disgrace, and a lifetime dream go up in smoke. O! how I suffered.

Murphy found his second wind, made up the 50 feet, and streaked across the finish line just inches behind the coach. In what seems like a needlessly dangerous maneuver, the jubilant officials reached down, hoisting Murphy and his bicycle onto the still rapidly moving train. His muscles tightened up like turkey gristle and he temporarily lost his senses.

283

"Carry me back to where my wife is," he said, apparently thinking he was about to die. Reporters and friends ignored his ravings, slapped him on the back, and shouted that his time was 57.8 seconds. Man had made 60 miles an hour on his own power. Charles would be known as "Mile-A-Minute" Murphy for the rest of his life. And it would be several years before Barney Oldfield could match that speed in an automobile.

NELL SAUNDERS   At Hill's Theater in New York City on March 16, 1876, Miss Nell Saunders defeated Miss Rose Harland in the nation's first public female boxing match. The winner received a silver butter dish.

LOUIS SOCKALEXIS   The Cleveland Indians are forever indebted to Louis Sockalexis of Maine, the first full-blooded American Indian to play big-league baseball. It was Sockalexis's doing that the Clevelanders came to be known as the Indians. Before his arrival they were called, unpleasantly, the Spiders.

Louis Sockalexis, namesake of the Cleveland Indians *(National Baseball Hall of Fame and Museum, Inc.)*

JOE "MULE" SPRINZ   June 3, 1939, was "baseball day" at San Francisco's Golden Gate Exposition. As the crowning event of the afternoon's festivities, manager Lefty O'Doul of the San Francisco Seals (Pacific Coast League) tried to persuade his reluctant team to shag a few balls dropped from a Goodyear blimp hovering 1,200 feet above the fairgrounds.

"The other players walked off the field," Joe "Mule" Sprinz recalls. "But I said to myself, 'God hates a coward.' The first ball O'Doul released fell into the stands. The second I never caught up with. When the third one dropped, I saw it all the way but it looked about the size of an aspirin tablet."

While the ball screamed earthward, the Seals's .300-hitting catcher circled confidently below, with his overstuffed mitt upraised. The ball smashed into the pocket with a sound like a rifleshot and the impact drove Sprinz's gloved hand back against his face with tremendous force. "My lips and nose were lacerated very badly, there were twelve cracks in my upper jaw, and I lost five teeth. But," he says proudly, "I wasn't knocked out. I should have been a fighter!"

The *Guinness Book of World Records* and other authorities claim that Sprinz held the ball long enough for a put-out. But we got the story straight from the Mule's mouth: "Naw, I stayed with it all the way but I can't honestly say I caught it. My best was 450 feet—one of the balls O'Doul dropped off the Tower of the Sun as a warm-up."

GEORGE HENRY SUTTON   Sutton is still remembered as the greatest armless billiards player in the history of the game. A native of Toledo, Ohio, he once racked up a 3,000-ball run.

ROBERT TIMMERMAN   Just before a crucial game against a team known as the Golden Eagles, football coach Robert Timmerman of Iowa's Dubuque Hempstead High School gathered his eleven in the locker room, stirred their passions with some fiery Knute Rockne prose, and then produced a live chicken dripping with a fresh coat of gold paint. He placed the squawking fowl on the locker room floor and ordered his charges to kick it around. They did, and the bird died.

On the field, Timmerman's psychological fireworks notwithstanding, Dubuque Hempstead lost the game 7–0. Worse than that, Timmerman was threatened with arrest, although the Iowa attorney general ultimately waived charges against him on the grounds that the state's animal cruelty statutes do not protect poultry.

BOB WATSON Bob Watson of the Houston Astros reached home plate during a game on May 4, 1975, scoring the one millionth run since the creation of the major leagues in 1876.

RALPH C. WILSON Buffalo sports fans know of Ralph C. Wilson: he's the owner of the Buffalo Bills. But Wilson is a favorite among connoisseurs of the overstatement. When O. J. Simpson injured his knee Wilson was moved to say, "It reminds me of something that happened in the past. It was two days after the bomb was dropped on Hiroshima. I was there, and the feeling I had then is the same way I feel today about O. J.'s injury."

Index

Abortion, 263–64; legalization of, 217
Acclimatization Society, 7–8
Accounting, first Ph.D. degree in, 157
Actor, worst, 195–96
Adams, John Quincy, 28
Adultery, 128–30, 137
After-dinner speaker, most effective, 67
Airline stewardess, first, 100–01
Airplane, first double-decker, 238; landing on Capitol steps, 161
Alcatraz Prison, 57
Alchemy, 249
American Fertility Society, 263
American Medical Association, 223
American Revolution, 57, 97–100
Amusement park, 60; first, 164
Anaesthesia, first use, 240–41
Animals, cruelty to, 132–33, 275, 285–86
Ant farm, 3
Apes, head transplants on, 254; language of, 232
Apocalypse, predicted, 217, 219, 225–27
Archaeology, 5
Architecture, octagonal, 232
Ark, modern-day, 225–27
Arkansas State Legislature, 127
Around the World in Eighty Days, 33
ASPCA, 133
Astrology, 212–13
Atheism, 220
Atlantis, 2, 5
Aura phenomenon, 244
Aviation magazine, first, 238

Baby carriage, invention of, 97
Bacon, Sir Francis, 183–84
Bakery, Erotic, 74–75
Baker's riot, 79
Balloons, as weapons of war, 114–16
Bank robbery, 36
Barbers, 49, 158
Baseball, 237, 273–81, 285–86
Barton, Clara, 230
Battle Axes (religious sect), 214–15
Bean soup, 70
Beard: prosecution for wearing, 209–10; longest, 206–07
Beauty contest, 205
Bees, 235–36
Begging, 157–59
Best-dressed, 167, 178–79
Bicycling, around world, 25–27; solution to energy crisis, 95–96; speed record, 282–84
Billiards, 273; greatest armless player, 285
Billy Budd, model for, 65
Bingo, as cause of insanity, 114
Birds, 7–8
Blackmail, 59–60
Bleeding, biblical control of, 240; radio control of, 229
Body heat, excessive loss of, 204
Boston Tea Party, oldest survivor of, 172
Bourbon whiskey, 71–72
Boxing, 63, 279–80
Brassiere, invention of, 110–11
Breasts, development, 267–68; size, 269
Brooklyn Bridge, leaps from, 14–15
Bryan, William Jennings, 3

Buffalo Bills (football team), 286
Buffalo Bill's Wild West Show, 208
Burial, alive, longest, 179; in sports-car, 181–82; reburial, 84

Cadillac Ranch, 172–73
Caldwell, Governor Millard, 63
Cancer, 74, 87, 138, 255
Cannibalism, 17, 76, 77–79, 84, 86–87
Carbonated water, invention of, 87
Carnegie, Andrew, 38–40
Caruso, Enrico, 212
Cash register, invention of, 159–60
Cats, raised for pelts, 152
Centenarians, 211, 260
Chastity belt, male, 116
Chess, 173–74
Chewing, health benefits of, 77
Chicago Exposition, 102
Chicago Federal District Court, 242
Childraising, 263
Civil disobedience, 133–34, 143–46
Civil War, 8, 40–41, 48, 84, 102–03, 114–16, 249, 271–72
Cleveland Indians (baseball team), 284
Cock fighting, 141
Cockroaches, 97, 229–30; in Capitol, 143
Cocktail, invention of, 76
Collections, 161; streetcar transfers, 9; string, 177–78
Columbia University, 157
Combustion, spontaneous, 210–11
Commuter, most dogged, 19–21
Complainer, most successful, 152–53
Comstock, Anthony, 264
Congressional Medal of Honor, awarded to a woman, 272
Congressman, U.S., first elected while in jail, 139; heaviest, 139
Conspicuous consumption, 39, 166–67, 170, 172–73, 180–81
Constipation, 255
Contraception, 258–59; father of, 261–62
Corbett, Jim, 62, 280
Cornell University, 64
Corpses, freeze-dried, 91–92
Cow, first airborne, 23
Credit cards, most, 168
Cremation, first U.S., 58

Crossword puzzle, invention, 125; longest, 126
Crystal Cathedral, 220
Crystal Palace Exposition, 93
Curve-ball, proof of existence, 273–75

Dancing, marathon craze, 173
Daredevils, 14–15, 28–29
Dartmouth College, 6
Deer botfly, 251–53
Dentists, 83, 87, 186–87, 235
Deodorant, invention of roll-on, 124
Derby-tipper, invention of, 96
Dewey, Admiral George, 18
Diet and sex, 261
Dirigible, first religious service in, 213
Divorce, 147, 156, 260
Dog, suit to obtain visitation rights, 147
Doughnut hole, invention of, 80–82
Drake, Sir Francis: heirs of, 42–44
Dream, longest, 205
Dwarfs, 202

Earmuffs, invention of 106–08
Einstein, Albert, 234
Eisenhower, Dwight D., 220
Elections, posthumous, 142
Electric chair, 54–56
Elevator, 101–02
Emory University, 49
Empire State Building, 281
Enemas, 255
Energy, forms of, 91; theories of, 237–38, 345
Entertainers, worst, 188–89
Epidemic, St. Louis cholera, 117
Eraser, invention of, 32
ESP, in chicken embryos, 44–45
Esperanto, 193
Euthanasia, 19
Execution, of animals, 132; of dead man, 176; for divulging fraternity secrets, 64–65; first in U.S Army, 52

Face-slapping, 143
False teeth, 235
Faraday, Michael, 240
Feces: use in heating, 91; use in violin making, 201

Federal Reserve Bonds, 57
Female Benevolent Society, 265
Feminism, 23–24, 123–24, 143–46, 258, 266–67, 270–72
Films, 193, 198
Fire-breathing, compulsive, 211
"Five Thousand Year-Old Man," 60
Flagpole sitting, 24
Flat earth theory, 253–54
Flood, Great Boston Molasses, 16–17
Flower, official New York State, 133
Fogg, Phileas: model for, 33
Food Poisoning, 67
Foot, fetishism, 173–75; most perfect, 161
Football, 273, 275, 277, 285, 286
Frozen food, invention of, 68–69
Fund raising, 150
Funeral homes, 182; drive-in, 165

Gardening, 142
Garrison, William Lloyd, 33
George Washington University, 251
Germs, obsession with, 246–47
Gladstone, William E., 2
Goat glands, transplantation, 257
Goldfish swallowing, 89–90
Gold Rush, 5–6, 84
Golf tee, invention of, 106
Gomez, Lefty, 274
Graham cracker, invention of, 79
Grant, General Ulysses S., biography in verse, 72; favorite bourbon, 72
Gravestone, Interpleader Act carved on, 130
Gravitation, 234–35
Greeley, Horace, 41, 79, 230
Griffith, D. W., 121
Gutenberg, Johann, 194

Hammerstein, Oscar, 188
Hangman, most celebrated, 139
Harding, Warren G., 128–30, 212–13
Harvard College, biographical project, 175–76; first black graduate, 106; youngest student, 8
Hawthorne, Nathaniel, 184
Health hazards, 7, 97

Hemorrhoids, prevention of, 103
Herschel, Sir John, 45–46
Hiccups, 243
Hindenburg, 213
Hoaxes, 45–47
Hollow earth theory, 27–28, 249–51
Homosexuality, in seagulls, 236
Horseback dinner, 67
Horses, diapers for, 133–34
Hotdog, invention of, 75–76
Houston Symphony Orchestra, 203, 277
Howe, Elias, 110
"Human Cork," 17
"Human Fish," 186
"Human Fly," 24
"Human Lightning Rod," 27
"Human Pin Cushion," 171
"Human Storage Battery," 204–05
Hypnosis, for bust development, 267–68
Ice cream cone, invention of, 82–83
Ice, first export, 161–64
Illegitimate births, 38–40, 128–30
Indian, first in major league baseball, 284; and John Johnston, 84
Imposters, 38–40, 54
Indoor baseball (see softball)
Insanity, terror as cure for, 247–48
Insects, 3; fastest, 249–51; official New York State, 133
Insomniac, most famous, 205–06
Insurance, 157
Internal Revenue Service, 135, 189

Jackson, General "Stonewall," 48
Jaw-wiring, as slimming aid, 83
Jazz, campaign to annihilate, 190
James, Henry, 77
James, Jesse: impersonated, 54
Jennings, Al, 53–54
Jesus, female reincarnation of, 216–17
Jewelry, ingestion of, 58
Johnson, Andrew, 272
Johnson, Samuel, 222
Jonson, Ben, 183
Junior League, founded, 108

Karezza, 268
"King of the Dudes," 180
Kissing, as cause of disease, 239; as cause of tooth decay, 255; punishment for, 261

Koreshan movement, 250
Kite flying, 121–25
Ku Klux Klan, founded, 121–23
Kuralt, Charles, 106

Landon, Alf, 258
Lawsonomy, 238–39
Lawsuits, for broken date, 135–36;
    for parental malpractice, 134
Leaning Tower of Pisa, half-scale,
    110
Lemuria, 244
Libel, 141–42
Library fine, largest, 169
Life Savers, invention of, 70–71
Lightbulbs, ingestion of, 88
Lights, as cure for disease, 233, 240
    244, 246
Lincoln, Abraham, 34–35, 72, 103,
    115
Lincoln Logs, invention of, 125
Little Cyanide Cook-Book, The, 74
Longfellow, Henry Wadsworth,
    164–65, 222–23
Longley, Governor James B., 107–
    08
Los Angeles Police Department,
    149
Los Angeles Superior Court, 181
Lowell, Percival, 253
Loyola University, 241–42

Machine gun, first practical, 102–03
Mack, Connie, 277
"Magic Spike," 242–43
Magnus, Karl, 275
Mah-jong, introduced to U.S., 151–
    52
Malnutrition, 70
Man, oldest living, 211
Mann Act, 233
Manure spreader, invention of,
    120–21
Mars, 253
Marshall, Chief Justice John: blad-
    der stones, 88
Masochism, 15
Mayor, first female, 143; in tennis
    shoes, 130
Marriages, most by one man, 259
Masturbation, 260–1, 263; preven-
    tion of, 80, 116
Mather, Cotton, 9, 132

Mayan language, spoken by Christ,
    5
McClellan, General George, 230
Melville, Herman, 65
Mencken, H. L., 230
Mexican War, 115
Micturation, 166
Military incompetence, 13
Milk, evils of, 87
Miss America, first, 205
Modesto (California), origin of
    name, 219
Monkey, arrest and trial of, 132
Moon, life on, 45–47
Moran, "Bugsy," 50
Morgan, J. P., 60, 212
Morison, Samuel E., 164
Mother Goose, original, 191–92
Mother's Day, first proposed, 112
Mountaineering, 23–24
Mozart, W. A., 194
Mummies, 60, 62
Music, 201–02; worst opera singer,
    193–94
Musicians and conductors, 203;
    topless, 201
Muggeridge, Malcolm, 213

Names, incidents related to, 63,
    155–56, 175; maiden retained
    after marriage, 123–24; unusual,
    171, 180, 182, 258, 263
National Bureau of Standards, 274
National Endowment for the Hu-
    manities, 108
Naturopathy, 255
Navy, U.S.: first mutiny, 64–65
Newspaper, hand-printed, 194–95
Newton, Sir Isaac, 234
New York Giants (baseball team),
    280
New York World's Fair, 25
New York Yankees (baseball
    team), 274
Niagara Falls, first spanned, 124–
    25; stunts, 15, 28–29
Nixon, Richard M., 138–39
Northwestern University, 221, 242
Novelist, first U.S., 186
Nudity, 201, 209; in religious ser-
    vices, 213–15
Nut museum, 10–12
Nymphomania, 147

290

O'Bannion, Dion, 50
Obesity, 83, 205
Octagon, architecture 231, settlement, 232
Oklahoma House of Representatives, 141
Orange Bowl, bar mitzvah at, 168–69
Orificial therapy, 246
Osteopathy, 228

Painters, 184–86, 189–90, 192
Parachute, first wedding in, 25
Parapsychology, 40–42, 44–45
Pasqual, Camilo, 275
Patent medicines, 245
Peanut, pushed up Pikes Peak, 182
Pedestrians, 6, 34–36; first woman to cross U.S., 17–18; reverse, 37
Penis, first artificial, 267
Perambulator (see Baby carriage)
Philadelphia City Council, 142
Philips, David Graham, 52
Photographs, color cystoscopic, 225
Phrenology, 230–31
Physician, least expensive, 229
Plants, emotions in, 224–25
Poe, Edgar Allan, 28, 46, 222
Poets, 180, 189, 193, 198–201
Poetry therapy, 196
Poisoning, 19, 65–66, 259
Police, 7; vehicle stolen, 66
Police woman, first, 148–50
Polygamy, 17
Pornography, 265
Populist party, 2–3
Postage stamps, first perforated, 32
Postal Service, on skis, 30–31
Potato chips, invention of, 72–74
Potato patch mania, 142
Poultry Hall of Fame, 86
President, forgotten, 127–28
Presidential candidates, unsuccessful, 4, 33, 134, 140
Prohibition, 62
Pronunciation dispute, 127
Prospecting, 5–6, 156
Prostitution, 146, 265, 269
Protests, political, 25, 139–40, 189–90, 217
Proxmire, William, 269
Psychiatry, 134, 190, 247
Psychokinesis, 44–45

Punishment, cruel and unusual, 134, 148
Purdue University, 21
Pyramids, in Arkansas, 4–5

Radio therapy, 228–29
Railroad: planned collision, 1; robbery, 53
Raleigh, Sir Walter, 183
Rats, 96–97, 146; bounty on, 146, sexual behavior of, 256
Recordings, for crying infants, 197–98; for plants, 203
Regurgitator, 183
Religious services, drive-in, 219, nudity in, 213–14, shouting in, 215–16
Restaurant, cheapest, 85
Rickshaw, invention of, 121
Ringling Bros. Barnum & Bailey Circus, 208
Robot, zither-playing, 120
Roller skating, 161
Roosevelt, Alice, 281
Roosevelt, Theodore, 119, 141–42

Safety pin, invention of, 109–10
Salary, highest, 156
Sand, ingestion of, 84–85
Scandal, 1904 Olympics, 281
Sculpture, of George Washington, 192–93
Seagulls, homosexuality in, 236
Self-assertiveness, 156
Sewing machine, 110
Sex, non-orgasmic, 268–69
Sexual responsiveness, 260, 262
Shakespeare, 7, 195; authorship of plays disputed, 3, 183–84
Shaver, Richard 243–44
Shoes, fetishism, 174; for actors, 188
Shopping cart, invention of, 103–06
Sidney, Sir Philip, 183
Silly Putty, invention of, 108–09
Simpson, O. J. 286
Sinclair, Upton, 223
Skiing, 30–31
Skulls, mail order, 154–55; retail, 231
Skydiving, from World Trade Center, 25
Smithsonian Institution, 192–93

Softball, 280–81
Spacecraft, edible, 74
Spectro-chrome therapy, 232–33
Spying, 40
Spiritualism, 40–42
Starlings, 7–8
Stein, Gertrude, favorite book of, 130
Streetcars, resembling horses, 116; transfer collection, 9
Strength, feats of, 15–16, 273
String, largest ball, 177–78
Striptease, 139–40
Submarine, invention of, 97–99
Subway train, first, 92–95
Suction and pressure theory, 237–38
Suicide, 7, 19, 169
Sullivan, John L., 279–80
Survival, extraordinary, 16–17, 204
Syphillis, 19, 222–23, 255

Taxation, income, 135; inheritance, 189
Taylor, Zachary, 127, 128
Teddy bear, invention of, 119
Telekinesis, 244
Telepathy, 224
Telephone, curing disease via, 222–23
Television, death on camera, 88, 169; invention of rerun, 193
Temperance, 143, 220–21, 245
Texas A & M University, 201
Theater, excesses onstage, 196–97, 203
"Three-Legged Wonder," 206–09
Tights, invention of, 109
Toenails, 241–42, 248
Toilet paper, invention of, 103
Toilet, pay, 124
Tokology, 268
Tomato, first public ingestion, 83
Touch typing, invention of, 117
Tower of London, first American imprisoned in, 57
Transplants, head, 254
Transvestism, 47, 48, 136, 141, 270–73
Treason, 52
Tree, official New York State, 133; ownership limited, 140
Trinidad, 18–19
Turtles, giant, 132–33

Twain, Mark, 231
Tweed, "Boss" William, 94
Typewriter, earliest, 93

Uncle Sam, the original, 150
Unicycle, transcontinental trip, 22
UFOs, 47, 223–24, 227–28, 235–36, 243–44
Union Theological Seminary, 151
U.S. Constitution, set to music, 192
U.S. House of Representatives, 70, 139
U.S. Mint, 56–57
U.S. Senate, 127
U.S. Senator, smuggles Bibles into U.S.S.R., 138
U.S. Supreme Court, 217
University of Arizona, 157
University of Chicago, 228
University of Georgia, 97
University of Illinois, 157
University of Michigan, 234
University of Missouri, 267
University of Virginia, 108
University of Washington, 269
U.S.S. Somers, 64–65

Vanderbilt, William K., 59
Van Buren, Martin, 136–37
Van Doren, Mamie, 269
Vaseline, invention of, 153
Vegetarianism, 79–80, 88–89, 134
Venus, 223–34, 236
Verne, Jules, 28, 33
Veterans of Foreign Wars, 84
Vice Presidency, nadir of, 137
Victim, greatest crime, 173
Violin-making, 201
Vomiting, psychotherapeutic applications of, 247
Vrilium, 242–43

Wagers, 47–49
Walking, transcontinental, 17–18, 37, 134–36; upside-down, 197
War of 1812, 13, 171
War of Griffin's Pig, 130–31
Washington, George, assassination plot, 52; false teeth, 235; statue of, 192–93
Washington Senators (baseball team), 275
Wash 'N Dry, 125
Weapons, 117–18

Weatherman, resigns over bad weather, 248–49
White, Stanford, 167
White House, three-fifths scale model, 176–77
Wiesner, Jerome, 266
Wilde, Oscar, 222
Wills, 23, 181
Winthrop, John, 132
Woodhull, Victoria, 33

World War II, 251
Worms, ingestion of, 198
Wright, Frank Lloyd, 125
Writer, highest paid, 202–03

Yale University, 48
Yap Islands, 22–23
Yoghurt, ESP in, 225
Zig-zag-and-swirl theory, 237